The Man Who Made It Possible:

Canon and TAKESHI MITARAI

Katsumi Kato

Shuppan Bunka Sha Corporation

Tokyo, Osaka, Nagoya

This book is a translation of *Yume ga kakenuketa: Mitarai Takeshi to Canon* published by Gendai Sozosha in 1983. Please note that some parts of the book have been translated in a manner that respects the originality of the original author in its expression, and that the information in the book has been translated in the same way as it was at the time of the original interview.

Published in 2024 in Japan by Shuppan Bunka Sha Corporation
4F Across Shinkawa Building, 1-8-8 Sinkawa, Chuo-ku, Tokyo 104-0033
https://shuppanbunka.com

Translation Advisor : Shion Kono

Cooperated by : ThinkSCIENCE

The Man Who Made It Possible:
Canon and TAKESHI MITARAI

Table of Contents

Foreword to the English Edition

Chapter 1
Voices Echoing in the Birch Woods

Chapter 2
Leaving Medicine, Wartime Hardships

Chapter 3

A Fresh Start, and a Dream of Becoming the World's Best

Chapter 4

Castle Building and the "German-Japanese War"

Chapter 5

Through the Depression

Chapter 6

The "Premier Company" Plan
and the AE-1 Revolution

Chapter 7

Within the International Community

Chapter 8
Takeshi Mitarai and Canon's Corporate Culture

Foreword to the English Edition

Foreword to the English Edition

In "Dream of a Boy: The Origin of Kazuo Inamori," published prior to this book, I was able to interview not only the founder of Kyocera, Kazuo Inamori, but also many of the company's employees, including factory workers. Similarly, for this book, I met with many people at Canon, from the top management to ordinary employees. In the afterword, I list the names of everyone who helped me with the research for this book. Reading through the book now, I am confident that I conducted interviews as I thought necessary. I visited subsidiaries not only in Japan but also abroad. I departed Narita Airport on November 3, 1981, and visited 13 cities across 9 countries in just 33 days. Everywhere I went, people told me it was a crazy schedule.

When the editor asked me to write a foreword for the English edition, which I realized would be read mostly by non-Japanese, I wrote down some random thoughts about things that left an impression on me at each place I visited. This may be of some help in comparing what happened more than 30 years ago with what is happening today. I should mention that it was my first time to visit each of these places.

I landed first in Amsterdam, where I exchanged traveler's checks for Dutch guilders, which was the currency at the time. I was told that the portraits and numbers printed on the bills were embossed so that people with visual disabilities could tell the value of each bill by feeling the number of circles.

When I looked in the gift shop at the hotel where I was staying, I found a fancy ceramic container next to a beautifully carved sugar spoon. When I asked the clerk about it, she responded, "pill box," without even smiling. I was impressed by her frankness and ease in responding. The low-dose contraceptive pill was first approved in Japan in June 1999, nine years after the application was filed. At that time, the pill must have had a shady existence in Japan. I think her attitude reflected the disparity between Japan and Europe in terms of the degree of women's liberation.

In the early 1980s, few Japanese companies considered the needs of people with disabilities. It was therefore quite extraordinary that Mitarai, a medical doctor, developed and commercialized a Japanese version of the Optacon*[1], an electronic reading device for people with visual impairments, as early as 1974. When Saburo Nagata, the director in charge of the project, visited Canon Amsterdam, a young man with cerebral palsy came to the office to ask for a Communicator, a portable device that enabled people with speech disabilities to type words and print them in order to communicate with others. The receptionist, a local employee, told Nagata, "Canon has become a full-fledged company." Nagata did not understand what she meant, but the manager in charge of publicity said, "If a company isn't a place where disabled people can visit without hesitation, it will not be trusted in Europe." I had never thought about the relationship between people with disabilities and companies until then.

Next, I traveled to London, where I visited Windsor Castle. The Royal Standard was flown, indicating the Her Majesty the Queen was present. It was on Sunday, and all the stores in the city were closed, so I went to Trafalgar Square via Piccadilly Circus. I was struck by the sight of pigeons flocking together, two gushing fountains, and the statue of Admiral Nelson standing atop a soaring pedestal, which was guarded by four bronze lions. It was too high to be seen from below, like an illusory image of Great Britain….

Later, I spent a few hours at the British Museum. There were many Buddhist statues, and the sheer number of Japanese *inro* (seal cases) and *netsuke* (miniature sculptures) was astonishing. The volume and diversity of the exhibits seemed to indicate a nearly pathological determination to collect the entire history of humanity, the same kind of passion that had led to placing the statue of Nelson at such an outlandish height, which to an outsider would seem absurd. In 2014, I had the opportunity to travel to Dar es Salaam, Tanzania. When I visited a museum and saw for the first time actual chains used to bind enslaved Africans, I was deeply affected. Both the Louvre and the British Museum are renowned for their collections of art and historical relics, but I suspect that neither mentions the existence of slavery.

My next stop was Paris. As I strolled through the city, I came to the Pont Alexandre III, a bridge with splendid decorations and statues. On the parapet of the bridge is a statue of a child straddling a giant fish, about to be impaled by it. Not far from there, I came upon an old, dignified building with a statue of a seated figure, and on the pedestal were the names of famous politicians such as Richelieu and Colbert. Wherever you go in Paris, you can feel the weight and depth of history, and the sensibilities cultivated in this city are embraced by people on both the left and the right, regardless of ideology.

I wanted to tour the Louvre, but I couldn't find the entrance. Unfortunately, it seemed that the museum was closed. As I wandered around, a group of Arab women and their children approached and surrounded me. One of the women tried to twist my hand into my coat with a terrible force. I finally shook them off and ran away like a rabbit. At that time, the Japanese media rarely reported on the refugee situation there.

My next interview was in Giessen, Germany. I was treated to a French dinner of venison and mushrooms at an old restaurant. A few tables away from ours sat the most strikingly beautiful woman I had seen in Europe. With her white skin, long hair, and straight posture, she looked as though she were playing the leading role in a dinner scene in a movie.

When I asked Kurt Hansen, a 41-year-old employee of Giessen, if he had been directly affected by World War II, he told me that he had lost his mother and that one of his relatives had been interned in East Germany and had never returned. We had dinner at a neighborhood restaurant called Gift of the Mountain, where we enjoyed wine, sea turtle soup, smoked salmon, and veal steak. The Italian waiter who brought us our food had a very pleasant demeanor, which delighted us. I couldn't help but compare him with the waiters at first-class restaurants in Japan, who are so polite that they make you feel uncomfortable.

When I went to New York and mentioned to someone that I was almost mugged in Paris, they said it was so common in New York that no one was surprised anymore. People even stole cars. A relative of mine, who was in elementary school at the time, had asked for a photo of the Statue of Liberty, so I took a picture from the boat and then went to the Jewish Museum. Although I had no particular interest in Jewish history at the time, I wanted to know what the Jewish people considered important. There was a special exhibit on the life of Kafka, who is widely admired in Japan. I was impressed by the thick sacred book whose cover was embossed in silver, but the fact that most of the exhibits were related to religious ceremonies showed the deep religiosity of the Jewish people. At that time, I was not aware of the conflict between the Israelis and Palestinians, and I have not been particularly interested in learning more about the Jewish people since I learned that Israel has persecuted the

Palestinians in various ways.

Between interviews, I was taken to a Japanese-owned teppanyaki restaurant for lunch. The waitress was a petite Japanese woman, which, oddly enough, made me feel relieved, as if I could relax my shoulders, perhaps because I felt tall women had been looking down at me every day.

That afternoon I was on my way to Toronto, Canada, and the immigration officer at the airport was a woman. She looked nice but asked me a lot of questions. We could not communicate well in English, so she finally gave up and let me go. I mumbled a swear word. Someone told me later that female officers in many countries, generally speaking, tend to ask too many questions, so that experienced travelers will choose a male officer, even if their line is long. I had gone to her line because it was shorter.

The central district of Toronto was brightly lit at night. But that doesn't mean people were working late. Some stores kept empty cash drawers open so that thieves wouldn't break them open.

My next stop was Los Angeles. From the airport, I took a cab to Little Tokyo. I met Mr. and Mrs. Yamada and Mr. and Mrs. Masumura, who, like Chairman Mitarai, are from Oita Prefecture. As Japanese immigrants, they were put in an internment camp during World War II. This, I discovered, was yet another war experience of the Japanese. Yoshio Katayama, a lawyer in San Jose, and Noriyoshi Kawasaki, who ran a Japanese restaurant in Portland, were also immigrants and had similar experiences. Haruo Odagawa at the Honolulu office, born in 1930, lost his brother in the atomic bombing of Hiroshima.

Shuichi Ando, president of Canon Australia, had been sent to an internment camp in Siberia. (My older brother, Jiro, was born in 1926, graduated from junior high school, and after serving in Manchuria, was sent to an internment camp in Siberia for two years before returning home safely.)

In Taiwan, I visited the Dr. Sun Yat-sen Memorial Hall. Although I had not expected it, one of the most striking features was the presence of several photographs (perhaps copies of newspapers of the time) showing the Japanese military acting as the aggressor against Taiwan during the war. I thought Japanese people should be more conscious of the fact that Japan's history as an aggressor has not been easily forgotten overseas. At that time, many Japanese were visiting the Beitou Hot Springs in Taiwan, which was known as a prostitution destination.

I also visited the National Palace Museum in Taipei, which is well known in Japan. Because Taiwan was the last stop on my trip, I couldn't help but compare it with the British Museum. The comparative difference in historical consciousness between the two institutions made me consider the differences between Asia and Europe. The basis for this was a book on my bookshelf, *Gendai Chugoku Ron* (On Modern China), published in 1954 by Yoshimi Takeuchi, a scholar of Chinese literature. Several lines of the text — which I had first read as a high school student when I was recovering from tuberculosis — came back to me as if they were rising from the depths of the earth: "In order for Europe to be Europe, it had to invade the East… For Europe, it was conceived as the progress of world history, or the triumph of reason… Europe advanced step by step, and the Orient retreated step by step."[*2]

The National Palace Museum, which merely displayed outstanding cultural relics, and the British Museum, which had displayed an almost pathological need to recreate the history of humanity. Somewhat unexpectedly, I wish to close this foreword with this trivial experience more than 30 years ago.

July 10, 2023
Katsumi Kato

*1 The Optacon used a camera to capture text and converted each character into a tactile representation using vibrating pins, which could then be read by touching the raised pins with one's fingertips.

*2 Source: *Takeuchi Yoshimi Zenshu* (Complete Works of Yoshimi Takeuchi), vol. 4. Chikuma Shobo, pp. 131–134

Chapter 1

Voices Echoing in the Birch Woods

Chapter 1
Voices Echoing in the Birch Woods

"Boys, be ambitious!"

In 1877, more than a century ago, the American William Smith Clark said goodbye to his students from Sapporo Agricultural College at Shimamatsu Station, about 24 kilometers southeast of Sapporo. He then rode off on horseback and disappeared into the white birch forest.

Sixty years later, Masatake Oshima, one of Clark's few remaining direct disciples, dictated to his son the preface of his book, *Dr. Clark and His Students*, to record Clark's footsteps as well as his idealism. It was 1937, the 12th year of the Showa Era.

On August 10 of that same year, a young male doctor named Takeshi Mitarai, who shared Clark's ideals, helped to found a small company, Seiki Kogaku Kogyo (Precision Optical Industry, Co., Ltd.), in Tokyo.

However, just over a month earlier, on July 7, a shot fired at the Lugou Bridge (also known as the Marco Polo Bridge) on the Chinese mainland began a series of events that intensified the Sino-Japanese war. These events and other changes in the world impacted the company and it barely survived by producing optical weapons and X-ray cameras until Japan's defeat on August 15, 1945.

After the Empire of Japan collapsed, many people had no homes to live in and little food to eat. However, instead of producing pots and pans, like so many other companies, Seiki Kogaku Kogyo decided it would continue to manufacture cameras.

Did Mitarai have a good chance of succeeding at that moment? Maybe not, but he had to try regardless. Soon after, he would announce his goal of "defeating Leica," referring to the German camera company, at a meeting of industry professionals. Although both Germany and Japan had lost the war, Germany's camera technology was far ahead of Japan's and the camera technology in Japan had yet to advance beyond the level of small-scale factories.

In 1950, Mitarai traveled to the U.S. for the first time, bringing with him a product he was confident would succeed. Still, he had to face the reality that many Americans did not want products with the "Made in Japan" label. The following year, he built the modern factory constructed from non-flammable materials he had long dreamed of and used it as a base for his business. There, he aggressively developed his management philosophy with the aim of making Canon the number one camera company in the world. Mitarai was at a forefront of it all.

In April 1921, at the age of 20, Mitarai left his hometown of Kamae, Oita Prefecture, a farming and fishing village where he had grown up, and made the journey to Hokkaido, far to the north.

"Be a Gentleman."

To get to Sapporo from Kamae, which is located on Kyushu, the southernmost of Japan's four main islands, he would first have to travel to nearby Saiki on foot or by boat. The journey on foot was about 28 kilometers through the mountain roads. From Saiki, he would take a train to Moji, cross the Kanmon Straits by ferry and then take another train bound for Tokyo via Kyoto. In Tokyo, he would board a train at Ueno Station and traveled to

Aomori, at the northernmost tip of the Honshu island. From there, he would take the Seikan ferry to Hakodate in Hokkaido and then take a train to Sapporo. The journey took at least two days.

There, Mitarai enrolled in the preparatory course for Hokkaido Imperial University and moved in to the Keiteki Dormitory. From his dorm room, he could see the Ishikari Plain as well as Mt. Teine, which rises over 1,000 meters and has snow even in spring. He was fascinated by the bright red sunset and the vast plains in the distance.

From the plaza in front of Sapporo Station, a wide road lined with acacia trees ran from north to south and a streetcar carried passengers up and down its straight path. Among the rows of low houses, the red-brick Fifth Building stood out. Near the preparatory school building in Kita Kujo, the road was stony and weedy, and cows were slowly grazing.

The university's campus occupied a vast expanse of land, with large elm trees standing among the buildings of the Faculty of Agriculture and the central lecture hall. To the north of the preparatory school building was a cornfield, from which the sound of leaves rustling in the autumn breeze filled the air. A group of students walked down the main street, the sound of their wooden clogs echoing through dimly lit evening, while other students belted the dormitory song. The fragrant smell of roadside baked corn stands wafted through the area (according to a text by Yoshiomi Sato in *The Fifty-Year History of the School of Medicine of Hokkaido University*).

The following names appear in the list of new members in the 92nd issue of the *Bunbukai Newsletter*, published by the university at the time:

Preparatory Courses
German, 1st year, Class A, Fumio Otsuka (Chiba Kisarazu Junior High

School)

German, 1st year, Class B, Shuzo Imai (Kyoto 4th Junior High School)

German, 1st year, Class C, Kumazo Nagata (Sapporo 1st Junior High
School) and Takeshi Mitarai (Oita Saiki Junior High School)

Kamae Village, where Takeshi Mitarai was born and raised, is located in the southernmost part of Oita Prefecture and faces the Bungo Channel. The shoreline is a typical ria coastline with a complex combination of promontories (capes or headlands) and inlets. Today, the town of Kanae stretches about 20 km diagonally from northeast to southwest and only 5 km from east to west. The mountainous terrain is complex and rugged, and land transportation has been inconvenient since ancient times. Although Kanae is now connected to Saiki City by two prefectural roads. It takes one hour by bus, following a mountainous route with many curves and passing through a mountain pass tunnel more than 300 meters above sea level. A mountain range, standing about 400 meters tall and running northeast to southwest, blocks the cold winter winds from the Kyushu island's interior, and it is a frost-free area with the average annual temperature of about 17°C. Very little of the land is used for farming, with 0.7% (62 hectares) used for rice paddies and 5.4% (510 hectares) used for fields, and about three-quarters of the area is mountain forest and wilderness (according to the History of Kamae Town, published in 1977).

The climates of Kamae and Sapporo are very different.

Of the preceding list of names, Otsuka would go on to work as a company doctor at Canon for 30 years and is now deceased, but both Imai and Nagata are still alive and well as of this writing. Mitarai was in the same class as Nagata because students were assigned to classes based on the alphabetical order of their family names. Mitarai had arrived at the University a week late for some reason, so his seat remained vacant during that time. Nagata, who was two years younger than Mitarai, was born in Sapporo in 1903 with cerebral palsy and had disability in both legs, but he had a gentle heart that fit with his slim build and modest demeanor. He became friends with Mitarai after lending him some of his notebooks.

Shuzo Imai (born in 1903 in Hyogo Prefecture) shared a dorm room with Mitarai, who was "like a big brother to him." Soon they and Otsuka began spending a lot of time together.

The University was filled with Clark's "Boys, be ambitious!" spirit of 1876-1877, which was appropriate for the carefree climate that could not be found on the main island of Japan. In addition, a new movement called "Taisho Democracy" was spreading across Japan. Mitarai and his friends enjoyed a carefree youth amid these developments.

After Clark was appointed to establish Sapporo Agricultural College, he read the rules and regulations for schools and dormitories issued by the Japanese. "Education under these conditions is not enough to create human beings. Be a gentleman, that's good enough," he declared, to the surprise of the school's professors (according to *The History of Keiteki Dormitory*). This episode symbolizes the freedom of Clark's spirit.

In Mitarai's time, the dormitory was self-governing. The dining hall operations were not outsourced to a contractor. Instead, the students selected the head of the cooking department as well as the members of the purchasing, furnishing, and accounting committees who would manage the hall.

Mitarai was already picky about food. One day, he invited Imai to go to the school farm to eat melons, which were shaped like big red pumpkins. Mitarai bought a melon, cracked it open, removed the seeds, and ate the yellow flesh inside along with the wine he had brought with him.

His picky taste led to some unfortunate incidents, however.

"The food in the dorms is terrible. Let's have *sukiyaki*," Mitarai said one evening.

It was a hassle to dress up to go out to eat. So, he sent Imai and Otsuka to buy meat, vegetables, tofu, and a hot pot. They put the food on an electric heater, and just as it was beginning to simmer, a man whom Mitarai disliked approached.

Not wanting to share their food with him, Mitarai put his cloak over the pot and went to Otsuka's room, one door down, pretending that he had some business to attend to. When he returned to his room, it was filled with smoke.

"What's going on?" Suddenly, there was a commotion and someone shouted, "Hey, the electricity is out!" Fortunately, Mitarai and his friends returned just in time to stop the electric heater from catching fire. Students were not allowed to cook in their rooms, and Mitarai would have been suspended or expelled if someone had found out about the incident.

Mitarai loved food and often went to restaurants. There was a soba noodle shop near the school as well as a fruit shop and a café and a restaurant that was famous because it had introduced coffee to Hokkaido (according to *The Beginning of Sapporo's History*). In addition, there was a shop that sold western-style confections. Mitarai and his friends often ate there, purchasing ice cream and cream puffs on credit.

(Even after reaching the age of 80, Mitarai's obsession with eating has not diminished. He claims this is the source of his health, and when he travels abroad, he is happy to eat the local cuisine and does not crave Japanese food).

The area known as Tanuki Koji (literally, "raccoon dog alley") was a playground for students, who would hang out there in the evenings. The name first appeared in history in 1873. In 1869, Yoshitake Shima came to Hokkaido to help establish what is today the city of Sapporo, and he created a government district on the north side and a shopping district on the south, divided by Odori Park in the middle. After Shima left, Toshimichi Iwamura oversaw its continuing development, but workers did not remain. So, he built a brothel in Susukino, as well as the government-run Tokyo-rou (a brothel). In 1873, Iwamura departed, and many people left the Susukino area when the economy entered a recession. Prostitutes, called "*goke*" or "*tanuki*," lured drunken customers to cheap drinking spots in the area, which has been called Tanuki Koji ever since. Stores, theaters, playhouses, photo studios, and amusement centers were also built in the area (according to the book, *Sapporo Fubutsushi* <Sapporo's Seasonal Tradition>, edited by Sapporo City Board of Education).

It was an entertainment district like Minami in Osaka, Kyogoku in Kyoto, and Kabukicho in Tokyo today — and the scenes there are still quite vivid in Imai's memory. Students walked around, wearing wooden clogs and singing the dormitory song in loud voices. There was a beer hall directly managed by Sapporo Beer, and one of the waitresses was an Ainu girl with thick eyebrows, well known for her beauty. A large mug of refreshing draft beer cost 10 sen (100 sen = 1 yen) and was served with salted beans. In the winter, Mitarai and his friends would gather around the red-hot stove. Steam would rise with a sizzle whenever someone put their snow-covered clogs near the stove. There was no curfew in the dormitory, so students could come and go as they pleased, and many came back at two or three o'clock in the morning. Students who had no money were still able to drink because there was always someone wearing a hat with white lines (a symbol of the preparatory school students) who would pay for their drinks.

"Miyako zo Yayoi"

"Miyako zo Yayoi," the timeless dormitory song of the preparatory course of former Hokkaido Imperial University (now Hokkaido University), conveys these "good times."

Miyako zo Yayoi no kumo murasaki ni

Hana no ka tadayou utage no mushiro

Tsukisenu ogori ni koki kurenai ya

Sono haru kurete wa utsurou iro no

Yume koso hitotoki aoki shigemi ni

Moenan waga mune omoi o nosete

Hoshikage sayaka ni hikareru kita o

Hitonoyo no kiyoki kuni zo to akogarenu

"In the city, in March, the purple clouds and the scent of cherry blossoms float over the feast,

The endless delicacy and the deep crimson rouge, the colors of spring come and go.

My dream grows like green leaves, and my heart is burning,

With all my heart, I am longing

For the north, where the stars shine brightly, and the human world is pure."

[The first verse of the song lyric, above, contrasts the luxurious cherry-blossom parties in March in a large city (presumably Tokyo), a symbol of extravagance and transience, with the clear, starry sky of Hokkaido where life is simple and people's hearts are pure. – Trans.]

These words were written by Yoshisuke Yokoyama, a student in the preparatory course at the time and a native of Shizuoka. The first verse of the lyrics express his longing for the "pure" lands of the north, and Mitarai felt the same longing. Even now, 60 years after his school days, Mitarai still finds himself humming this song in the bath. The rest of the song always reminds him of the scenery of the Ishikari Plain and Mt. Teine.

He could see the geese flying over the bountiful Ishikari Plain, the flocks of sheep returning to the barn as Mt. Teine dimly glows in the twilight, and the leaves of the elm trees rustling in the wind, and the North Star hanging high in the sky. The moon hangs in the cold sky over the coniferous forests, and even the sound of the sleigh freezes as the snowflakes dance over the field.

When the heat haze arises on the pastures, green buds sprout on the laurel trees, grass grows in the field, flowers bloom along the banks of the stream, and a skylark is singing.

The lyrics conclude with a thought for Clark: "We cannot but be proud of our glorious dormitory, where we cultivate the lessons of noble ambition."

(Mitarai even hoped to have this dormitory song played at his own funeral, and the impact of his time at Hokkaido Imperial University symbolized by this song is hard for anyone else to measure.)

This dormitory song was composed in 1912, ten years before the famous dormitory song of the First High School (the predecessor of the College of Arts and Sciences, the University of Tokyo), "Aa, Gyokuhai ni Hana Ukete," was composed. The lyrics, "Once a man arises, he should do something great with his life," "Let us save our people who are adrift in the muddy sea," and "If anyone hinders our way, there should be no hesitation to cut him down with the sword of destruction," there is an elitism built as a mixture of bold heroism and selfish careerism, but do not reflect the real world at all.

Compared with this, "Miyako zo Yayoi" describes specific scenery, and even though the young people living in Sapporo are described in the song as "gushing out their surging blood" (in other words, "channeling their youthful energy"), there is no sense of looking down on the common people. Facing the vastness of nature, it may have been difficult to create a sense of elitism, as the First High School students would have done.

The lyrics from the second to the fourth verses are as follows:

Yutaka ni minoreru ishikari no no ni
Karigane harubaru shizumite yukeba
Yogun koenaku bokusha ni kaeri
Teine no itadaki tasogare komenu
Ooshiku sobiyuru erumu no kozue
Uchihuru nowaki ni hae no haoto no
Sayameku iraka ni kuon no hikari
Ogosoka ni Hokkyokusei o aogukana

When the wild goose sinks far into the fields of Ishikari, where the crops are bountiful,

Sheep return to the barn without a flock's voice, and the mountaintop of Teine glows in twilight.

The elm treetops rising majestically, the sound of leaves shaking in the wind, the clapping of roof tiles, and the eternal light,

I look up to the North Star solemnly.

Kangetsu kakareru shin'yojurin
Sori no ne korite mono mina samuku
No mo seni midaruru seihaku no yuki

Shijima no akatsuki hihitoshite mau
Aa sono sakuhu hyohyotoshite
Susaburu hubuki no sakamaku o miyo
Aa sono soku kozue tsuranete
Juhyo saku sourei no chi o koko ni miyo

The cold moon shines over the coniferous forests, the sound of sleighs is freezing, and everything is cold.

The snow, clear and white, falls crazily all over the field, and snowflakes dance incessantly in the dawn of silence,

Oh, look there at that north wind aloof, the blizzard swirling in the opposite direction,

Oh, look here at the magnificent place where the treetops of that azure sky are strung together and the ice trees bloom!

Mkiba no wakakusa kagerou moete
Moriniwa katura no shinryoku kizashi
Kumoyuku hibari ni enreisou no
Mashiro no hanakage sayuragite tatsu
Ima koso ahurenu seiwa no hikari
Ogawa no hotori o samayoi yukeba
Utsukushikarazuya saku mizubasho
Haruno hi no kono kita no kuni sachi oshi

A heat haze rises above the young grass in the pasture, and the forest is sprouting fresh green of laurel,

A skylark is flying above clouds, and the shadow of the pure white flower of the Enrei grass is wavering and standing.

Now is the time for the clear light of spring to overflow,

Mizubasho (skunk cabbages) in bloom, so beautiful, on a spring day in this northern country.

Fluttering Cloaks in the Wind

Sports such as tennis, table tennis, skiing, and skating gave the students many opportunities to let out their "surging blood."

The first issue of *Frate*, the journal of the Hokkaido University School of Medicine Alumni Association, was published in 1925 (the year before Mitarai entered the university). Issues published between 1926 and 1928 contain records of intramural tennis and table tennis league matches, in which Mitarai's name appears six times.

Skiing was a rare activity for students from the mainland, so they borrowed skis from other dorm residents who had them. Imai became a skater and even won first place in an intercollegiate competition.

On one occasion, Mitarai rode a horse. When he was a sophomore in college, he visited a ranch in Niikappu. A cavalry regiment had sent students to a training camp to make them feel closer to the military, and Mitarai decided to participate because he thought it would be a good experience. One evening, he was riding back to the barn, and about 100 meters out, his horse began running so fast that Mitarai had to cling tightly not to fall off. It was lucky that he didn't break his neck as they raced inside.

They also learned a type of Japanese classical music called *nagauta*, which was popular at many universities. Mitarai invited Imai to join the *nagauta* group, but Imai pleaded with his "older brother," "I have a bad voice and no musical talent, so please don't make me." But Mitarai insisted, saying "No, you have to," and thus Imai was "forced" to join the group. The teachers were women and most of the students were young girls. "Sweat was pouring from my armpits as I learned with them. It was an interesting experience," Imai remembered with a laugh.

Mitarai, Imai, and Otsuka went on a one-week trip not carrying any money. It was the fall of the second year of the preparatory course. In the following year, the three of them would go their separate ways, Otsuka to Chiba Medical College in his hometown, and Imai to the Faculty of Agriculture and Mitarai to the Faculty of Medicine at Hokkaido Imperial University ("Hokudai" for short).

On the first day, they headed south to Tomakomai. Because they were traveling without money, they decided not to stay at an inn but instead to crash in the sewing room of a women's college. Mitarai was in charge of negotiating this. A teacher at the school was impressed, asking, "Are you a student at Hokudai? Please use the room." The fact that they were going to be students at Hokudai gave us credibility. In Hokkaido, it was cold at night in the fall. They gave 50 sen to an errand boy and asked him to light a charcoal fire.

They went to Muroran and then back to Noboribetsu, where they stopped at the most luxurious inn. Mitarai asked the owner, "Where is the best hotel around here?" He scratched his head and said, "Well, I don't know where it is, but my place is…" After hearing this, the trio stayed at another hotel. However, it kept raining and they had to stay there for three days in a row. They ate a lot of local delicacies from the mountains and the sea, but they had no money to pay for them. A friend in Sapporo had to send them 20 yen by wire to pay for everything.

On the way back to Sapporo, the three friends went to Tomakomai again and then to Lake Shikotsu. They boarded a train carrying lumber for Oji Paper, but a sign warned that the passengers' lives were not guaranteed. They tried to stop at the lakeside, but they had only 3 yen in their pocket and it cost 1 yen and 20 sen per person for lodging. They negotiated to pay 1 yen each without meals because they had bread with them. To their surprise, they were served *sashimi.* When they went to bed, they thought they could see the stars through the ceiling of their room but soon realized that the ceiling was covered with flies. Needless to say, they didn't sleep very well that night.

As they waited at the station to catch the 8 o'clock train, a train coming from the opposite direction showed no sign of stopping. The driver smiled as he looked at the three people on the platform. If they missed the train, they would not be able to return to Sapporo. They literally had no cash on them. The passing train was now in the middle of an uphill slope, and their train was about to stop. With his cloak fluttering in the wind, Mitarai ran after the train on the tracks. There were four bars attached to the back of the uncovered freight car. He reached for them and jumped on. Imai, who had been trained in skating, had no problem getting on. Finally, Otsuka made it. The passengers watching the race between the train and the humans were delighted.

"Don't Besmirch the Family Name."

Here, it is worth mentioning the Mitarai family, which has a long history. Takeshi's older brother Nobuo (born April 29, 1890), is 11 years older than Takeshi and still going strong as the 15th head of the Mitarai household.

Osakishimo Island in Hiroshima Prefecture is also called Mitarai Island, and it is said that after the Mitarai family was defeated in a battle on the island, some of them settled in the village of Kamae in Kyushu. An enormous amount of old documents from the pre-Meiji period, when Mitarai's family served as the great village headman, are preserved in the Mitarai family in an unorganized state.

A festival is held on Yakata Island that floats at the entrance of Kamae Bay. According to local legend, if the Mitarai family does not go to the festival, the door to the island's shrine will not open. (Oita Prefecture Local History Study Group, Oita Prefecture Local History, No. 63, Someya Takio, *Folk Customs in Kamae-ura*).

During the Edo Period (1603–1868), the Mitarai family had a 21.6-meter-long, 3.6-meter-wide path leading from the gate to the front door of their house. The villagers would take this path to get water from the well on the Mitarai property.

Genta, the grandfather of Nobuo and Takeshi, was born in 1842 and called himself Yataro Nobuyoshi. He loved learning so much that he walked from Kamae to Saiki to attend a scholar's school and eventually became a skilled calligrapher. He also liked to drink *sake* from morning to evening. He sometimes made his own *sake*, and the remains of a well he used for this purpose can still be seen in his residence. However, Genta was not good at making money and borrowed large sums of money from many people. He had to sell many of the forest that had been on his family's property for generations in order to repay the debts.

He lived a life of luxury and once had a chef come all the way from Nagasaki so that he could eat delicacies from the mountains and the sea. He had a stroke that left him bedridden for 13 years and died in May 1906, when Takeshi was five years old. He remembers only a few glimpses of his grandfather's life.

Genta first married a woman named Shina, and they had a daughter named Tora, but Genta left Shina and took Tamo Ishida as his second wife. She was a large, beautiful woman who excelled at sewing and cooking and was also a talented illustrator. Genta was a bold man who talked about luxuries such as soups made with crane or suppon (softshell turtle) meat.

The son-in-law welcomed into the Mitarai family was Taizo, the fourth son of a foot soldier of the Saiki Domain who lived in Saiki Village. Born in 1861, about seven years before the Meiji Restoration, Taizo Kaneda entered the Mitarai family as an adopted son in July 1881 and inherited the governorship of the household in December 1883.

Taizo had the responsibility of rebuilding the Mitarai family. He was extremely strict in his treatment of his children, as if he were a samurai warrior. Nobuo, the eldest son, couldn't remember his father ever relaxing, and the children naturally became reserved in front of him. Nobuo couldn't recall ever being spoiled by his father.

Taizo never expressed any likes or dislikes about food, and didn't allow his children to do so either. Nobuo was a man of great frugality and patience, and he never wore socks except at New Year's. However, he was extremely fair to his children, and when he received food from other families, he would divide it equally among all members of the family, serving it on small plates.

He abstained from gambling and horse racing, and in order to rebuild his finances, he did not invite any guests to his home, except for Buddhist services, for ten years. He never haggled over his debts and always paid the interest in full. Nobuo remarked that he had nothing to be ashamed of.

His wife Tora was born in 1864, and grew up as the daughter of a village headman. Like a princess, she was served by her maid, but she excelled in silk farming and weaving, and made all of her children's *kimonos* herself. Nobuo's son, Fujio (born in 1935), remembered his grandmother, saying, "She got up early every morning to comb and dye her hair. She was small but always neat and had the look of a princess. She was fashionable and well-groomed until the day she died."

Takeshi was often admonished by his mother that he must never do anything to tarnish the family name. The young Takeshi did not understand why she said such things, but even though he was very young, he knew that his mother was proud of her family. Takeshi was a quiet, obedient boy who was loved and cherished by his parents.

Takeshi attended Kamae Elementary School, where he played while wearing *zori* (traditional Japanese sandals), caught spiders, fished, and learned to swim by watching and learning from others. He was the head of his class for six years, and on his graduation day, he read a speech that began, "When I entered this school, I was a child who did not know the east from the west." The opening passage was still vivid in his memory.

Descriptions of the Mitarai family frequently appear in *History of the Town of Kamae*.

According to that book, Takamasa Mohri arrived in Saiki as a head of the 20,000 koku domain*[3] in April 1601, a year after the Battle of Sekigahara. In 1604, "Gendayu, a fisherman from Kamae-ura, offered Takamasa sardine fish," according to *Tsuruhan: A Brief History of the Saiki Domain*. This Gendayu is said to have been the great village headman from the present-day Kamae village.

In the mid-eighteenth century, bad weather, including floods, led to a series of poor harvests, and the Mohri Domain forced the merchants and wealthy peasants in the castle to pay a supplementary allowance. *History of the Town of Kamae* records that the Mitarai family donated 50 ryo and 100 ryo separately (100 ryo was equivalent to 5 million yen today), and was given permission to carry two swords and wear *montsuki* formal attire.

In addition, in the mid-nineteenth century, the Mitarai family invited many literati to stay at his house as guests, and during the stay, the literati selected "Eight Places of Scenic Beauty in Kamae (*Kamae hakkei*)" and its accompanying poems, which are celebrated to this day. Among these guests were Akizuki Kitsumon, and his son, both of whom were professors at the Saiki domain school Shikodo, which Gendayu attended. The original copy of this "Eight Places of Scenic Beauty in Kamae" is preserved in the Mitarai family. In 1894, Taizo wrote a Chinese poem about the scenery of Kamae and submitted it to *Tsurutani Soshi,* a magazine about Saiki published in Tokyo. These episodes show that Gendayu and Taizo were traditional-style literati.

In January 1907, the township was implemented and Taizo became Saiki Town's first mayor. However, in July of the same year, Taizo had heart trouble and died at the age of 51.

---

[3] The domain of 20,000 koku would produce roughly 3 million kilograms of rice annually, and is a medium-sized domain.

In his will, which was left to his eldest son, Nobuo, he wrote, "Takeshi has a promising future. I want him to go to college." Nobuo carried out his father's wishes.

Taizo's original family was a wealthy family in Saiki. Taizo's brother and the head of the family, Naomi Kaneda (aged 65), offered to take care of Takeshi, so the young man moved to the Kaneda home and attended Saiki Junior High School. Takeshi's impression of his uncle was that he was "a respectful, honest man without a smile." Naomi's only son Minoru had died of tuberculosis, and his 25-year-old widow Naka was raising her three-year-old daughter and serving Naomi's elder wife. Minoru's older sister had returned home after a divorce, and she treated Takeshi with a lot of ill will. He experienced the grief of being a fatherless child, but he fought off the loneliness and went to school so as not to worry his mother. His only relief was that Naka took good care of him, like an older sister. (Takeshi never forgot her kindness and would return the favor some forty years later, as a man joined Canon and played an important role in the company.)

After the last class before the summer vacation, Takeshi wanted to go straight home. Not wanting to wait any longer to see his mother's face, he tried to cross the Katada River, which was flooded by heavy rain, and arrived home soaking wet.

According to Minoru Yamada (now living in Los Angeles, California), who was born in 1901, the same year as Takeshi, and who also attended Saiki Junior High School and was taken good care of by Tora, "The Mitarai family is a first-class family from Kamae—one may even say an aristocratic family." The lower class ate potatoes, the middle class ate half barley rice several times a year, and the Mitarai family ate rice every day. In fact, Nobuo's child, Fujio, cannot remember ever eating barley rice.

However, "Takeshi was a quiet and unobtrusive man, and he was not haughty about his family background," said Yamada.

During this period, Takeshi's personality was influenced by a new mathematics teacher at his junior high school, Sakichi Kishino, who was born in Gifu Prefecture in 1887. He had been assigned to the school immediately after graduating from Tokyo Normal School and appeared before Takeshi and his classmates in his school uniform, only exchanging gold buttons (for students) with black ones. Over the next three years, Takeshi's math skills did not improve, but Kishino never became angry. In later years, they would both be business owners. Junior high school lasted five years, but Takeshi contracted tuberculosis in the second semester of his fifth year and returned to Kamae to recuperate and to prepare for the university entrance examinations. However, he did not take the exam until 1921.

His friends had gone on to prestigious high school, but he was not interested in following in their footsteps. Instead, he took the entrance examinations for both Jikei Medical School and Hokkaido Imperial University because his older brother Nobuo was a graduate of Jikei Medical School and because Hokkaido Imperial University accepted the entrance examinations from Tokyo. At that time, the results of university entrance examinations were published in an official gazette, and he enrolled in Jikei Medical School because it was announced first. However, several days later he found out that he had also been accepted to Hokudai and, after consulting with his brother, decided to go to Hokudai.

The Emperor's Birthday Celebration Play

After completing the preparatory course, Otsuka entered Chiba Medical College as planned, but Imai and Nagata changed course. It was Mitarai who prompted the change.

They were both in the agriculture department, but Mitarai didn't think they would have much luck if they continued there. "We won't be able to make a living with a degree in agriculture. Let's change to medical school," he said. Without a second thought, Imai said, "Let's do it." First, Mitarai persuaded Nagata's mother to let him study pediatrics. Then he went see to the Dean of the School of Medicine, the same person who had operated on Nagata's leg when he was a boy. Mitarai convinced the dean to approve their request for a transfer to the Faculty of Medicine of Hokkaido University.

According to Nagata, "He is quick to make decisions and swift in his execution. When he has an idea, he is persuasive. The course of my life changed when I met him."

Imai said, "He understood everything about society from that time."

In his second year of the preparatory course (1922), Mitarai was nominated as the business manager of the dormitory committee (second only to the chairman), and in his third year, he was nominated as the head of the middle dormitory (there were four dormitories: South, North, Middle, and New), and then as the chairman. When he was the dorm director, he performed in plays.

It was customary to have a party at the dormitory on the Emperor's Birthday, which was then called "Tenchosetsu," the word with a nostalgic resonance for people above a certain age.

First, there was a luncheon or dinner party, with the student supervisor and a few teachers in attendance. The dormitory chairman congratulated the committee members, and then, after three chants of "*banzai*" for His Majesty the Emperor, everyone sat together at the dining table for a feast. Later, entertainment would be provided by the Keiteki-za (the theater troupe of the dormitory). Before the party was discontinued in 1923, it was the largest social event of the year, surpassing even the commemorative festival (according to the book *History of Keiteki Dormitory*).

The final event in 1922 consisted of contemporary plays (*shingeki*), and the program was as follows:

- *The Assumption of Hannele* by Gerhard Hauptmann, translated by Kaoru Osanai

- *The First World* by Kaoru Osanai
- *Heroes of the Sea* by Kan Kikuchi
- *Night on the Border* by Ujaku Akita
- *Shunkan* by Hyakuzo Kurata
- *The Launderette and the Poet* by Yobun Kaneko
- *Horrible Father, Horrible Daughter* (Author unknown)

Mitarai and his team performed *Night on the Border,* which had first been performed at the Meiji-za Theater in Tokyo in May of the previous year.

The main character of this play, Ohno, is a man who made his fortune by exploring the wilderness of Hokkaido, and from his hard life experiences, developed a philosophy of neither accepting help nor offering it to others. One night during a snowstorm, a father and son come to Ohno's house seeking shelter. Ohno's wife and daughter try to let them in, but Ohno follows his philosophy and turns them away, and the father and son freeze to death. The same night, robbers attack the Ohno house and tell Ohno that if he doesn't kill his wife and daughter, they will kill him. When Ohno hesitates, the robbers move toward his wife and daughter, but Ohno finally confronts the robbers. It is later revealed that the robbery is a dream that reflects Ohno's emotional conflict, and the play ends with Ohno reconsidering his philosophy.

It is said that the play's author, Ujaku Akita, was influenced by the socialist ideology of the time, but the script has a strong humanitarian sensibility. Mitarai played Ohno, while Gen-ichi Ogawa (now professor emeritus at Hokkaido University), who was in the same class, played his wife, and Fumio Otsuka played the robber.

Mitarai was an avid reader of literature. Mitarai encouraged Imai to read Hyakuzo Kurata's *The Priest and His Disciple*. Also, one of Mitarai's favorite books was *Views on Love in the Modern Era* by Hakuson Kuriyagawa. It was published in 1922 and captured the hearts of many young people with the words "Love is best" at the beginning of the book. In 1933, the book was included in the Kaizo Bunko collection of pocketbooks, indicating that it was still popular more than a decade after its publication.

Recently, Mitarai recited a scene from the book smoothly and without hesitation, as if he had just finished reading Hakuson's book. "The wife is covering up her head and cheeks (with a towel), and is heading to Kyoto with a load of vegetables from the cozy countryside. Those two were probably united on the night of the *Bon* dance. What a happy couple." In the original work, the passage is as follows.

"At dusk in Kyoto, a young couple were seen pulling a cart along the streets. On top of the empty cart was a cute little child of two or three year old in a basket. Having earned their bread for the day, they were now hurrying home. The man and the woman sometimes look back at the child, and the child in the basket smiles back to them. Their beautiful love must have been consummated in the middle of a summer night in a mountain village in Rakuhoku, after a Bon dance or something like that. The child was a precious angel given to them by the god of love. Even though they were poor, they were happy people who were 'in love and working.' I would like to bless the parents and a child as a true family living sincerely while praising and praying for them."

It is clear that the story remains ingrained in Mitarai's memory.

But that's not the only thing that left a deep impression on him. An "incident" during his dormitory chairmanship days remains a vivid and painful memory.

There was a guy from Aomori Prefecture in Mitarai's class who stole some books from the dormitory library and sold them to a used bookstore. It may have been for tuition fees, but stealing is stealing. Because it was a self-governing dormitory, he had to be punished as a dorm resident regardless of how the school viewed the matter, and the final decision was left to the chairman of the committee. Mitarai understood the man's plight, so he struggled over what to do. Although he thought it was too severe, he reached a conclusion, which he described as follows: "It's humiliating to be expelled by the school authorities. As a friend, I advised him to voluntarily submit a notification of withdrawal." Although the man withdrew from the school, Mitarai regrets his cold decision, even though it was made under the authority of the chairperson, and it has lingered in his mind for a long time.

Mitarai and his friends became university students in 1926, the 50th anniversary of the founding of the University, and they graduated in April 1928. He never had to find a part-time job to pay for his tuition because his older brother Nobuo sent him money. Nobuo was like a "loving father" to him, and he always felt a deep sense of gratitude toward him.

Dormitory life during his preparatory course years was a special time for Mitarai, and his efforts to demonstrate his autonomy as dormitory committee chairperson gave him experience as a leader. This would become the foundation for his management skills as a corporate manager. Mitarai enjoyed his seven years of student life, including three years in the preparatory course and four years in the medical school. "My personality was nurtured at Hokudai," Mitarai recalled.

After graduating, he interned at the university's obstetrics and gynecology department, learning by watching actual births. Whenever there was news of an impending birth, he rushed to the delivery room.

The first time he received a salary was when he became an instructor at an obstetrics school affiliated with the University. Among the three assistant instructors, only Mitarai became a full instructor, perhaps because Dr. Seishichi Ohno expected him to be a good teacher. "I think I was a lax instructor because I had just started learning," said Mitarai.

The salary of fifteen yen a month was enough for Mitarai and his friends to go out drinking.

As a young doctor, Takeshi Mitarai's future looked bright. His ambition was to eventually become a professor. He also wanted to study abroad.

One day, however, he happened to catch a glimpse of a certain teacher's lunch box, which contained only bread and milk. Mitarai groaned. "Is this the life of a professor?" He began to wonder whether he should continue working at the university. Feeling a need to control his own destiny, he left the university on the grounds that his brother needed his help at the hospital in their hometown.

In December 1928, Mitarai told Nagata and Imai that he was leaving on the train for Tokyo that very night. They were surprised, but both of them knew that once Mitarai had made up his mind, there was nothing they could do to change it. Nagata paid for part of his train fare. It was December 14, the very day that the famous 47 Ronin (lordless samurai) of the Ako Domain invaded Kira's residence. He passed the employment examination and joined the Department of Obstetrics and Gynecology at the Japan Red Cross Hospital in April of the following year, where he remained until 1935.

Chapter 2

Leaving Medicine, Wartime Hardships

Chapter 2

Leaving Medicine, Wartime Hardships

Trend of the Times

In 1933, Mitarai became involved with cameras while working as a doctor for the Japanese Red Cross Society.

He became acquainted with Saburo Uchida, the husband of one of the parturient women he examined at the hospital. Her brother, Goro Yoshida, was a camera enthusiast and he asked Uchida, who was working at Yamaichi Securities at the time, if he would be interested in working as a camera maker.

It had been five years since Mitarai left Hokkaido Imperial University, and although the nurses and patients called him "Sensei (Doctor)," the lingering passion of his student days remained in his mind and body along with his memories of the harsh cold of the Hokkaido winter. After work, when he would go to a bar and pour beer with Uchida and Yoshida, it seemed like only yesterday that they were sitting around the bright red stove at the "directly managed" beer hall in Tanuki Koji (Raccoon Alley).

"Japan already has fine warships, and our textile industry will soon surpass Lancashire in Great Britain and soar onto the world stage. But there is something missing. Japan has no precision industry. This will put Japan behind the rest of the world."

(In fact, in 1933, Japan's cotton fabric exports surpassed those of the United Kingdom, making Japan the world's largest exporter of cotton fabric, and it was also the world's second largest producer of rayon. At the same time, Japan's export growth caused tensions internationally, with other countries accusing Japan of "social dumping," using its low wages as an economic weapon, according to *Comprehensive Chronology of Modern Japan* published by Iwanami Shoten.)

When Mitarai thought about it, he realized that the microscopes he regularly used at the university were made by the German companies Zeiss and Leitz. Although Germany's economy had been devastated by World War I, it had made good use of its precision industry to produce world-class cameras.

When the 33-year-old doctor thought about it this way, he was unconsciously forming a plan that would influence the major trends of the times.

World War I began in July of 1914, when Mitarai was in his second year of junior high school, and in August of that year Japan occupied Qingdao in the German-held Shandong Peninsula. Although the war ended in 1918, Saiki Bay was a military port, and the movements of the Imperial Japanese Navy excited the imagination of boys living in the area. Young Takeshi watched the ships from the top of a mountain and dreamed of becoming a naval officer and emigrating to Brazil on the other side of the Pacific Ocean.

In September 1931, the Mukden Incident, also called the Manchurian Incident, occurred. At the end of that year, Tsuyoshi Inukai, the president of the Seiyu-kai political party, became the prime minister of Japan. Mitarai felt a connection with Inukai because their given names—Takeshi and Tsuyoshi—were both written with the same Chinese character. The following year, however, Inukai was assassinated by naval officers (the May 15 Incident) and Japan withdrew from the League of Nations in March 1933.

Consequently, people were forced to consider Japan in the context of the rest of the world and to think about Japan's future. Diverse ideas and practices aimed at reforming Japan emerged, ranging from left-wing to right-wing.

The enthusiasm for cameras in Uchida, Mitarai, and their colleagues was for them a response to the times, a combination of risk-taking spirit and idealism.

In November 1933, Seiki Kogaku Kenkyusho (Precision Optical Instruments Laboratory) was founded in Roppongi, Azabu, Tokyo.

Early that same year, "the Leica Portrait Photography Exhibition of Literary Artists" was held in Ginza, but what kind of presence did Leica have in Japan at that time?

According to *Cultural History of Ginza Photography* by Koji Morooka (published by Asahi Sonorama), the capabilities of Leica's camera were unknown, and it was surprisingly expensive: 520 yen for a 50-mm $f/3.5$ lens and 520 yen for a 73-mm $f/1.9$ replacement lens. For comparison, 1,000 yen was enough to buy a house. Professional photographers in Japan used an assembled box camera with a tripod and a lens costing a total of 36 yen. This is the cheapest model, and there are more expensive ones, but the difference with the one-thousand-yen Leica set was like night and day.

It is believed that Leica cameras were first imported to Japan in 1926, and Leica attracted broad interest in Japan in August 1929 (the year Mitarai worked for the Japanese Red Cross Hospital), when the German airship *Graf Zeppelin* landed in Kasumigaura and a photo of its commander, Dr. Hugo Eckener, appeared with a Leica camera on his chest in a Japanese newspaper.

A camera called Baby Pearl costing between 25 and 40 yen was released in June 1934 by Rokuosha, the predecessor of Konica Corporation. Toshio Yamazaki, who joined Seiki Kogaku in 1937, was paid 50 sen (half of 1 yen) a day, or 13.50 yen a month at that time.

"Terrifying" Cameras

It was during these times that Seiki Kogaku Kenkyusho (Precision Optical Instruments Laboratory) was born with the aim of researching and producing high-end 35-mm cameras. Headed by Saburo Uchida, the laboratory in Roppongi consisted of a western-style room, which was used as an office and assembly plant, and two other rooms, which were used by the craftsmen as a dormitory.

The company employed about ten people, including Takeo Maeda, Uchida's former colleague from Yamaichi Securities, who oversaw clerical work. In the spring of 1935, five or six boys were hired from Maeda's hometown of Yamura in Yamanashi Prefecture, along with five or six assembly workers, seven or eight machine finishers, and several servant boys, bringing the total number of employees to around 25. Most of the assemblers had previously worked in clock shops, but some had worked in tinker shops or bicycle shops.

From 1934 to 1935, Seiki Kogaku Kenkyusho was struggling not to infringe on Leica's patents and to produce a camera (Tatsuhiko Arakawa has written a detailed examination of the trends of the time in his book, *Nikon Monogatari* [*The Nikon Story*]).

In 1934, thanks to their hard work, they were able to place an advertisement for the KWANON camera in the June issue of *Asahi Camera*. This was the first time that the name of a camera made by Seiki Kogaku Kenkyusho was publicized, and the advertisement read, "Igo Submarine, Kawasaki Army Type 92 Fighter, KWANON Camera – all the best in the world," referencing two world-class products made in Japan. The cameras were priced at 200 and 285 yen. An article in the August issue of *Nihon Shashin Kogyo Tsushin* (Japan Photo Industry News) reported that there was "momentum for domestic lens production and that Nippon Kogaku offered a

50-mm $f/3.5$ lens to Seiki Kogaku Kenkyusho. In September of 1935, Ohmi-ya Shokai began selling domestically produced Canon cameras with a case for 270 yen.

At Seiki Kogaku Kenkyusho, Maeda worked as both a sales representative and a clerical worker, preparing meals and making miso soup while listening to the motor sound of machines. He went from one factory to another in Tokyo with drawings and materials to place orders for various ground and pressed products, but no one would make the 50 or so parts he needed. After visiting ten shops, one or two of them saw Maeda's distressed face and accepted his order.

In February 1936, Ohmi-ya Shokai began selling Hansa Canon cameras under the company's trademark "Hansa." The price was 275 yen, much higher than the 20 or 30 yen price of other domestic products. Kimio Yamada, who joined Seiki Kogaku Kenkyusho that year, remembers that every day or two, Maeda would bring a finished camera wrapped in a purple wrapping cloth to Ohmi-ya Shokai. When the February 26th Incident (a failed coup d'état by young Japanese Army officers) occurred that year, Yamada and his family packed their belongings and prepared to evacuate the area. (Army Captain Koji Muranaka, a classmate from Sapporo First Middle School of Kumazo Nagata, who had been a friend of Mitarai since Hokkaido Imperial University, was involved in February 26th Incident).

Sales of the Hansa Canon were good. In June 1936, the head office and factory were moved to a new location at 2146 Nakane-cho, Meguro-ku, Tokyo, and the company was renamed Nippon Seiki Kogaku Kenkyusho. Only one truck was needed to move all the equipment.

According to Hanataro Taniuchi, who joined the company after the relocation, the building was modern, more like a research institute than a factory, and had an idealistic atmosphere. Surrounded by fields of tomatoes, cabbage, green onions, and other crops, the Seiki Kogaku building stood alone, with a good view to the Ookayama area.

In November of that year, Shuji Tokunaga (born in 1914) and Muneo Hirai (born in 1918) joined the company. Tokunaga was good with his hands and had wanted to make his own camera. He joined the company after hearing a rumor that a company was making imitations of Leica cameras. Hirai had previously worked as a technical apprentice at a watchmaker's shop.

As for the actual work, Tokunaga remembers that he was given a small cardboard box containing all the parts except for the lens and helicoid. But no one told him what to do, so he kept a screwdriver, a file, a drill, and a tool for making screws close by and kept putting the cameras together and taking them apart. Eventually, the screws would get damaged, so they would melt the metal with an alcohol lamp and solder the parts together. The work was quiet with only the sound of the compressor spraying paint – tokotokotokotoko…. The hardest part was dealing with the broken screws and adjusting the shutter so that it would slide down smoothly without getting caught on anything.

Tokunaga also did the focusing by himself. A glass plate (about 45 × 35 mm) with one side frosted to about 0.5 mm was gently inserted into the body of the film's focusing surface. It was so thin that it would break easily if not handled carefully. A 25× telescope was mounted on a wooden stand, the camera was placed on the same stand with its bulb fully open, and the focal length was adjusted to the glass surface. There was a chart ahead, so he turned the helicoid and read off one meter, then two meters, and so on. There were graduated washers of the scale from five-hundredths, and he added or subtracted them, placed them in the lens, put them back together, and looked through. If the lens was clear at one meter, the next step would be five meters, and so on, until the helicoid was aligned with the scale on the lens. Then the focus adjustment was complete.

The peephole for the focus adjustment was located on the back of the camera body. He didn't know who had started this method, but it might have been Nippon Kogaku. It worked fine.

When a part broke and he went to get a new one, others complained, "They cost tens of sen each!" However, the production of some parts was outsourced, and other parts were made by inaccurate machines that somehow produced the right shape, so it required true craftsmanship to assemble these parts and make a functioning camera.

There was no measuring device for shutter speed, and even though the maximum speed was 1/500, and the following scales were marked 200, 100, 60, 40, 30, and 20, it was only good enough to get the half chance of 1/500th of a second.

It was fortunate that the black-and-white film at that time had such low sensitivity. If it had been more sensitive, the images would have turned out black. According to Araki, "It was a terrifying camera, now that I think about it."

Even so, he took the finished product to Ohmi-ya Shokai as soon as it was ready. It was only when he saw the pictures taken by the customers that he could confirm the results of his work, saying, "Oh, they look great."

X-rays to Overcome a Difficult Situation

There was a limit to such manual camera manufacturing. Therefore, Uchida proposed that the research institute be re-organized as a company, and

Mitarai wholeheartedly approved, becoming the founder of the company.

Mitarai was responsible for raising funds for the new company. From the spring of 1937, he started asking relatives, acquaintances, and friends to become shareholders. Among them was Manabu Atsugi, who was then a vice president of Oishi Hospital and a close friend.

"Are you all right?"

"I'm not sure if it's a good idea or not, but I think it will grow in the future. Help us as if it were a postal savings account."

His brother Nobuo and his friend Shuzo Imai also became shareholders.

It was decided that there would be no president, but that Uchida would be the executive director, and Mitarai would be an auditor who would visit the company once a month or so.

On August 10, 1937, Seiki Kogaku Kogyo (Precision Optical Industry, Co., Ltd.) was officially established, with capital of 1 million yen (for some unknown reason, "Nippon" <"Japan"> was dropped from the company name), and a reception was held at Meguro Gajoen, a fancy hotel. The building in Roppongi was used as a dormitory, and the employees in the dormitory cooked their own meals there. One thing they looked forward to was the soba (buckwheat) noodles they were treated to on their way home from overtime work, so when they arrived at the hotel, they felt like they had gone from paupers to princes.

Mitarai was also asked to participate in the management of the company as a director, but he declined the position because he had become director of the Department of Obstetrics and Gynecology at Seibo Hospital in October 1935 and then obtained the doctor's degree in May 1937 for his thesis on the "Relationship between poison gas and miscarriages during World War I," and he was planning to eventually establish his own practice.

Although the company had capital of 1 million yen, it initially received only about 40% of that amount, and not all of it was in cash. A substantial portion was an in-kind investment that overvalued the research laboratory's facilities. It was not until the second half of 1938 that the company was able to pay a 5% annual dividend to shareholders.

The times were changing swiftly. On July 7, almost a month before the company was founded, the Sino-Japanese War began, with the Lugou Bridge (Marco Polo Bridge) Incident. This was followed by the occupation of Nanjing in December, the proliferation of thousand-needle stitches (a good luck charm for soldier going to war) and comfort bags (gift packets to be sent to soldiers) throughout Japan. The establishment of a special excise tax (July 1937) severely hurt the camera industry, and the expansion of areas where photography was prohibited (under the Military Aircraft Protection Act) negatively impacted camera sales. On the other hand, the ban on the import of foreign goods in October boosted the manufacturing of cameras domestically, and thus the company experienced both highs and lows.

The company's machine equipment included a lathe, two bench lathes, and a milling machine. There were 60 employees, and the monthly production target was 45 units. The company's employees worked overtime and managed to complete the production, but parts were not always available when needed. Sometimes the company had to outsource production, but only when they had enough money to pay the outsourcers. Maeda scrambled to collect parts and went to Ohmi-ya Shokai to borrow money at the end of each month.

The highest salary was 12 yen plus room and board in the company dormitory. Although the company provided work clothes and bath tickets, to many employees it was as if there were no salary. If someone saw a shiny object on the street, they would run to see if it was a 50-sen coin, but it usually turned out to be a bottle cap. On payday, Maeda would leave in the morning, and when he returned after dark, the employees would look at him as though he were a god.

(In 1936, the average daily wage for general laborers was 2.41 yen for manufacturers and 1.99 yen for carpenters. The average salary from 1935 to 1937 for industrial workers was 2.01 yen men and 64 sen for women, and cigarettes cost between 8 and 20 sen, according to *100 Years of World Prices*, by Jiro Iwasaki.

The biggest problem, however, was the lens. Since the company's days as a research institute, lenses had been supplied by Nippon Kogaku. But as the war in China expanded, peaceful industries were being converted to produce military equipment, and camera lenses and related products were no longer a priority. Maeda had to visit Nippon Kogaku two or three days each week to get the lenses he needed.

In 1938, the year after the company was founded, Seiki Kogaku began researching lens design, and in 1939 they created the Serenar Lens.

Susumu Tazawa, who joined the company (Seiki Kogaku) in 1938, recalled that there were about 130 employees at the time, many of whom were involved in military-related work, and that they made a machine that recorded changes inside gas masks on photographic paper. Yone Mori, who joined the company the same year, was surprised to see a small, dimly lit room with clerks working in a chaotic manner, while five or six people were working right next to them, making noise with files and hammers.

Cameras were utilized by the Navy for weaponry, and as a subcontractor of Nippon Kogaku, the company made rangefinders to measure the altitude of airplanes, photophones (which transmit sound via light), and even balloon bombs, but the company's financial situation was not good.

As a doctor, Mitarai conducted detailed medical examinations for his employees. It was not just simple percussion and auscultation, but as detailed as a physical examination like the ones for army conscripts. Muneo Hirai, who joined the company in November 1936, was afraid of the examination because it was conducted by a big shot. Seeing Hirai's hesitation, Mitarai told him, "I'm going to see you as a doctor today, so you don't have to be afraid of me."

Mitarai had to diagnose the company's condition as well, and the diagnosis was not good. "In the third year of its establishment, the company was on the verge of collapse," Mitarai remembered. The solution to this problem was to produce an X-ray camera.

At the time, more than 100,000 people were dying from tuberculosis each year, so it was important for the government to take measures to combat the disease. However, most cases could not be detected by percussion and auscultation with a stethoscope. It was not uncommon for a person who had passed the military physical examination to be found to have tuberculosis within six months or a year. Moreover, during that period, an infected person often transmitted the disease to many other people. Therefore, the company proposed the medical departments of the army and navy to "use medical equipment that could perform more precise examinations."

A history of group medical examinations is relatively short. According to the chronology in the article "History of the Development of the Indirect Radiography Camera" written by Susumu Tazawa (August 1980), Professor Yoshihiko Koga of Tohoku University conducted research on indirect radiography using a Contax camera in 1935, succeeded in this endeavor in 1936, and conducted the world's first group medical examination.

Koga and Mitarai were friends, and when Koga asked if they could develop the product at Seiki Kogaku, Mitarai readily agreed. It was a matter of life and death for the company, so the question of whether they could do it was beside the point. There was no choice but to go ahead with the project. The paper by Tazawa mentioned above describes the situation during this time.

> In February 1940, Dr. Seijiro Yokokura of the Japanese Imperial Navy examined an X-ray indirect imaging machine equipped with a Tenax camera with a Zeiss Sonnar 50-mm $f/1.5$ lens, which the Navy had imported from Siemens in Germany. He intended to produce a similar device domestically according to his own specifications. Seiki Kogaku took up the challenge and began designing and manufacturing the machine in June of the same year, completing it in December of 1940. The pioneering product produced in Japan was a naval-type 35-mm indirect camera with a Sonnar 50-mm $f/1.5$ lens, which was equipped with an X-ray machine that included a stand.

Fumio Otsuka, Mitarai's former classmate in the preparatory course at Hokkaido Imperial University, was in charge of preventive medicine at the Army Ministry, and Dr. Yokokura served as major general of military medicine and the director of Yokosuka Hospital. Mitarai negotiated the contract to supply the X-ray machine with these two men. In July 1939, Mitarai became the director of Seiki Kogaku, believing that the title of auditor was no longer appropriate, considering the work he was doing on behalf of the company. In 1941, the company introduced a general X-ray indirect radiography system, manufactured several hundred units per month at most through 1942, and produced and delivered an army model in 1941. (Otsuka later became Canon's chief health advisor and contributed the company as company physician).

Mitarai Becomes President and Introduces a Monthly Salary System

In 1940, the war intensified even further, and even photographers were mobilized to work at munitions factories.

At Seiki Kogaku, the employees chanted the Imperial Rescript to Soldiers and Sailors during the morning assembly and worked all night long, wearing white headbands with the rising sun flag or with the word *kamikaze* written on them.

That year, Mitarai opened a hospital in Mejiro, Toshima-ku, Tokyo.

He had always desired a life of freedom without constraints, but this was not possible with hospital work. The only way to have real freedom is to open your own business, he thought. "I'll do it the way I want to."

However, the changing times did not allow him to do so.

On December 8, 1941, the year after the hospital was formally established, the Japanese army landed on the Malay Peninsula and the navy attacked Pearl Harbor, beginning the Pacific War.

The advancing Japanese forces occupied Guam and Hong Kong that year, Rabaul in January 1942, and Singapore in February. Saburo Uchida, the chief executive officer of the company, was assigned to Singapore as a magistrate.

A magistrate was appointed by the Japanese government to administer the local government in Southeast Asia under the Japanese military regime, and had considerable authority.

At that time, Michitsura Ishihara was in charge of general affairs, while Harumi Shibata, a high school classmate of Uchida, was in charge of accounting. The two men, annoyed by Uchida's absence, asked Mitarai to take over the role of president, even if he only came to work once every two weeks or so.

Thanks to Japan's wartime policy encouraging families to have more children, Mitarai was extremely busy with his day job at the hospital. Therefore, he refused their request. However, the two did not give up, and they visited Mitarai in his office every evening after work to discuss the company's direction. "If things continue as they are, our employees will be left on the street," they told him. Eventually Mitarai relented and on August 14, 1942, the board of directors informally approved Mitarai's appointment as president, and on September 10, it was officially decided at an extraordinary shareholders' meeting.

When Mitarai started looking into the inner workings of the company, he found that some executives had not been doing their jobs properly and problems were piling up. The man who had always made quick decisions now looked up to the heavens and sighed. In this position, he had to break through barriers, but Mitarai was a novice manager who didn't know anything about technology or accounting.

When one stands on a knife's edge, it is necessary to reveal one's entire self. Mitarai decided to address his employees. "As you all know, I am a doctor by training. If you want to deceive me, it would be as easy as twisting a baby's arm. I have no choice but to trust you. If the accountant wants to cheat the books, he can. If the factory manager says he bought a 10,000-yen machine for 15,000 yen, I won't be able to tell the difference. However, it is obvious to me that the company will go out of business if you continue to do so. As president, the responsibility for that lies with me. It is also obvious that if we want this company to prosper, we must all give our best and act with sincerity."

Thus, he began his life with two jobs.

From then on, the 43-year-old Mitarai woke up at 5:00 a.m., had breakfast, went to the office, presided over the morning meeting, finished his work, and then went to the hospital around 11:00 a.m. to see his patients who were waiting for him. They were told he had been out making house calls, and they complimented him on his hard work. He would take off the cap he wore at Seiki Kogaku, put on a white lab coat, and sit down in his chair. He would put aside the difficulties he was facing as a company president and turn to the patient sitting in front of him. "What seems to be the problem?"

Mitarai, then forty-three years old, used to tell his wife, "Be prepared for us to end up in the streets at any time."

As president, Mitarai had to make some difficult decisions. In February of the following year, he asked the problematic executive and plant manager to step down, saying, "I don't really understand your way of doing things."

In June, he adopted a monthly salary system. At that time, there was a clear distinction between "employees" and "workers" at all companies, with employees usually entering through the front gate and workers coming through the back gate, and Seiki Kogaku was no exception. In addition, employees were paid a monthly salary, while the workers were paid on a piece rate. From Mitarai's point of view, such a system was unacceptable. One day, as Mitarai was walking around the factory premises thinking about what to do, he overheard a worker say, "People like us with no education can go only so far."

Shigeru Shinagawa, who joined the company in 1941 and was assigned to the Machinery Division, described the contracting system in those days. "The work was done on a contract basis, and everyone has a craftsman mentality – even a master mentality. There was a great deal of competition for good-priced work, and workers ended up having incredible conflicts. They did not teach other workers how to do their jobs, and mentoring the younger workers and managing health and safety in the workplace were of secondary importance. Young boarders were paid on a daily basis and given a small amount of money for helping out, regardless of whether they were contracted or not."

Mitarai decided to send some of his employees to a training program before they transition into a monthly salary system. At that time, Pilot Mannennhitsu (Pilot Fountain Pens; currently Pilot Corporation) and Otsuka Seika (Otsuka Shoe Company) were the pioneers of the monthly salary system, and they stayed overnight to see how employees came to work in the morning. Both Mitarai and Shuji Tokunaga recalled not being able to sleep when they visited Otsuka Seika because of the strange smell of the tanning chemicals. They also attended lectures on spiritual at Kinkei Gakuin (Golden Cock Academy).

On March 24, 1943, the board of directors officially adopted the monthly salary system, and one morning soon after, Mitarai gathered his employees to share his thoughts. "This may be my layman's opinion, but I don't think your lives will be stable if you are paid on a contract basis. I visited two companies and asked their managers about it. They said that the outsourced contracting system was an exploitation of labor and that a monthly wage system would respect the employees as people. That resonated with me. As it is now, if someone becomes ill, they don't receive an income. Especially now, during wartime, I would like to believe that everyone can have a stable life if they work hard. But that is just my opinion about life. My idea may not necessarily be a good one. If you disagree with me, please do not hesitate to let me know."

He had the titles on all ID cards changed from "worker" to "employee."

In the end, some quit because they felt the monthly salary system created a lukewarm work environment, but some came back later to reconsider.

Around this time, the issue of a company merger arose.

The First Step toward Expansion

In the spring of 1943, there was talk of a merger with Yamato Kogaku Seisakusho (Yamato Optical Manufacturing Co., Ltd.), also located in Tokyo. The company had about 200 employees and manufactured binoculars, telescopes, surveying instruments, and so on.

According to Hidetaro Kaneko, an employee of Yamato Kogaku at the time, the company's facility stood alone in a field, just like Seiki Kogaku, as farmers were leading ox carts along an old highway of Nakasendo (a central highway during the Edo period). As the war progressed, the surrounding vegetable fields were gradually replaced with munitions factories, and Yamato Kogaku was converted to produce munitions. Seeking ties with the munitions industry, Shoei Seishi Co. Ltd. acquired Yamato Kogaku with the help of Yasuda Bank (later Mizuho Bank – Trans.), and Yasuda Bank brought to Mitarai a proposal to merge Yamato Kogaku with Seiki Kogaku, which had a similar business and scale. Mitarai thought it was a timely proposal and asked the board of directors to approve.

Despite some initial reservations, they eventually agreed and decided to absorb Yamato Kogaku at a board meeting held on June 15, 1943.

At the time, many industrial operations were being reorganized to support the war effort, while non-military industries were being closed under government guidance. In addition, many companies underwent mergers, with the aim of concentrating the capital of financial institutions and trading companies.

Given this trend, the merger of Seiki Kogaku and Yamato Kogaku was not at all unusual. However, corporate mergers always present challenges, including finding the right balance in executive and managerial personnel, maintaining employee work efficiency and compatibility, and managing capital. It was only natural that the leadership of both companies would have a spirited debate. Seiki Kogaku's hesitancy was understandable, especially given that it had only been in business for a short period of time and the company's foundations were still in the process of being solidified.

However, Mitarai had a spark of inspiration and conviction. "Without effort, there is no prosperity." This was the first step toward expansion.

On March 15, 1944, the acquisition of Yamato Kogaku was officially completed and it was renamed Seiki Kogaku Kogyo Itabashi Factory. The new company was capitalized at 1.75 million yen and had 350 employees at the Meguro Plant and 200 at the Itabashi Plant.

Fleeing Under Air Raids

With the merger complete and the confusion within the company under control, it seemed that the company had finally come together under Mitarai's leadership. However, things would soon change.

The first air raid warning in Tokyo was issued on March 5, 1942. In August 1944, a mass evacuation of school children began, and Seiki Kogaku, which had become a military-managed factory, was ordered to evacuate its plant. The first group of workers traveled to Maeda's hometown of Yamura, in Yamanashi Prefecture, at the end of 1944. The second group evacuated in April 1945, after the Tokyo Air Raid on March 9 and 10 in which 230,000 houses were destroyed and 120,000 people were killed or injured.

According to the memoir of Nobuo Terai, an employee at the time (currently living in Wakayama City), the optical equipment assembly team rented Mr. Maeda's *geta* (wooden clog) factory in the nearby village of Takara to assemble cameras. The team consisted of fourteen people, including seven young men and women from the local community. The seven employees from Tokyo and their families each rented a room in a farmhouse. Over the course of a month, the move began with a commuter pass from Toritsu Daigaku Station to Yamura.

Tokyo was bombed almost every day, and there were no vehicles available for moving. So everyone had to carry their belongings on their back. Terai's wife was seven months pregnant, so she only wanted to bring a tub. With a large *furoshiki* wrapping cloth on her back and a tub hanging from her neck in front of her big belly, she resembled Chindon-ya (a group of commercial performers). But this life-threatening relocation was no laughing matter.

Every day, 40 to 50 students from youth schools,*4 who remained in Tokyo were sent out to defend the factory. One of the students, Shigeru Shinagawa, recalled that during the air raids only one bomb fell near the company's premises.

Kumazo Nagata's Hospital in Mejiro was burned down in air raids on April 12 and 13, 1945. When an incendiary bomb hit the back of Seibo Hospital, where Mitarai used to work, he rushed to Nagata's home and said, "It's all over, you must evacuate." After that, Mitarai had his wife carry their baby on her back and evacuate to an acquaintance's house in Nanamagari-zaka in Kanagawa Prefecture, while he himself fled with the hospital nurses to the Musashi High School area, chased by fire.

Nagata himself had a physical disability and could not easily travel from place to place, so he remained alone in the hospital and left his fate to the heavens. Everything burned to the ground except for what he had put in an air-raid shelter, but Nagata survived. Mitarai Hospital was also burned down.

---

*4   Youth schools provided social education for young people who had graduated from elementary school, which was compulsory education at that time, and who were engaged in work without going on to secondary schools such as junior high schools, high school girls' schools, or vocational schools.

Wild Rocamboles, Silkworms, and Roasted Salt

Everyone was hungry.

Before Takeharu Ando joined the company in 1939, he was a dormitory student at the youth school. One day, he went to the dormitory head, Michitsura Ishihara to complain about the food in the cafeteria, which did not have enough rice in a bowl and contained too many soybeans. He was irritated by the air raids, and his dissatisfaction with the food made him go into a rage, but Ishihara, who was a big, burly man, somehow managed to calm him down. Shigeru Shinagawa also had a hard time going out on the night watch to defend the factory, but the best thing about being a night watchman was getting a puffed sweet potatoes.

However, what awaited the evacuees was not a company job, but days of labor to secure food for each day. "One gou and eight *shaku* (324 ml) of soybeans and two *shaku* (36 ml) of rice a day." The amount of food rationed in Yamura remains clearly in Ryoichiro Yamagata's memory even now, more than 30 years after the war. Yamagata (born in 1916) had worked for Tokyo Keiki (Tokyo Measuring Instruments) after graduating from Yokohama National College of Technology, and later joined Yamato Kogaku, becoming an employee of Seiki Kogaku after the merger.

The two *gou* (360 ml) of soybeans and rice were divided between breakfast, lunch, and dinner. On their days off, the evacuees would dig up yams.

They grated them and poured them over the boiled soybeans. They even dug up a school tennis court and planted daikon radish seeds and ate a bitter, pitted, pint-sized radish. In 1945, the schoolchildren, who had been mobilized to do labor at the same time as the evacuation, were unable to work, so they cleared the mountains and planted sweet potatoes. One of the ingredients for miso soup is sweet potato vines. They also grew wild spinach, which was used as a metaphor for poor food but was delicious.

Soon, the seasoning salt ran out. Someone lamented that without salt, they would all die. "Well, there lies the problem. What should we do?" A local man brought a lump of salt that had been burnt in Tokyo during the war, and that saved his life.

Morimasa Kaneko (born in 1916) also lived in Yamura. Once every three days, he would go to Tokyo to pick up barley and miso from the company (Seiki Kogaku). He would take the first train at 5:00 in the morning, when the train was not crowded, and arrive at the office at 10:00 a.m. On one occasion, he was bombed on his way home and didn't return to Yamura until the middle of the night. There was nothing to wear, so all the evacuees of the company made *geta* (wooden clogs) together. Whenever they tripped over a stone, they fell down. That was how much their physical strength had been drained. Kaneko lost all of his upper teeth due to dental abscess caused by malnutrition.

Unsure of what to do, Yamagata consulted with Ikeda, the plant manager. Ikeda asked an acquaintance at Nakajima Hikoki (Nakajima Aircraft Company) if they could get food by working on airplanes. When Ikeda consulted someone at Nakajima Hikoki that there were about 200 evacuees, including mobilized students, he was told that they would all bring machinery and food. Ikeda, feeling that it was a good idea, consulted with Mitarai, but Mitarai dismissed the idea, saying that it was outrageous to ask Nakajima Hikoki for machinery and food because they were getting work from Nippon Kogaku, and that Ikeda and other evacuees could not get food from them.

Even if they had wanted to work, they would not have been able to assemble the pieces because the materials were not available when they were needed or in sufficient quantity. The students also tried to avoid working because they think it would be a loss if they worked. They were reluctant to carry sand for concrete, so their managers promised them one cigarette for every cart of sand they delivered. The income from the factory was almost nothing, so there was no point in evacuating the area.

"Cut the pipe of the tripod of the enlarger at an angle, go to the graveyard, put it over the wild rocambole, turn it around, and pop it out from the other side."

The only vegetables that Tokunaga and the others who had evacuated to the village of Takara deep in the mountains, about 4 km from Yamura, could eat were wild rocamboles. The farmer they were staying with gave them boiled barley to eat but there was no salt to season it. They chose days when no air raids were expected, got up early in the morning, and went to Omori in Tokyo. There, they would collect seawater in large bottles and then get a little bit of rice from the town office. When they returned to Yamura, they would boil the water and cook the food.

Most of the employees who had evacuated to Yamura were too weak to do the work of assembling X-ray machines and cameras. Some even hurt themselves when they tried to carry their luggage.

Shoji Suzuki (born in 1913) was also at Takara at the time after joining the company only in the fall of 1944. "The locals have potatoes, barley, and a little rice, so they make porridge. We can hear them slurping it through the sliding doors. They don't have to slurp it, but they are nasty old women," he recalled. The corn was taken to the water mill in the village to be ground into flour, which was then kneaded and baked to make a kind of rice cake.

The employees were given rations of salt from the town office under the guise of making pickles together, which they licked, added to something like rice cake made of corn flour, or in dissolved dried wasabi seasoned with salt, and served as a side dish.

One of Katsuo Ando's children died of malnutrition, and Tokunaga made a coffin for him.

The farmers in Takara raised silkworms, and the sound of silkworms eating mulberry leaves sometimes kept the evacuees awake, but Suzuki thought the insects could be used as a source of protein. Once the threads are taken from the chrysalis, there should be no need for the rest, he thought.

Thinking it was better to cook them first, he tried boiling the silkworms. The head was somewhat firm, but the body was bloated and he couldn't season it, so he finally gave up trying to use it as food.

Once while Suzuki was traveling to Tokyo, someone on the crowded train tapped him on the shoulder. He turned around and saw that it was the company president, Mitarai. After chatting for a while, Mitarai asked Suzuki if he had brought his lunch with him. Suzuki replied that he did not. "You never know when or where an air raid will occur, so you have to take your lunch with you," Mitarai said.

Suzuki had been living on corn flour and didn't have money for lunch, but he couldn't say so. "I had a full meal this morning, and it's better to go light," he answered. After a while, Mitarai tapped Suzuki's shoulder again. "I have some food for lunch here. My wife went to a lot of trouble to make it for me. You should eat half of it." "No, it's OK," Suzuki said. "I don't mind skipping lunch. I'm young and healthy." Mitarai replied, "Young people are the ones who need to eat right."

Mitarai pulled out an old aluminum lunch box and began to eat while standing. Suzuki looked outside, hoping his stomach wouldn't growl. Then another tap. "Eat this," Mitarai said, leaving half of it neatly cut as if with a knife. "No, I'm full," Suzuki replied. "Don't lie to me," Mitarai said.

Now the people near Suzuki were looking at him, so he said "Thank you" and accepted the food. It was just brown rice topped with bonito flakes, but both were delicious after not having had either for such a long time. Suzuki was truly moved to tears. The mention of rice made everyone crazy about, as it was a difficult time to get it.

"I was deeply moved and thought that I would have no regrets if I followed him, and that I could help him realize his ideals, even if only a little." Suzuki was over 30 years old and Mitarai was in his mid-forties.

"We're Going to Lose the War."

Mitarai's family was also evacuated. The hospital was designated as a relief station, so he made his wife and children evacuate to an inn in Otsuki, Yamanashi Prefecture. On Saturdays, Mitarai would visit the evacuation site, where his children were waiting and crying with their mouths open. His oldest son Hajime (born in 1938, the year after the company was founded), who was still in elementary school, could hardly wait for his father's arrival, although he was more excited about the food he would bring than his father himself. They usually had *suiton* (a wheat flour dumpling dish), but when their father came, they were served rice. The women would get one serving and the men would get two. Later, his sisters used to bully Hajime because of their food grudge.

Instead of rice, they often ate grass stalks or bamboo bark wrapped with pickled plums and shiso.

In July 1945, charges were dropped against a member of the Yokohama Farmers' Union vigilante group who beat to death a worker who had stolen some potatoes. The decision was made because his actions were judged to be in self-defense (Iwanami "Chronological Table"). This incident symbolizes the how bad things were at the time.

Nobuo Terai wrote in his journal that he saw American B-29s flying in formation over Yamanashi, headed toward Tokyo, and in less than ten minutes the sky in the east turned red.

Mitarai's wife once saw a Japanese plane confront a B-29 but it was quickly shot down. The sight of the formation flying in the sky was so peaceful that it was hard to believe that they were returning from an air raid.

When Mitarai's eldest brother Nobuo, who was living in Oita Prefecture, learned that 30,000 Japanese troops had been defeated in the Mariana Islands on July 7, 1944, he thought, "This is it." They had no more planes, no more artillery, and their ships were being hit every day off Fukashima Island in Kamae. "We're going to lose the war." A man who was fishing for sea bream off the coast was hit by debris from the wing of a downed American plane, leaving a pool of blood inside his boat.

Around the same time, a nationalistic student who had been mobilized to work at the Mitsubishi Nagasaki Shipyard was shocked when he saw the actual conditions of the work site.

Ryuzaburo Kaku, born in Oita Prefecture, Japan, had graduated from Qingdao Middle School in Qingdao, facing Jiaozhou Bay, Shandong Province, China and enrolled in the Fifth High School in Kumamoto Prefecture in 1944. He did welding work on a secret military submarine where he was mobilized to work at Nagasaki Shipyard. Kaku had believed that Japanese science and technology were on the cutting edge, as evidenced by the battleships *Yamato* and *Musashi*, but when he arrived he saw that none of the large presses and rollers were in operation.

When he asked the factory staff why, he was told the machinery had been imported from England and no longer worked because they could not get replacement parts. Kaku was astonished. Even though Japan's technology was advanced, it was only good at making hulls and it lagged behind the enemy in the machinery industry, which was the foundation of Japan's technology. The Japanese government was calling for a hundred-year war, but Japan couldn't even make its own machinery. "We're going to lose," he concluded. "We will lose very soon."

But he kept this to himself.

August 15, 1945

And then August 15, 1945 came.

In March of the same year, Tomomasa Matsui (a former Shoei Seishi employee), who was a second class sailor at Chitose Airfield in Hokkaido, heard a recorded announcement from Emperor Hirohito that was broadcast on the radio.

They were supposed to be celebrating the completion of a runway. When they were told to gather together, he thought they were going to have a drink. He couldn't understand what the radio was saying, but some of the junior officers started crying and yelling, and others fled on horse-drawn wagons with sacks of rice, fearing that the Soviet army would soon come ashore. The situation quickly descended into chaos.

Yoshio Okada, who joined the company in 1939, was in Central China at the time. When he returned from a punitive expedition in China, he was told by the remaining soldiers that they had lost the war. The non-commissioned officers and others cried, but Okada was happy that he could return home early. He did not return home until a year later, malnourished from eating two meals of rice porridge a day.

Shigeru Ohnishi, who joined the company in 1939, was sent to a prisoner-of-war camp in Siberia and did not return to Japan until 1948.

"Is this the end of Seiki Kogaku?" Tokunaga wondered in Takara, as he struggled to hear the broadcast on his simple four-tube radio. He knew that Japan had lost and he thought that, somehow, this meant the end of the company, and the end of the road for himself as well.

Yamagata, in Yamura, was in training for a marching squad. The evacuees were all unsteady because they hadn't slept much due to the air raids. Yamagata went out on behalf of the employees to attend the marching squad, but he was sitting on the river bank, still woozy from the previous night's air raid. When called to assemble, he went to the place, then he was told to go home and listen to the radio. That evening, Japan's defeat was announced. Someone brought out a Japanese sword and slashed it against a pillar.

Suzuki, in Takara, cried because he never thought Japan would lose. Everyone who heard the broadcast cried. In fact, shortly before August 15, 1945, a woman visited a fortune teller in town. "All of Japan will soon speak softly, like the cries of mosquitoes," she was told.

Kaneko, in Yamura, had taken a train to Ryuo, one station away from Kofu Station, to get food with Maeda and the other, and heard the broadcast at a farmhouse. When the engineer learned of the defeat, he stopped the train at the station near his house and went home, leaving many passengers stranded.

Fortunately, Maeda knew how to get home. Unlike the other two, Kaneko had military experience and was a fervent nationalist. He felt desperate and said, "This is a big deal."

Maeda responded, "It is a pity that we lost, but there is another way to live from now on." Such a thing was completely inconceivable to Kaneko. He had always thought that the war would end with Japan as the victor, so he thought Maeda was disloyal. Kaneko felt that he was quite different from the others; he was just 29 years old.

Muneo Hirai, in Takara, wondered what would happen but was optimistic. "We've made it this far, so we can keep going. I won't be fired."

Shigeru Shinagawa, who was staying in the dormitory of a youth school in Tokyo, heard the broadcast in the yard of his office. He was so shocked that he invited two or three of his dormmates to go to the Imperial Palace to pray. He was deeply disappointed that Japan had lost.

The Mitarai family had almost run out of food at their evacuation site. If the war had lasted any longer, he might have lost half of his children.

Hajime, his eldest son, didn't understand the meaning of the broadcast. He just watched as everyone listened. All he felt was his empty stomach.

"We're Still Fighting."

The young people who joined the company after the war commiserated Japan's defeat in various places.

Ryuzaburo Kaku (age 20), who narrowly escaped the atomic bombing of Hiroshima on August 6, finally left his dormitory on August 14 after being summoned back to the shipyard. However, he was in no condition to work, and he first had to restore the foundry, using prisoners of war from both the British and Dutch armies. Each student oversaw about 20 people, who removed stones mixed in with the sand. This was continued for 15 days. The shipyard didn't let them hear the recorded announcement from Emperor Hirohito when it was broadcast on the radio.

However, Kaku knew that there had been some kind of broadcast, and rumors circulated that Japan had been defeated. Meanwhile, leaflets were posted stating that the Nagasaki Garrison of the Imperial Army would fight even if separated from the mainland, and soldiers with guns with swords were walking around. That night, rumors circulated that the Japanese had retaliated with a new type of bomb and Washington D.C. was reduced to ashes. Kaku and his fellow workers were again holed up in their dormitory from the 16th, as they were told they would be considered war criminals if they used prisoners of war as laborers.

He thought his life would be over when he was 20, but he suddenly brightened up and thought, "Oh, there are no more air raids, now I don't have to run to the shelter anymore." And he felt a strange sense of confidence that he had been right. While everyone else around him cried, Kaku did not. He was perhaps unique among his generation.

Hiroshi Ito (born in 1925), one year Kaku's senior, was in a similar place. He had graduated from high school in March 1945 and enrolled in the Department of Engineering Science (Aerospace) at the Second Faculty of Engineering (currently Faculty of Engineering) at the University of Tokyo in Chiba Prefecture. When he returned to his hometown of Nagoya for summer vacation, he heard a broadcast at a temple where he had been evacuated.

From the broadcast, he concluded that the "special bomb" in Hiroshima must have been an atomic bomb and that Japan could not continue to fight against such a weapon. "Soon, I will be able to study freely," he thought.

The next day, on the 16th, he returned to Chiba. His dormitory, which housed 300 students, was located in a potato field just in front of the school building. The head of the dormitory was a staunch pro-war man and had organized a rally to "fight till the end" at a dormitory students' convention on the thirteenth or the fourteenth. Now, as Ito walked from Chiba Station, he saw many students coming out of the dormitory. The aviation students were particularly hostile. "Japan has lost, but we will go underground and fight," they declared. They were afraid that if enemy forces moved into Japan, the engineering students might be killed, and since they would be forced to stop their research anyway, they had no choice but to do it in secret. Ito returned to the dormitory alone.

Hiroshi Kawaguchi (born in 1916) graduated in 1941 from the Department of Military Engineering at the Second Faculty of Engineering (currently Faculty of Engineering) at the University of Tokyo, the same faculty as Ito, and was commissioned as a lieutenant in the navy and assigned to the naval arsenal in Maizuru, Kyoto Prefecture. Until the air raids in the first week of August 1945, he had no feeling that Japan would be defeated, and thought, "We have to do it, we have to."

He even thought that the recorded announcement from Emperor Hirohito broadcast on the radio might have meant they should try harder. However, when he found out that it was in fact a surrender, he shed tears of regret with the other mobilized students. After the broadcast, they continued to work hard. The young men, still in high spirits, did not listen to their captain's orders and sailed away in a submarine. They took down the usual flag of war and wrote "*Hachiman Daibosatsu*" (Great Bodhisattva Hachiman) on a long white banner with a picture of a skeleton on it. Kawaguchi and his crew waved the Hinomaru (Japan's national flag) from the dock as they departed. However, they circled around and came back at midnight.

Shuichi Ando was born in 1922 and went to Manchuria as a student under the student mobilization order. The unit he was fighting in was defeated in Ganan, a town on the border of Manchuria and the Korean Peninsula, and he was captured and sent to Siberia.

Hayao Nakahara (born in 1930) was in his third year of junior high school. He was soon accepted into the Naval Academy, which he had long dreamed of attending, and before he knew it, he was on his way to Etajima in Seto Inland Sea.

Some were defeated days late.

Tetsuro Tamanuki (born in 1932) was on Karafuto (Southern Sakhalin), the southern half of a large island north of Hokkaido. Karafuto was occupied by Japan at the time. He was mobilized as a junior high student and drafted into military service, mowing grass to feed horses deep in the mountains. On August 8, Soviet troops rushed across the border. Believing that the Soviets would not enter the war, most Japanese troops had gone south, leaving Sakhalin poorly defended. The civil defense forces fought back, and it was not until August 18 that Tamanuki and the others learned of Japan's defeat. They were far from the fighting, but if Japan's defeat had been delayed for a week, the island might have suffered the same fate as Okinawa.

The military instructors had taught them that if the Soviets invaded, they should fight one on one and kill their enemy, and everyone was willing to do so. Because bamboo does not grow on Karafuto, the instructors told them they cut down a tree that resembled bamboo, made it into a spear, attached a sickle to the handle of a grass cutter, and told them to kill the infantry that would come after the tanks. Some of the older students died near the border.

Chapter 3

A Fresh Start, and a Dream of Becoming the World's Best

A Fresh Start, and a Dream of Becoming the World's Best

Decisions in the Midst of Confusion

"The time will come."

Mitarai took August 15 as such.

It was the recorded announcement from Emperor Hirohito broadcast on the radio (the Imperial Rescript on the Termination of the War), which Mitarai heard amidst the cicadas, that was the impetus for him to leave behind the era of subcontracted factories, which lasted from August 1937 to August 1945, and to take a bold step forward in the field of precision industry that Japan had long specialized in.

"We are keenly aware of the inmost feelings of all our subjects. However, it is according to the dictate of time and fate that we have resolved to pave the way for grand peace for all the generations to come by enduring the unendurable and suffering what is insufferable." – Emperor Hirohito, August 15, 1945

"The time will come."

What was it that resonated in the heart of Takeshi Mitarai, a man in his mid-forties amidst burnt ruins – the landscape that, one might say, is the starting point of the postwar history for the generations born before 1935? It was similar to the sense of liberation he felt when he first saw the wilderness of Hokkaido.

However, because there is no definitive record of the events that took place after August 15 until the company was officially re-incorporated, it is difficult to accurately reconstruct the events of that time.

The situation in Japan was in flux and the government was in turmoil. It is quite possible that the people interviewed for this book misremembered things, given the situation at the time. Even if a company's policy had been established, it might not have been accurately conveyed down to the lowest-level staff. It is also unclear when and in what form General MacArthur and the General Headquarters of the Allied Powers (GHQ), the new rulers who replaced the military, communicated their intentions to companies regarding the resumption of production at Japanese plants.

August 15 was a Wednesday, but Mitarai was in Yamura. He gathered everyone on the grounds of the Yamura School of Commerce and Industry to hear the Emperor's recorded announcement on the radio, and announced that the factories in Yamura and Takara would be closed that day. Mitarai immediately went to Tokyo and, after consulting with Michitsura Ishihara, decided on the temporary closure of the company.

According to Shigeru Shinagawa, many of the employees who were farmers in the rural areas returned to their hometowns, while about 10% of the employees remained behind to maintain the factories.

A few days later, all the evacuees were gathered in Yamura, and Mitarai appeared with Ishihara and told them that he had closed the head office. Ryoichiro Yamagata recalled him saying, "We will temporarily close the head office, and we will decide who will stay and who will not." Then, Yamagata and Ishii, the general affairs manager, put circles and crosses on the list of the employees.

Mitarai took this step because the monthly salary system that he had implemented based on his beliefs was a failure. Because workers were paid even if they took a day off, many of them would take a day off to go shopping for food. This experience led him to question his belief that people are inherently good. By suspending the company's operations, he wanted to start over with a group of honest, hard-working people.

Tokunaga thought that they would eventually resume producing cameras when Mitarai said, "Let's meet again when we can resume production." In the meantime, he went home to Nagano Prefecture.

Suzuki remained in Takara to return the machinery and other items that had been brought to the evacuation site back to Tokyo. It was not until September that he returned to his wife's parents' home in Hiroshima Prefecture.

Terai's wife gave birth on August 28, and she didn't leave the evacuation site until mid-September. Before she departed, she ate the sweet potatoes she had planted when she came to the village, which by now had grown to the size of his thumb.

What were the Allied forces doing at the time?

August 28: Allied advance troops arrived in Atsugi. GHQ was established in Yokohama.

August 30: MacArthur arrived in Atsugi.

September 2: GHQ ordered the total suspension of munitions production.

September 7: The Engineering Bureau of the Ministry of Commerce and Industries informed Nihon Shashin Kanko Zaiyo Tosei Co., Ltd. (Japan Photosensitive Materials Control Corporation) of the GHQ directive.

September 8: U.S. troops began to move into Tokyo by jeeps.

September 11: GHQ arrested 39 war criminals, including General Tojo.

September 15: The Hibiya Dai-ichi Seimei Sougo Building was designated as GHQ Headquarters.

September 22: The "Initial U.S. Policy toward Japan after the Surrender" was formally announced.

September 25: The GHQ Memorandum on the Operation of Manufacturing Industries was released.

In September, the Hattori Clock Shop and Toshiba Building in Ginza were confiscated by the Occupation Forces for use as a PX (post exchange), and the streets were quickly flooded with black market goods. Among these items, Japanese cameras were very popular with the Occupation Forces.

Terai returned to Tokyo and stayed at the dormitory, but a few days later the Occupation Forces arrived to tour the camera assembly plant. He was told by the company to hide all the cameras they had made while they were in the evacuation zone. Specifically, he was to put the cameras in a wooden box and bury them in the air-raid shelter of the dormitory. The cameras may still be there today.

(The item on the previous September 7 regarding the Engineering Bureau of the Ministry of Commerce and Industries is based on a description on page 589 of Konishiroku Shashin Kogyo's 1973 book *One Hundred Years with Photography*. The directive included the following: "Factories subject to the Munitions Company Law that manufacture air weapons, naval vessels, gun powder, liquid fuel, and their important materials and parts, as well as controlled factories, must carefully manage their equipment and materials. However, it is permissible to use the equipment and materials of plants that do not fall under this category for the manufacture of civilian products, and it is also permissible for plants that have traditionally manufactured both military and civilian products to manufacture civilian products using materials other than military supplies." Konishiroku, which "had been spending its days helplessly since the end of the war," applied to convert its factory to produce civilian supplies and resumed business activities on October 1.)

"We Will be the World's Best"

On October 1, 1945, with all 156 employees gathered in the lens room of the Meguro Plant, Mitarai announced that Seiki Kogaku Kogyo would resume operation as a camera company.

"It is a great pleasure for me to see you all here under peaceful skies, having passed through the unspeakable hardships of the war, air raids, and evacuations. I am sure that all of you must have rubbed shoulders with each other and rejoiced to see your colleagues, superiors, and subordinates in good health. However, there are those who lost their young lives at the front, those who lost their parents in air raids, and those who lost their children because they did not have enough to eat. I would like to pray for their souls once again.

"On reflection, when I think about us and our families who have gathered here, we all have been busy trying to secure food on a daily basis, and we are forced to live with only the clothes on our backs. I am sure that we are filled with anxiety about what will happen to Japan in the future and what we should do. All of the big business leaders who reigned over the Japanese economy as *zaibatsu* [financial cliques] are looking to the left and to the right and are in a panic. The leaders of our country, who should be guiding the people, are themselves lost. They were so overbearing during the war, but when I look at them today, I can't help but laugh at how they have changed.

"So what should we do at this time? It is true that Japan lost. We lost miserably. We were devastated. But we lost in terms of quantity.

"When American officers came to us for cameras, they all said, 'These are wonderful,' 'These are very beautiful,' 'I can imagine that something like this was made in Japan because the Zero fighter aircraft is really excellent. It is a marvel that Japan was able to create something like that. And it's no wonder that they can produce such a high-end camera, which could be called the heart of the precision industry.'

"I was moved by their words. I still am. We lost the war, but not due to a lack of brainpower. I am very determined. We will never be defeated.

"Many companies are staying alive by making pots and pans and building bicycles. Some have suggested that we do the same. However, you don't need a brain to make pots and pans. Also, Japan, with its limited natural resources, cannot continue to rely solely on pots and pans forever.

"The Americans are praising our technical ingenuity. The camera, which requires fewer materials, is a perfect product for Japan to produce. If we grit our teeth and continue our research efforts, we will eventually be the best in the world with our magnificent cameras. If this were key industries, the government would help us. But it's not, so we have to help ourselves. And that is the only way for us to survive. If you agree with me, please join me. I will consider you my comrades and friends. Let us work together, everyone, hand in hand."

At this moment, Mitarai must have given up his career as a doctor once and for all. If the hospital had not been destroyed by air raids, or if the old Japanese ruling system had not collapsed in defeat, his medical practice could have continued, and Seiki Kogaku might have been lost to history among the confusion of the postwar period, without ever growing beyond a small factory.

By deciding to pursue their own path and focusing on the camera business, Mitarai set the ideological foundation of Canon as a technology-driven manufacturer for decades to come.

One *Sho of Sake* per Contract

However, ideas and dreams tend to be realized only through a series of trivial and prosaic details. The reality is that Seiki Kogaku was extremely poor, and the postwar period was a time of "thievery."

During the war, the white wax used for gluing lenses was rationed, and the company was careful to preserve as much as possible because no one knew when they would be able to get more. Only a handful of employees knew about the company's supply and they took precautions to guard it. That's because power outages were a common occurrence due to electricity restrictions, and since white wax could be used to make candles, it was often used as barter for food. So many other things were stolen that Yamagata had to ask Mitarai to instruct the employees to stop stealing.

Yamagata was tasked with installing the machinery and equipment that had been evacuated to the Meguro Plant. First, he needed gravel for concrete, and considered buying gravel from the miners at the Tama River, but the Occupation Forces were also mining there so he could only buy gravel in between. A driver of a gravel truck told him, "I'm a government employee. I get paid the same even if I do your work."

In the end, it was decided that each contract would be for one *sho* (about 1.8 liters) of *sake*, and with the *sake* that Mitarai and Ishihara had rationed, Yamagata was able to use about three *sho*. For Yamagata, who loved to drink, exchanging *sake* for gravel was the most painful thing he ever did. This was around the end of 1945.

Around the same time, four employees transferred from Nippon Kogaku. One of them was Yoshiharu Sago (born in 1914), who had joined Nippon Kogaku in 1935. He had been designing periscopes for submarines, but he was informed by telegram that he would be joining Seiki Kogaku due to downsizing after the war. At Seiki Kogaku, his job was to design the parts for the camera body, which were called 'hardware' in this industry. Since his house was close by, he walked to work in clogs and had his boxed lunch delivered by his children. When it was cold, he placed a potbelly stove on the creaking floor and cut logs to burn for warmth.

From October to November of 1945, many people who would later play important roles in the company, including Shunji Wako, Masanori Seki, Hidehiko Taguchi, and Masana Kuroki, were transferred from Nippon Kogaku. This reflects the enthusiasm that Mitarai had for re-launching the company.

Then, in January 1946, Hiroshi Kawaguchi, an engineer who had been working at the naval arsenal in Maizuru, Kyoto Prefecture, joined the company. Traffic was bad, with cars running on firewood burned in a furnace at the bottom of the car, and the windows and seats of the train, which had been burned out in an air raid, had been replaced with wooden boards. For these reasons, he decided to look for a job within walking distance of his house, and a relative introduced him to Mitarai. When they met, he had the impression that Mitarai was a very kind and caring person.

During the war, the ceiling panels in the factory in Meguro, Tokyo were still removed to prevent incendiary bombs from burning the building, which allowed the wind to blow in and dust to collect. Now it was winter, so they burned leaves and wood chips in oil cans to stay warm. There was not enough newspaper and their nostrils became blackened.

Kawaguchi was assigned to the newly established Manufacturing Engineering Department, which consisted of a manager, one young employee, and Kawaguchi. Their first job was to install window glass. They cut glass that had been removed or broken during the war into strips with a glass cutter and tried to fit them into the windows. They had no idea about what to do without any machines.

The actual work involved centering the lathe with a level and kneading cement to set it in place. The lathe used a belt to change the speed of rotation, so Kawaguchi had to go up to the ceiling to hang the belt on the step-wheel.

The assembly of cameras resumed around February 1946. The cameras were called "J-type" cameras, but in essence, were assembled from ready-made parts, leading to strange cameras, including one with a viewfinder but not a rangefinder. According to Shuji Araki (né Tokunaga), the first cameras that actually sold were made in May or June of 1946, while Kawaguchi noted that they were making two cameras per month in June.

A service station was established in Ginza, and Shigeru Shinagawa, a former student at the youth school, was dispatched there in October 1946. Products were sold, but they were delivered in batches to the Central Purchasing Office (CPO) of the U.S. Army, which had seized the Shibusawa Warehouse in Tokyo. From there, they were distributed to PXs in various regions.

Kinji Kikuchi, who joined the company in 1950, was immediately put in charge of sales. Every day, he checked the lenses that were delivered from the factory in backpacks, accepted them, and shipped them out to customers. He went to the CPO each day to get orders from the U.S. Army. If the order was not filled when the name was called, it would be canceled, so he would pack up in the morning and wait patiently. If they took the order form to the bank, they could use it as collateral and cash it in. Deliveries were made using the only three-wheeled motor tricycle available at the time.

This means that no products had been produced for at least six months since the company re-launched. So, how did they survive during that time?

"Please Give Me Chewing Gum."

Hyozo Sakurai, who joined the company in 1945, went around recruiting people as a member of the General Affairs Section. He asked people who had previously worked for the company to rejoin, but most of them refused, saying, "We can't work for a salary we can't afford to eat."

According to Hiroshi Kawaguchi, "It seems that the company sold rather expensive items with the materials they had on hand and used the proceeds to cover their salaries. With a starting salary of 170 yen, we could not afford to eat, but we had to live on with that amount of money."

Yosiyuki Hayashi, born in 1913, transferred from Shoei Seishi to Yamato Kogaku and then joined Seiki Kogaku. "The salary had increased at places that made pots and pans. We made cameras, so our wages were low. There was a big gap in wages. The president often persuaded us that we should grit our teeth and do what needed to be done. However, even if we wanted to hire someone, they would refuse when they heard about the salary. We had a lot of trouble getting new people."

Masanori Seki (born in 1920), who transferred from Nippon Kogaku, also thought about quitting several times because of the low pay. "All I can do to make a living is to sell my possessions. There doesn't seem to be a future for me."

Tomomasa Matsui (born in 1917), who returned to the company in November 1945, was in charge of the accounting department. To cover the payroll, he had to sell the company's automobiles, X-ray machines, and sometimes even machine tools. When he went to the bank to borrow money, they asked him, "Is it even possible to make and sell cameras nowadays? Wouldn't it be better to make pots and pans?" To borrow money, he had to submit a list of items that he would sell to pay back the loan.

When Matsui was asking for a loan of 200,000 yen at the bank, it was nothing compared to the larger companies who were inquiring about loans for 10 million yen.

When he finally got the money and went outside, he found a bunch of kids clinging to an American soldier and begging for chewing gum. Matsui was annoyed. As an elementary school student, the first English that Hajime Mitarai learned was "Please give me chewing gum." The English phrase had spread among the children, and Hajime benefited from it.

The company survived in part by starting a few side businesses. One of these, Akatsuki Musen (Akatsuki Radio), was created in October 1945. Mitarai saw that radio was the only source of information and entertainment. Fukutaro Tsuji (born in 1921) had joined Seiki Kogaku in 1939 but left to work for another company during the postwar holidays, but within a week he received a notice from Seiki Kogaku that he would be coming to work for the company, and after much hesitation, he returned to his old home in October 1945. His job was to create the articles of incorporation for Akatsuki Radio and to establish the company with a capital of 195,000 yen. There was a general affairs manager above him, but Tsuji also oversaw accounting as the manager of the miscellaneous section. Mitarai concurrently served as president.

Since there was a shortage of 5 to 6 million radios nationwide, the business temporarily boomed and the number of employees grew to 200. The machinery and equipment were disposed of from the military, and the products were delivered to the radio control company, a rationing company, at the official market price. The price for a standard four-tube radio was 42.50 yen. Since it was not possible to make a profit at the normal rate, the company would also sell it on the black market for 500 yen. The exchange rate with rice was also good, and one radio could net more than one to (about 18 liters) of rice. Due to inflation, the cost of materials changed every day, and a rectification plate that cost 12 yen could be sold for 80 yen in Kanda, Tokyo. Eventually, GHQ forced the company to close, and money once again became tight. Tsuji sold the remaining 1,000 radios, carrying them on his back all the way to the snowy Tohoku region in northeastern Japan. Tsuji would spend a month in bed recovering from exhaustion after he had found new jobs for the female employees and tied up all the loose ends.

There is one thing Tsuji still feels sorry for Mitarai all these years later. When Tsuji asked for help because he could not pay his employees' salaries, Mitarai brought him 150,000 yen wrapped in a white handkerchief and said, "Take this and pay them," but Tsuji could not pay him back.

Kashiwa Yakugyo (Kashiwa Pharmaceutical) was also established around the same time, but this was related to his friend Fumio Otsuka from the preparatory course at Hokkaido Imperial University. Otsuka was a section chief of the Medical Bureau of the Army Ministry during the war, and was looking for postwar employment opportunities for others who had worked in the Bureau. Mitarai himself had a desire to produce medicine that was not yet on the market, and eight former army medical officers (former majors) joined the company. In addition, Saio Mitsui, who joined the company in April 1946, doubled as plant manager and head of the materials department.

The company built a facility to cultivate lactobacilli as an intestinal regulator, and the product was well received, but it was an equipment industry, and there was no plan or money to pay for it. Also, the pharmacist quit, and the company dissolved around the same time as Akatsuki Radio.

Although Mitarai had created these side businesses to make money during an emergency situation, neither were profitable, and he only heard reports about their operations, realized it was premature to diversify the company's business, and decided to dissolve them.

"Deficits for Households, Businesses, and the Nation"

In 1947, the company was still struggling.

In March, a young man who had graduated from a vocational school entered the company as a stopgap measure because it was close to his home and because it was difficult to find a job elsewhere. "I'll be happy if I can get a job anywhere," he thought. "I don't know when I'm going to get out of the company, so I'll just go somewhere else sooner or later." He was surprised to find that the glass factory had such a low ceiling that he could hardly hold his head up, and the machinery and equipment were covered in rust. But everyone worked diligently and he was paid on time.

Eiji Hashimoto (born in 1922), a survivor of the Philippine front who opened a camera store in Tokyo that year, recalled, "At that time, there was a difference between those who were so despondent that they stopped caring and those who were so desperate that they worked as hard as they could." Later, he would become the president of Nihonbashi Camera Sales Co., which had close ties to Canon.

Before the war, he worked for Murakami Shokai as an apprentice but was unable to return to his job when he came back to Japan after the war.

His only customers were from the Occupation Forces. He rented two *tsubos* (around 6.6 m²) from a man who had a store in the area that sold kelp and other non-controlled goods. Much of the area around the store had burned down, Tokyo Station was visible, and only the department stores Shirokiya and Takashimaya had survived.

He handled only British, American, and German products. Cameras that were bartered were acquired from brokers (middlemen). Most of them were German-made: Carl Zeiss, Rollei, and Leica. He also sold Kodak Retina. Inflation quickly increased the price. He was unmarried but worked hard to support his family.

In the Philippines, the grim reaper was right beside him. He was one of only two survivors from his unit. When he rolled up his right sleeve, you could see the mangled flesh of his forearm. He had been hit by a bomb and carried on a stretcher by a medic, who turned around and never came back. Two hours later, his unit was wiped out. He was unaware of Japan's defeat until he descended the mountain in mid-September.

Business was good at the tiny two-*tsubo* store. The rent of 100 yen a day was hard to pay, especially for such a small space, but inflation made it a little easier. Eventually, he created a a small factory manufacturer and exported products through the British company Jardine Matheson (see later in Chapter 4), but he stopped production in 1955.

"You can't choose to live or die, and you don't know what the future holds, so you have to live by the stars." This was Hashimoto's philosophy.

The subtitle of the "Report on the Actual State of the Economy" (the first "Keizai Hakusho" [Economic White Paper]), which came out in July of that year, was "Deficits for Households, Businesses, and the Nation."

Unionization and Incentive Pay

Postwar society was undergoing a massive change.

The Emperor's visit to MacArthur on September 27, a little more than a month after Japan's surrender, heralded the changes that were to follow. On

October 6, the Special Higher Police was abolished; Kyuichi Tokuda, Yoshio Shiga, and other members of the Japanese Communist Party were released from prison; the Yomiuri Shimbun newspaper was involved in a labor dispute at the end of October (President Matsutaro Shoriki resigned in December); on November 6, a proclamation ordering the dissolution of the *zaibatsu* (financial cliques) was issued; and on December 9, agrarian reform was instituted. On December 22nd, the Labor Union Law was promulgated and went into effect on March 1 of the following year.

On May 1, 1946, the first May Day events in 11 years was held. 500,000 people gathered at the Imperial Palace Square. Two days later, the prosecution began its opening arguments in the International Military Tribunal for the Far East. On May 12, Setagaya Ward residents held a 'Give us rice' demonstration to Miyagi Prefecture. On May 19, representatives of May Day for Foodstuffs (officially known as the People's Convention for the Acquisition of Rice), staged a sit-in in the Prime Minister's official residence. In 1946, there were 17,200 unions (4.93 million workers) and 622 strike actions (510,000 participants), compared with just 509 unions (380,000 workers) and 95 strike actions (35,000 participants) the previous year.

In July 1946, the Seiki Kogaku employees' union was formed at a time when the labor movement was becoming militant, and Mitarai became concerned. Mitarai believed that a company should be composed of labor, capital, and management and that it would be dangerous if any one of the three was not in harmony with the others. Although he thought the formation of a union was "premature," he recognized that the times were changing and concluded that it would be wrong to fight it.

At the same time, it was fortunate that the core of the union's membership consisted of employees who had joined the company in its early days and had endured the wartime hardships. Matsui, the first union chairman, was the head of the accounting section, Morimasa Kaneko was one of the two vice chairmen, and Ryoichiro Yamagata and Shoji Suzuki were among the six permanent committee members who drafted the founding documents.

Some complained that they couldn't afford to buy food with their current wages and suggested going on strike to demand higher wages. Suzuki's proposal was as follows.

"Workers must unite and defend their interests. However, it is not enough to simply fight against the capitalists. It is meaningless if the workers do not prosper together with the company, and it is equally meaningless if the company collapses and only the union remains. Therefore, the issue is the distribution of profits. Labor and management are united in the pursuit of profits. We will prosper together with the company."

The Seiki Kogaku union did not join the national organization and subsequently changed its name to the Employees' Union.

To motivate workers, an incentive system was introduced at the suggestion of Yamagata and others who were familiar with the spirit of craftsmanship in the field. Many workers felt that they would not be able to make a living if things continued as they were, and this system was the only way to increase wages and make the company more profitable.

As a result, everyone's salary increased visibly month by month. Incentive pay was given at mid-month, and the monthly salary was paid at the end of the month. The mid-month portion grew each month and everyone worked very hard. "The union did not have to tell management to raise their salaries. It was a good policy," said Susumu Tazawa.

The administrative department calculated the ratio of incentive pay to the main salary, and the average of the Itabashi and Meguro Plants was used as the basis for the main salary (according to Tomomasa Matsui).

Mitarai himself said, "The times have changed. Before, the *zaibatsu* (financial cliques) had the upper hand, but now they have been broken up. Let's be diligent in getting there, as a technology company, without any bare bones and without anything else."

They were well aware that although the government would take care of the major industries such as steel and electricity, no one would care if a camera company went bankrupt. Matsui, the union president, said, "No one will do anything, even if this factory collapses. If we don't do it, no one will take care of us. But we have the skills. Let's work hard and make a profit."

"You'll see."

The world would not weep if a camera company went bankrupt. Indeed, financial institutions were originally reluctant to move into the camera business. They felt it was too risky. A Fuji Bank representative often asked Mitarai if he was sure they could make a profit producing cameras.

This was also a concern during the prewar fundraising for the establishment of the company. Before the war, Mitarai could still make a living as a doctor, but after the war, Mitarai had reached a point where he could no longer retreat. Did he really have a chance?

At a dinner party in 1947 to commemorate the 10th anniversary of the company's founding, to which outside parties were invited, Mitarai made his determination known.

"I have been with you for the past ten years since the establishment of our company. Thanks to your support, I think we have finally emerged from the period of confusion. You may laugh, but we are now doing our best to "defeat

Leica." Right now, we are not even close, but I am sure that one day we will be able to achieve this goal. I firmly believe that there is no other way for our country to survive than to compete with the rest of the world with our brains and export products made using our brains."

The gathered guests could not believe their ears when they heard Mitarai say the words "defeat Leica." People thought, "What kind of nonsense is this?" In fact, Masao Nagaoka, then president of Nippon Kogaku (and son of the physicist Hantaro Nagaoka), who was present at the time, is said to have remarked, "He talks like that, but how can he do such a thing? He is a funny guy." This was around the time that Matsui was calling on union members at Seiki Kogaku to "catch up with Nippon Kogaku in terms of salary."

There was nothing strange about Mitarai's beliefs. Nor were Nagaoka's beliefs mistaken, either. If Nagaoka had uttered Mitarai's words, they would have been true, but this was during the period when Seiki Kogaku still bought almost all of its lenses from Nippon Kogaku. According to the book *Forty-Year History of Nippon Kogaku Kogyo*, Seiki Kogaku purchased 950 lenses from the company in 1946 and 1,000 lenses in 1947. This was also a time when Nippon Kogaku employees still had a sense of what their parent company was like before the war.

Later, Mitarai learned of Nagaoka's comment from someone else, and he thought, "We'll see." It was in March of the following year, 1948, that Seiki Kogaku stopped buying lenses from Nippon Kogaku.

It is difficult to predict what the relationship between certain individuals will produce. Before World War II, when Mitarai became president, Hideo Araki of Nippon Kogaku was a friend of Mitarai's older brother, Kameta (surname changed to Takabayashi, now deceased). Both had studied law at the

University of Tokyo and worked for Mitsubishi Electric. Kameta had asked Araki look after Mitarai when he became president, and Araki had supported Mitarai from behind the scenes (based on Mitarai's own words).

In May 1946, Araki became president of Nippon Kogaku, but he was soon expelled from public office and resigned from the company in January of the following year. If Araki had remained president, it is doubtful whether Seiki Kogaku would have taken up the challenge of starting full-scale in-house production of lenses a mere three years after the war. The company's progress as a leading manufacturer would have been even slower.

Accordingly, this episode illustrates how one person's beliefs, however ridiculous they may seem from the outside, can be a driving force to change reality when they are unleashed with confidence.

However, to realize the ideal, it is essential to make a series of daily and practical efforts. The development of Mitarai's measures from 1947 to the beginning of the 1960s is quite remarkable.

Katakana Company Name and Dance

August 15 came.

But it was not in 1945. It was in 1947, at a meeting of the board of directors, Mitarai suddenly said, " 'Seiki Kogaku' does not work in the international market. Since we are selling Canon cameras, I think we should change the name of the company to Canon Camera.

American soldiers often called saying, "Canon, Canon," and although Seiki Kogaku Kogyo was thought to have more weight as a company name (at least, it was felt that way at the time), "Canon" was much easier to remember. The main objection came from outside the company. Ryosaku Konagaya (who joined the company from Nippon Kogaku in December 1945) had difficulty registering the company name because there was no precedent for a company name to be registered in katakana, the set of Japanese characters often used to write words of foreign origin.

Tokyo Tsushin Kogyo (Tokyo Telecommunications Engineering Corporation), which was established in May 1946, was renamed Sony two years later; Hayakawa Electric became Sharp in 1970; and Takachiho Seisakusho, which was established in 1919, became Olympus Optical in 1949. Nichi-Doku Shashinki Shoten (Japan-Germany Camera Company), which was established in 1928, became Chiyoda Kogaku Seiko and then Minolta in 1962. Nippon Kogaku Kogyo and Konishiroku Shashin Kogyo, both of which have long histories, show no signs of change and maintain the appearance of long-established companies. (As of 2024, these companies are named Nikon Corporation and Konica Minolta, Inc., respectively – Trans.)

Such a change may not seem like a big deal now, but at the time, it was a decision that was a cut above the rest. In another surprise, Mitarai learned ballroom dancing at the end of 1945 or 1946.

When a dance school opened in Jiyugaoka, Tokyo, Mitarai decided to take dance lessons, bringing all his family members. Mitarai thought that he might have a chance to meet Americans sooner or later, and that they would understand each other through dancing even if they did not understand each other's language.

At first glance, the company may have appeared to be America-oriented, but its quick rebuilding after the war and the new company name show that it was confidently charting its own path.

"With Us in Our Joys and Our Sorrows."

At that time, Mitarai had an idea about *naniwabushi* (a genre of traditional popular music) being very popular on the radio.

"Japanese people today are looking for a sense of moral obligation and humane feelings."

At the time, Canon was still little more than a collection of workers from various companies and backgrounds. One group had been making cameras by hand since the prewar days of Seiki Kogaku Kogyo. After the war, a group from Nippon Kogaku joined the company. And then there were the engineers from the military. Furthermore, the prewar group included people from Yamato Kogaku, who had a different spirit compared with those who had started at Seiki Kogaku. One of Mitarai's challenges after the war was to figure out how to lead such a mixed group.

In addition, postwar society was rife with blood-chilling incidents.

Forty-year-old Yoshio Kodaira raped and murdered seven women between 1945 and 1946. In March 1946, the kabuki actor Nizaemon Kataoka and his family members, five in total, were murdered by a writer living in the house over a food grudge. In 1948, a couple from Kotobuki San-in in Ushigome, Tokyo were found to have murdered 103 infants since 1944 and had been collecting their child support and rations. On January 26, 1948, 13 employees of the Shiinamachi branch of Teikoku Ginko (Imperial Bank) were poisoned.

Many who worked as military subcontractors during the war had amassed huge fortunes by diverting military supplies during the anarchy of the postwar period. One cannot be blamed if they thought it was foolish to work diligently — there was no work to be done. Around 1942, there were around 40,000 street prostitutes in the six major cities in Japan, and the annual number of vagrants in Tokyo exceeded 11,000.

In January of 1947, the company decided on guidelines for regular salary increases, and in November, two months after the company changed its name to Canon Camera, a ceremony was held to celebrate the 10th anniversary of the company's founding and to honor long-time employees. In the fall of 1948, the company held a special party, to which all employees and their families were invited to receive awards for their many years of service, followed by a performance at a theater, which became a regular event held at the Teigeki (Imperial Theatre), Meijiza, and Kabukiza theaters.

In January 1950, the first housing association was established. At that time, company housing programs were prevalent, and the accountants thought, "Don't be ridiculous." Even if an individual builds a house, the interest will not be treated as an expense. No write-offs are allowed. But with company housing, both were permitted. And in case of an emergency, the property could be sold. That would have been a good argument, but Mitarai had a different idea.

"Everyone should own their own house. Let's form a housing association. Each one of you should make an investment for this purpose. Let's think of it as a savings account and participate in it. Then, as a company, we can borrow money from the bank and sell the land to everyone."

The term "familialism" is associated with prewar feudalistic patriarchal tyranny, and it is fair to say that it had a negative connotation during the rise of postwar democracy. Mitarai dared to take up the word and call it "new familialism." Owning your own house and trips to theatres were the embodiments of this new system.

It can be said that the idea of "sharing joys and sorrows together" was also included, and the company tried to realize this idea of mutual support in the form of a housing cooperative association. Company housing is a form of dependence on the company, whereas home-ownership is a form of self-sufficiency.

While these humble and mundane efforts continued to accumulate, several technological innovations were quietly but surely being promoted within the company.

"Scattered and Reunited"

On March 1, 1948, two engineers from the Navy — Suzukawa and Agari — joined the company. Both had been approached by Hiroshi Kawaguchi, also from the Navy. As mentioned earlier, Kawaguchi's first job after joining the company in January 1946 was to install window glass, but his first true engineering job was to design a jig for drilling holes in the back cover of the camera.

The process of making cameras was slow, and Kawaguchi was surprised to see such a large difference between the drawings and the finished product. The drawings did not include tolerances, so there was no way to know what would be produced, and each component was handmade and thus not interchangeable. No one knew how the parts would fit together or when the product would be ready. To turn the process into a daily production, it was necessary to revise the blueprints and standardize the way things were made.

Kawaguchi thought that the company needed to hire a skilled engineer to further develop the company, and advised the factory manager, Wako.

Hiroshi Suzukawa was born in Aichi Prefecture in 1916. After graduating from high school, he enrolled in the Department of Technology of Arms at the Tokyo Imperial University in 1937, the year Seiki Kogaku was established. The following year, he became a Navy-commissioned student, and upon graduation in 1940, he joined the Navy as a lieutenant. In 1943, he was responsible for technical repairs at the Penang Island base in Malaysia, and at the end of the same year, he returned to the Kure Arsenal and was placed in charge of designing the Kaiten, a suicide attack weapon.

After the war, when he was in his second year of designing camera shutters at Nihon Koki Seisakusho, he was approached by Hiroshi Kawaguchi, who was born in 1916 but was his junior at university (also in the same Department of Technology of Arms, which was renamed the Department of Precision Engineering after the war). Suzukawa was also a Navy-commissioned student and majored in torpedoes, the same as Kawaguchi.

Because he had been involved in shutter production, he had acquaintances at various camera companies and could have worked anywhere he wanted but decided to join Canon after meeting Mitarai. At the time, he thought he could build a life-long career based on what he had learned at university. He wanted to work in a cutting-edge field where he could make use of his knowledge of precision technology and where it would lead in the future. This was just before he turned 32 years old.

When Mitarai met with Suzukawa, he thought the conversation would last an hour at most. However, Suzukawa asked so many questions one after another, such as "What are your plans for the future" and "What is your camera policy," that Mitarai wasn't sure how to answer them.

By chance, Yoshiya Agari appeared in the president's office, where the two were talking. Born in 1917, he had graduated from Kiryu Technical High School (now Gunma University). He was also a Navy-commissioned student, one term ahead of Kawaguchi and a classmate of Suzukawa's.

He worked with Kawaguchi in Maizuru, Kyoto Prefecture for three years on torpedoes. After being transferred to Kure in Hiroshima Prefecture, he went to the south, where he was interned, and when he returned to Japan in 1946, he was malnourished, nothing but skin and bones. He went to Takasaki, Gunma Prefecture and reported to Kawaguchi for demobilization. It was there that Kawaguchi approached him about joining the company. Because of restrictions on moving to Tokyo, he was not able to join right way, but when he finally arrived, he was reunited with Suzukawa.

Thus, as if destined by fate, the old acquaintances were together again. With the aim of standardizing the drawings, a study group was formed with five members, according to Agari's memory. In addition to Agari, Kawaguchi, and Suzukawa, there was also Masanaka Koyama and Rentaro Uchida (nephew of Saburo Uchida), who had also been commissioned by the Navy.

Because former military personnel were banned from holding public office, they could not become union officers, and GHQ had prohibited meetings of several people, so they gathered only after regular hours and voluntarily worked overtime. Because they did this in secret, it is said that the company's upper management did not know much about what these engineers from the Navy were doing. However, it was a blessing in disguise that the people involved with torpedoes were gathered in one place, given that "torpedoes are top-notch precision equipment, and their internal structure is far more sophisticated than that of cameras," according to Agari. Thus, it can be said that Mitarai was in good hands, and his dream of defeating Leica attracted top talent. Shuji Araki (né Tokunaga), who had been with the company since before the war, still remembers Suzukawa telling him after he joined the company, "Let's make drawings with limits on them."

Joining this group was Hiroshi Ito, for whom the end of the war represented the opportunity to study freely.

He graduated from both the same high school and the same university as Suzukawa. When he joined the company in June 1948, it gave Canon a combination of marine and aviation engineers.

Thus began the creation of work process diagrams based on limit gauging, in other words, the standardization of manufacturing. The idea was to make it possible for non-experienced craftsmen to work by following process diagrams. Although the skilled workers who had their own set of tools could do it with the current drawings, it would not allow for modern mass production. The study group was the first step in changing the structure of Canon, which until then had been little more than a small factory, and laid the foundation for modern production technology.

Mitarai invested several million yen, a large sum of money at the time, to purchase a set of measuring instruments. Since all the drawings were changed, the products had to be made exactly as shown in the drawings, so the measuring instruments were given to the in-house staff and subcontractors who processed the parts in order to check them. From then on, the parts for the products were interchangeable.

Unique Lens Design

As the modernization at the company progressed around Suzukawa, Tadashi Nakamura (born in 1927), joined Canon after graduating from Tokyo Academy of Physics (currently Tokyo University of Science) in March 1949. His job was to inspect the lenses.

He thought the company was a bare-bones operation, but it seemed like everyone in Japan was still just barely getting by, so there was no time to be discouraged. Leica lenses were really good, and he wondered why Canon couldn't produce something of similar quality.

He didn't have shoes, so he had to commute to work barefoot or wearing wooden sandals.

He knew about Mitarai's dream of defeating Leica. "That's a lot of work, and we can't catch up with them in a short time," he thought. However, the company was filled with a can-do spirt, not out of a sense of obligation imposed from above, but rather from a collective determination to push ahead. Nakamura worked like a horse, trying to find a way to produce high-quality lenses at low prices.

Ito was in charge of designing lenses. In college he had learned about the flow of gas, not light. Even when he went to ask his optics teacher for help, Ito was so ignorant about the actual lens design that he couldn't tell him the f-number (a number indicating the light-gathering ability a lens) of the newly released lens. At that time, the only lens designer at Canon was Kuroki, who had come from Nippon Kogaku, and his method was to disassemble German lenses, examine the materials, measure the curves and thickness, and make them as close to the German lenses as he could. Consequently, there was little awareness of how to design a new lens.

Ito borrowed a book on lens design published in Germany and studied it by taking photographs. Around that time, there was a small incident. Among the 50-mm $f/2$ lenses that Canon had produced after the war, there was one that took extraordinarily good pictures. This was because one of the six elements that made up the lens had a slightly different refractive index than was intended. It was the result of a mistake by a worker in the lens kiln, but once the first lot was gone, the lens could no longer be produced. Ito redesigned the lens and produced the $f/1.9$ lens, which was released in February 1949.

At that time, only one employee was responsible for lens design calculations. She would determine the angle and location of the light entering the lens, and if the lens consisted of six elements, she would use a logarithmic table to calculate where on the film surface the light would strike through the six curves. A veteran designer can do about 20 calculations a day. Since there were two designers, each did calculations for ten lenses. It took several days to determine the curve of one lens and to calculate its out-of-focus condition (aberration). After making considerable effort to save money, they were able to reduce the number of lenses to seven or eight and came up with a method to simplify the calculation. (Today, of course, computers have dramatically reduced the time needed to perform these calculations.)

Later, when the ƒ/1.8 lens was produced in August 1951, Tomomasa Matsui and others were so pleased that they could produce a wonderful Canon original design that it brought tears of joy to their eyes.

"Is It Finally Over?"

It is a wonder that Mitarai thought about the need to bring in new people, one after another, during the postwar period of poverty. All he had in mind was that "as long as we have human resources, the company will grow." So, in a way, Japan's defeat was a golden opportunity for Mitarai, and he seized it. He did not ask Nippon Kogaku to transfer employees to Canon. In later years, when Nippon Kogaku started to make their own cameras, they asked Mitarai to please return Wako to them, but he brushed them off. "Stop joking around."

In contrast to the culture of valuing school background that is common in large companies with a long-established business tradition, Mitarai's philosophy was based on the principle of meritocracy: "To hell with academic background. From now on, those with ability will advance."

He did not particularly care about excessive labor costs. If Mitarai had had such reservations, the company might not have developed. He said, "All good people should come here." That was his strength as an amateur in business. (This forced individuals in charge of accounting to scramble around in search of funds.)

In February 1949, a British film company shot footage of Canon's factory for a movie entitled *This Modern Age*. In June of that same year, Canon's monthly production exceeded 500 units for the first time, and in September, the company won first prize at a national camera exhibition in San Francisco. In October, the company moved its headquarters to the Ono Building in Ginza, Tokyo, and in November, the company was approved for listing on the stock exchange. But once again, the company's modern katakana name was a problem.

Mitarai was grilled by the bigwigs at the stock exchange.

"Mr. Mitarai, we don't really care for katakana company names. Can't you do something about it?"

"With all due respect, but I prefer names that are easy to say. The name fits well with the word 'camera.' We sell our products in the U.S., and 'Canon Camera' is easy for Americans to say. I am thinking mainly of exports, so please understand my reasons for using katakana."

Some said that it might be mistaken for a cannon, but if he had taken that kind of thing into consideration, he would never have been able to do anything. He felt as if he were a defendant on trial, but he had a conviction.

"Without natural resources, all Japan has is its precision industry, which requires the use of brains. Katakana is better than kanji for exports."

Meanwhile, a recession was underway. In December of the previous year, the U.S. had ordered the implementation of nine economic principles in order to control inflation and promote economic restructuring in Japan, and J. M. Dodge, Chairman of the Detroit Bank, was dispatched to Japan in February

1949. As the financial advisor to MacArthur, Dodge personally prepared the budget for that year.

In April, the exchange rate was set at 360 yen to the dollar, and strict measures were implemented to control inflation, including cutting various subsidies and cutting back on people's livelihoods in order to boost exports, leading to a recession known as the Dodge deflation.

Sales of cameras, which had been brisk, came to a halt, and Canon's inventory grew, piling up in the corners of elevators because there was nowhere left to put them. However, with the incentive pay system, any reduction in production would immediately impact the company's bottom line and reduce worker pay. The plan to produce 1,000 units per month was canceled, and wage cuts of 5% for section managers and 10% for general managers were implemented. However, these measures were not enough to keep the company from burning through its cash reserves, and without new financing, Canon went bankrupt.

One day, the department heads gathered in a room at the head office in Ginza and made the decision to drastically reduce production, saying " we've worked very hard, but there is no prospect." Some of them thought, "It is finally over." But a few days later, on June 5, 1950, the Korean War started, which jump-started the economy. The stockpile of cameras that had accumulated soon ran out, and the company began to increase production again.

Around that time, some employees felt that the company was focusing too much on high-end cameras. "Why don't we make cheaper products?" Some of the finished products did not meet the specified accuracy standards, so selling them at a lower price would eliminate waste, they argued. Also, if the quality is too high, the product will last a long time and there will be little demand for replacement cameras. Mitarai brushed this off as well.

"Canon is trying to catch up with and surpass Leica. Our goal is to be the world's number one camera maker. If we sell products that don't pass strict standards just to make money or if we make products that don't last long, we'll never be number one. We have to make products that no other company in the world can imitate."

In April, before the war broke out, Mitarai had offered a five-year guarantee of quality, and with his determination to "become the best in the world" and his confidence in his company's technological capabilities, he finally realized his long-held dream of visiting the United States.

But did the trip turn out well or badly?

Chapter 4

Castle Building and the "German-Japanese War"

Castle Building and the "German-Japanese War"

"We Will Not Sell Out the Castle."

In October 1949, the year before the Korean War started, GHQ announced that trade would be privatized from December for exports, and from January of the following year for imports. Therefore, Mitarai was firmly convinced that he had to keep a close eye on the U.S. market from then on. And he did.

The president of a small Japanese company going to the U.S., which wielded absolute power in occupied Japan, was an extraordinary thing for the company's employees. They worked until around midnight each day to make the cameras that Mitarai would take to the U.S., according to Muneo Hirai, who joined the company in 1936. After finally switching to modern production technology, they were even able to add a flash synchronization device, which, according to Hiroshi Kawaguchi, was quite ambitious. Leica's synchronization device had a complicated way of aligning the shutter dial with the synchronization contacts, requiring the bottom lid to be removed each time, but Canon's new camera eliminated such inconveniences, and it was "a work of art" in every respect, in Mitarai's words.

On the day of his departure in August 1950, a table was set up in the garden of the Meguro Plant and people toasted with a glass of *sake* poured from a large bottle. All the employees were proud of their president's impending trip to the U.S. and lined up at the front gate to see him off, and some went out into the street and shouted "Hooray!" Local shopkeepers also came outside to wish him well. About Canon 100 employees gathered at the Haneda Airbase, which was still tiny, to see him off, waving the company flag in their hands. This was before the signing of the Peace Treaty and before Japan Airlines was established.

An international trade fair was being held in San Francisco, and a consortium of Japanese manufacturers was going to exhibit cameras and lenses there. Mitarai was a representative of the industry, and as such, he was authorized by GHQ to go to the U.S. When Hajime and his mother went to see his father off, they were stopped at a checkpoint by an American MP (military police) and doused with the insecticide DDT, and Hajime thought, "Dad is going a long way." Accompanying him was Hidehiko Taguchi (born in 1906), who had joined Nippon Kogaku after the war along with Wako and Seki. They boarded a Boeing Stratocruiser, a double-decker aircraft with four propellers, that Mitarai worried might fall into the sea during the flight.

When he opened a camera magazine on the plane, Mitarai was surprised at the words that jumped out at him.

"Exclusive Canon Distributor, Skinner Company"

Skinner Trading Company was responsible for Canon's products at the exhibition in San Francisco, but it was not the sole U.S. distributor.

Mitarai visited Skinner as soon as he arrived in San Francisco. President Skinner told him, "I went to Tokyo as a buyer and talked with the sales representative there, and we started this business two years ago." They had been passing themselves off as a special contract store. An American lawyer told him that if the contract had been in effect for two or three years and Canon did not raise any objections, it was the same as having agreed to it, but if it went to court, they would lose, so they should cut their losses and pay the $100,000 penalty to cancel the special contract store. Mitarai demanded that Skinner import and sell a minimum of 300 units per year as long as they were the special contract store, but it had neither the ability nor the money to do so. In the end, the agency contract was canceled for $100,000.

The person who had negotiated the deal with Skinner was Yoshio Katayama, a second-generation Japanese-American lawyer (now living in San Jose, California). Katayama had met Taguchi, who had previously gone to the U.S. as an employee of Nippon Kogaku, when he was working at the Patent Office in Washington, D.C. in 1939. Taguchi had sent a letter to Katayama before traveling to the U.S. with Mitarai.

Katayama's first impression of Mitarai was that he was "A very nice gentleman. Although company presidents tend to be overbearing, President Mitarai was very humble." He said this in fairly good Japanese.

Later, Mitarai visited Chicago. While looking at a local newspaper, he saw the headline "Twenty-nine-year-old President Born at Bell & Howell." The article was about Charles Percy, who would later become a U.S. Senator. "That's America," Mitarai thought.

Mitarai decided he wanted to meet Percy and asked a PR firm to introduce him and also provide an interpreter. He met Percy as well as the vice president and other company executives at the Chamber of Commerce in Chicago. When they met, Percy looked closely at Mitarai's clothing and asked, "Excuse me, but where did you get your shoes made?" "In Japan," Mitarai replied. "How about your clothes?" "In Japan." Percy also asked if there was a subway in Japan.

Mitarai was surprised at how Americans perceived Japan, but he was hopeful that such a young president would listen to what he had to say with an open mind. He was hoping to find a reliable distributor somewhere in San Francisco, Chicago, or New York, so he cut to the chase. He said, "Japanese products have a reputation for being cheap and poor quality. We come from a small country, so we are like a frog in a well that knows nothing of the ocean, but we would like to hear your honest opinion about how this camera will be perceived in the U.S."

"I just became president, so I can't reply right away," Percy said. "It looks like a fine camera, though. Please give me some time to think about it. Are you going back to Japan soon?" "No, I will stay until I hear from you." Mitarai gave him the camera, accessories, and a telephoto lens, but Percy said he needed a month's time.

They spent a month going to Niagara, rode a boat on the Hudson River, visited machine tool manufacturers, among other activities. The amount of foreign currency available for their stay was limited to $30 per day for Mitarai and $25 for Taguchi. It was a large sum in yen, but in the U.S., it was barely enough. Hotel rates usually ranged from $8 to $10, but they stayed in a sort of "boarding house" for just $2 or $3 a night. Then they returned to Chicago and met with Percy again at Bell & Howell.

"Everyone in the company examined the product from both a technical and sales standpoint. The engineers concluded that it was several orders of magnitude better than Leica. If this were made in Germany, it would sell like hot cakes. But I am sorry to tell you, Mr. Mitarai, since this is made in Occupied Japan, it will not work in our country."

At that time, Japan was not Japan, but rather "Occupied Japan."

Percy said he would be willing to distribute the camera if it were branded as Bell & Howell rather than Canon.

Mitarai immediately refused. "No matter how weak I might be, I was 'the lord of one country, one castle,' and I could not sell out my castle," he said. It was a foolish thing to say, he thought to himself, such nonsense! (When he used the expression "one country, one castle," he told me, "This is what those of us who were born in the Meiji era have in the bottom of our hearts." This was the only time that he uttered the phrase "born in the Meiji era" during the interview. This reflected his pride in Canon and his strong patriotic spirit.)

If he had only considered the short-term gains, it would have been wiser to accept Percy's offer. Instead, he chose "self-pride," which was very typical of Mitarai. Seeing Mitarai at that time, one could only conclude that he would surely succeed.

The interpreter for the meeting was Tokuyoshi Kawasaki, who was born in Shimane Prefecture in 1909, immigrated to the United States in 1924, and after the war, organized the Chicago Resettlers Committee by Japanese-Americans living in Chicago. Kawasaki had never heard of Mitarai, nor Canon. But he was struck by Mitarai's passion to work with a leading American company. He felt the "humility and unbreakable determination" in Mitarai's words.

Kawasaki saw that Percy was a smart man, but Kawasaki said bluntly, "As for myself, I'm not interested in him." And when he saw Mitarai confidently displaying a blueprint and a camera, he thought his back was against the wall. Mitarai's eyes were sparkling. Kawasaki had the impression that this was a historic moment.

Kawasaki wanted Mitarai to succeed. But the negotiations were not successful, and Mitarai returned to Japan with the stigma of "Made in Japan" weighing heavily on him. The camera that Mitarai had brought with him cost $245, while the Leica cost $380, but its performance was just as good, if not better. Although he was disappointed, he returned home with a newfound confidence in his company's technology.

After this trip, Mitarai traveled abroad frequently, but wherever he went, he was struck by the patriotic displays and love for the national flag in each country. These experiences inspired Mitarai to display the Japanese flag and the company flag behind the podium and sing the Japanese national anthem at important company events.

(Minoru Yamada, who had attended the same junior high school as Mitarai in Saiki, went to the U.S. around 1919 to work, and they met again in Los Angeles during Mitarai's first trip to the U.S. From then on, whenever Mitarai visited the U.S., he brought strawberries and cherries from Yamada Farm, and the two old friends played *go*, a board game, at the hotel).

Hit by a Bolt Out of the Blue

Along with disappointment and confidence, there was one more thing that Mitarai brought back with him: it is nationalism. It was not exclusionary nationalism, but rather a kind of patriotism, a thought about what Japan or the Japanese people should be. And there was "documentary evidence" to prove it. To explain it, we must go back to the story of Tomomasa Matsui, the soldier who was at the Chitose Airfield at the end of the war.

Another of Matsui's fellow soldiers who was sent to build the runway was Shinpei Ikejima (born in 1911). After the war, Ikejima became editor-in-chief of the monthly magazine *Bungei Shunju*, and his friendship with Matsui continued. One day, Ikejima told Matsui that he was going to hold a roundtable discussion on the poor perception of "Made in Japan," which would be covered in the next issue of *Bungei Shunju*, and the president of Nippon Kogaku would be attending. Matsui said to him, "Don't be a stranger. Please invite Canon instead of Nippon Kogaku."

'Nikon' was the obvious choice, considering the situation at the time. David Douglas Duncan, an American photojournalist who covered the Korean

War as a correspondent for Life magazine, used a Leica camera with a Nippon Kogaku lens, and the sharpness of the image proved the high quality of lenses made in Japan. The December 14, 1950 issue of *Nihon Shashin Kogyo Tsushin* (Japan Photo Industry News) reported that an article in the New York Times had praised Nikon's quality.

Mitarai attended the roundtable, along with Yoshitaka Mikimoto, President of Mikimoto Shinju Ten (Mikimoto Pearl Store (currently K. Mikimoto & Co., Ltd.), Yoshitaka Sagi, Director of Ando Shippoten (currently Ando Cloisonne Co., Ltd.). It was only a few months after his visit to the U.S., so the experience was still fresh in his mind. An article about the roundtable was published in the magazine's February 1951 issue.

In the magazine article, Mitarai recalled the shame he felt when he was confronted with "what Japan should not be" in the U.S. He mentioned two experiences.

First, a binocular supplier in San Francisco told him, "Japanese manufacturers are not serious. They are unreliable." A pair of Japanese binoculars that had been initially priced at $75 was quickly marked down to $23. For Mitarai, it was "like being hit by a bolt out of the blue."

Then, in New York, a Japanese trader with U.S. citizenship told him how unreliable Japanese manufacturers are, and as an example, he mentioned canned food that contained nothing but water. Mitarai's face turned red with anger "I wanted to crawl under a rock."

Based on these experiences, he stated, "The distrust of 'Made in Japan' will not disappear overnight. We will have to reap what Japan has sown over a long period of time." Here, Mitarai was not speaking as the president of a private company, but as a representative of Japan playing a role in the U.S.-Japan relationship. The expression "the lord of one country, one castle" was not just about pride. And even though he was a representative of Japan in terms of ideology, it was as the business manager of a private company that he "reaped what Japan had sown." But he would have the opportunity to change things once he returned to Japan.

Arguing with the Ministry of Education

At some point a leader must make a statement and then back up that statement. He throws the words up into the air and chases after them. That is the destiny of a leader. This is true whether he is aware of it or not.

Mitarai had refused to sell out the Canon brand to make a deal with Charles Percy, the brilliant 29-year-old president of Bell & Howell, saying that he was the "the lord of one country, one castle." Now Mitarai had to prove it.

"How could we fight against *that* country?" Mitarai asked upon returning to Japan. This recognition of America's mightiness was compounded by the poor reputation of "Made in Japan." Adding insult to injury, a fire broke out at one of their factories while he was away in the U.S., but thankfully it was only a small blaze. What greeted Mitarai on his return from the steel and concrete landscape of America's cities was the paper-and-wood houses of Japan. He realized they would need to build a solid castle that would not burn. Otherwise, he would not be able to sell his products to "*that* country." The day would come when thousands of cameras would be sent to America. But for that to happen, he would need a new factory, not one that would go up in flames like a matchbox.

The first step for Japan, and for the further development of Canon, is to build trust and to erase the stigma of "Made in Japan." After returning to Japan, Mitarai desired a modern factory made of reinforced concrete. But, alas, he had no money. So he wondered if there might already be such a factory suited to his needs.

Sometimes, when you truly need something, it can come from the most unexpected places. This is probably what most people would call "luck."

At that time, Jardine Matheson, a large British trading company based in Hong Kong, was trying to sell Japanese products to the rest of the world, and was interested in cameras. Naturally, they approached Nippon Kogaku about selling their cameras. However, the negotiations fell apart, and they turned to Canon next.

Mitarai said, "We have the technology and you have the money. We would like to borrow some money from you." As part of the distributorship agreement, Jardine Matheson offered to lend Canon $300,000, which is about 100 million yen. (Canon had secured funding to increase its capital to 50 million yen in March of that year.) Just before signing, however, Mitarai held out five fingers. Matsui, who had been negotiating the deal, panicked and pulled on Mitarai's sleeve. Mitarai said, "I know." Mitarai thought to himself, "Three hundred thousand or five hundred thousand, it's all the same. If the other party says no, that's the end of the story." Pollocks, Jardine's Tokyo Branch Manager, was surprised and reluctant to give an answer. Mitarai said, "I will pay you back. Look into my eyes, and you will see that there is no room for any falsehoods." And with that, Pollocks agreed. The contract was concluded in November 1951. Canon agreed to sell at least 70% of its monthly production to Jardine for five years, and it would repay the loan in monthly installments of six million yen over 30 months beginning in November 1952. (Incidentally, Canon's production output in 1952 was approximately 960 million yen, or about 80 million yen per month.)

Mitarai immediately set about acquiring a factory in Shimomaruko, Otaku, Tokyo that had been used to manufacturer aircraft instruments during the war. Sumitomo Bank was in charge of selling the factory.

However, the Ministry of Education was interested in converting the factory into a fisheries university, and the bank wanted to accommodate the Ministry of Education as much as possible. Canon could pay immediately, but the Ministry of Education needed to go through a budgeting process, which would take a year. The bank wanted to look good to both sides, so in the end, Mitarai and Eizaburo Naito of the Ministry of Education decided to discuss the matter.

"We are working in a ramshackle factory, but we're focusing on exports. For that reason, we need a fireproof facility," Mitarai said.

"The factory is near the ocean, so we'd really like you to let us have it. In fact, we visited the factory two weeks earlier than you did, so we have priority."

"But have you made a formal offer to purchase it? Isn't the usual practice to sell to the party who makes an offer first?"

"Well, we're certainly no match for a crafty businessman like you," Naito replied.

"Now wait a minute. Crafty means cunning. I may be old, but I am doing things fairly and honestly. It's extremely rude for the director general of the Ministry of Education to say something like that."

"You're right. I take it back."

"Students go on to work for the Ministry of Education, but they also join our company. Therefore, we are equal in terms of serving the country. And what's more, you are a year away from being able to pay."

To this, Naito could not say anything back. Mitarai did not relent, partly because he resented the idea that the ministry had priority simply because they had visited the factory two weeks earlier.

"The Ministry of Education and we are both equal."

"That Would Destroy the Company…" "You'll See."

Morimasa Kaneko, one of the wartime evacuees, had worked at Takasago Tekko (Takasago Iron Works) before joining Seiki Kogaku and always passed by the Shimomaruko Plant on his way home. He was impressed by how beautiful the building was and dreamed of working there one day. Naturally, he was delighted when the company sent him to visit the factory after they had decided to buy it. Even though the company was growing rapidly, he wondered what they were going to do with such a big facility.

Kaneko was not the only one. Those who saw the site wondered if they could actually use such a large space, and everyone felt uneasy standing in front of the large structure, with its fresh air raid scars and boarded-up windows.

Borrowing $500,000 from Jardine Matheson was an unprecedented move and it became the talk of the industry. Everyone thought it would crush Canon.

An editorial in a business magazine read, "We understand the company's aims, but we hope it will not be fatal." When Mitarai read this, he felt a fierce urge to say, "You'll see!" He was so disgusted that he didn't forget the author's name for more than a decade.

Soon, the workers from the head office in Ginza and the factories in Meguro and Itabashi were brought under the same roof in Shimomaruko. At the relocation party, Maeda gave a tour to the owner of Murakami Shokai, who remarked, "You have a lot of space, but do you expect to fill it up just by making cameras?" Even with 700 employees, the space was so large that the office department had trouble deciding how to arrange the desks.

Another article read, "Until now, Canon has been able to get by under the amateur management of a doctor, but …" "Don't call me an amateur," Mitarai thought, "I have my own way of going about things. Say what you want, you'll look back one day and see that I was right. It doesn't matter how big the space is. Even if it's empty now, we just need to create a suitable structure. After a year or two, it will be fully developed." Mitarai was confident that he had done exactly what he was supposed to do.

When Tadashi Nakamura joined the company in 1949 and learned of Mitarai's goal to defeat Leica, he thought it was impossible. Nevertheless, he felt that there was an atmosphere of eagerness within the company to move forward because Mitarai's spirit permeated the company, and was true at the new facility in Shimomaruko as well.

But now, Mitarai's decision was being questioned publicly, and Nakamura knew that many employees were concerned. Mitarai knew he needed to project strength and confidence. On the day of the unveiling ceremony, he declared in front of the guests and employees gathered in the auditorium, "This is the best day of my life," which inspired his employees.

"Now that we have set sail, please place your trust in me as the captain of this ship. Some say the waves are rough and dangerous. What if we don't make it?" Mitarai felt that way. He was also determined to repay the debt to Jardine within three years, and in November 1954, when he had paid off the loan, he gave all employees in his company an average of 10,400 yen in celebration money (at that time, the salary base for government employees was 15,500 yen, while the starting salary in the private sector was 9,000–10,000 yen for a college graduate). Meanwhile, in January 1953, the company purchased an additional 1,250 square meters of land owned by the Tokyo Metropolitan Government along the Tama River adjacent to the plant, and in December, it acquired another site to build a training center. Mitarai had succeeded in giving substance to the phrase "the lord of one country, one castle."

"We Don't Want a Section Chief Who Can't Dance."

In the meantime, and following the establishment of the company's first housing association in 1950, Mitarai continued the initiatives for "new familialism," but it is in order to strengthen the defenses of the "castle" in Shimomaruko.

As previously mentioned, Mitarai started taking dance lessons soon after the war. It was actually as a way to get all of his employees to learn to dance, with the company president taking the lead. However, once they tried, he realized that it was more difficult than it seemed. Then he decided to create "Canon Ondo" (Canon dance song), to the tune of a traditional Japanese bon dance (often performed at a summer festival).

The lyrics were written by Yaso Saijo and the music was composed by Masao Koga — a very popular combination. The dance was choreographed by Kiitsu Sakakibara.

The lyrics conveyed Canon's distinctive features, such as: "Canon is the flower of the country"; "Now a blonde girl from a foreign country takes a Canon camera home as a souvenir"; "Canon cameras, which we are proud of, let us take picturesque photos, now a major export, putting Japan on its back"; "the Canon lens is so bright, there is no shadow in the home in the photo"; "A neat finish of precision camera, there is deviation with it"; "Let's build a new and prosperous Japan with the hands that assemble cameras."

Canon ondo wa kokusai ondo
Sasa odoreya hogarakani hogarakani

Teburi soroete odori no uzu ga
Nobirya kokui mo mata nobiru
E kokui mo mata nobiru

Canon Ondo is an international ondo
Come on, dance happily
A whirlwind of hand gestures and dancing
If it grows, the national prestige will also grow
The national prestige will also grow

The company song, with lyrics by Zenmaro Toki and music by Nobuo Iida, was to be sung in the spirit of "three 'self's' " (*san-ji*), i.e., self-motivation (*jihatsu*), self-governance (*jichi*), and self-awareness (*jikaku*) that was instilled in Mitarai as a student: "The flower of self-motivation blooms in the garden of self-governance, and self-awareness grows in the garden of cooperation. We vow "three selves" at Canon Camera." (Later, when the company name was changed from Canon Camera to Canon Inc., some of the lyrics were changed accordingly.)

The company even made yukata (*summer kimonos*) for the Canon Ondo, asking company employees to suggest patterns and then supplying the fabric for yukata to all employees.

A Bon Dance festival was held on the banks of the Tama River each year on the eve of the company's anniversary, and cost an average of about 1,500 yen per employee, with the total cost ranging from 1.4 million to 2.8 million yen. Once it even exceeded 4 million yen.

The executives, of course, had to learn the dance. Some were not very good, while others felt that dancing was not part of their job description.

However, Mitarai insisted that everyone participate. Mitarai scolded one executive with a serious face, saying, "you are so poor at dancing," while a section manager was told, "We don't want a section chief who can't dance the Canon Ondo."

Tadashi Nakamura (who joined the company in 1949) thought the Canon Ondo was a good thing. Even though the operations were now under one roof in Shimomaruko, there was still a rivalry between Meguro and Itabashi workers, and there was a feeling that the direction of the company was not aligned in some regards. The dance helped to resolve that. In addition, "It gave employees and their families the impression that the company was on an upward trend" according to Nakamura.

Hiroshi Suzuki (who joined the company in 1950) became the official first secretary section chief after the relocation to Shimomaruko. He got the impression that Mitarai was a man full of vitality who never wavered in his opinions. The factory work started at 8:00 a.m., but Mitarai arrived at 7:00 a.m. every day, making the rounds of the factory before the board of directors meeting, which started at 7:30 a.m. If anyone was around, he always said "hi!" to them.

Tsuneo Misawa (who joined the company in 1946) was pleased with how clean the inside of the factory was, and when approached by Mitarai at the factory, he casually remarked, "I think my family would be very pleased if I showed them this place." Mitarai simply said, "I see." But later, Misawa was surprised when Mitarai mentioned it during his New Year's address to the employees the following year, saying that he would like to invite employees' families to visit the factory. "The world is so harsh, but this company is different" said Misawa who was thrilled by Mitarai's warm words.

Birthday parties for employees began in 1953. Each month, Mitarai and the other executives would host the 70 to 80 employees who were born that month and serve cake. In addition, after the company's New Year's ceremony, they distributed cakes, lottery tickets, towels with the company name on them, theater tickets, and other items to the employees as New Year's gifts. On the Coming-of-Age Day, a commemorative tree was planted with a gift to the appropriate employees. Furthermore, the company organized bus trips in the spring, family recreational events (mainly theater performances) in the fall, movie nights, and other activities.

Meanwhile, starting in July 1950, the company had implemented a "trichotomy system" to distribute profits among investors, management, and labor. If the profits at the end of the fiscal year exceeded forecasts, an additional one-third of the difference was paid to each. (Kyocera Corporation, founded in 1959, implemented the same system for a while.)

In July 1953, a reward system for reducing defective products was introduced with the aim of eliminating waste. The total number of defective products caused by errors in parts processing, operations, and management was calculated, and a reward was given if the number of defective products was reduced by a certain percentage or more. This system led to a significant reduction in the number of defective products.

"How Are You Doing?"

However, no matter how good a system is, it will not survive without human trust between the leader and the members of the organization.

In this regard, the employees who joined the company before the War or between 1945 and 1955 recalled that Mitarai always told them to take care of their health.

Muneo Hirai, who had his "physical checkup" performed by Mitarai during the war, was repeatedly told, "Don't overdo it. If you have time during your lunch break, you should lie down and take a rest."

Masanori Seki, who had transferred from Nippon Kogaku after the war, had been convalescing from tuberculosis from 1941 to 1945. Knowing this, Mitarai always looked at him and said, "Seki-kun, how are you these days?"

Shigeru Nishioka's younger brother once developed peritonitis from appendicitis, and when he mentioned it to Mitarai, Mitarai said, "That is a serious disease. You have to be patient to recover." One day, when Mitarai was riding his bicycle to the Meguro Plant, he passed Nishioka walking to the plant and called out to him, "Hey, Nishioka-kun, what ever happened to your younger brother?"

When Mitarai returned to Oita, he hosted a party and invited Ryosaku Mitarai (no relation), one of his classmates from junior high school. When Ryosaku called to tell Mitarai that he couldn't attend, he said, "I'm happy just to hear your voice. Take care of yourself."

Mitarai paid special attention to the health management of his employees and focused on eliminating tuberculosis from the company, a disease that had become widespread after World War II. He made efforts to detect tuberculosis at an early stage by using the indirect X-ray camera developed by the company, and as a result, the percentage of the employees who contracted of tuberculosis rapidly declined. As soon as he found a possible tuberculosis infection, he would immediately put the employee in a sanatorium and tell them, "There's no hurry. Take all the time you need to recuperate."

But there was also a flip side.

Mitarai was famous, almost to a fault, for his punctuality. According to Yoshio Katayama, an attorney living in San Jose, California, "He was very prompt, very nice. That's a good thing."

The company's first secretary, Hiroshi Suzuki, remembered that Mitarai always had a full schedule, which included a steady stream of meetings. He was very concerned with punctuality and would refuse to meet with someone even if they were just five minutes late. Even if the sushi he ordered for lunch arrived five minutes late, he wouldn't eat it.

When Suzuki was reading the newspaper, Mitarai would often say, "What are you doing? It's time to work. When it's eight o'clock, you do your job." He also told him to stop holding unnecessary meetings, not to work overtime, and to use the allotted time to the fullest.

Mitarai was also averse to mid-year gifts and banquets. Entertainment expenses related to the sales department had to be approved by Mitarai. He didn't think it was wrong to entertain the customers, but rather that the focus should be on finding a better way to do business.

When the sales representative was visiting retailers throughout Japan, he planned to hold a banquet in Kyoto, where it is common practice to invite *maiko* (apprentice *geisha*, who are studying the art of conversation, singing, and dance) for such occasions. Mitarai objected and the sales representative was put in a difficult spot. In the end, the venue was changed to a hotel where *maiko* were not permitted.

The accountant had similar problems. Mitarai said, "Don't send mid-year and year-end gifts to banks. We borrow money from them so that they can live." The accountant had no choice but to send the gifts in secret and was severely scolded when Mitarai found out.

Around this time, Mitarai, who was now in his fifties, began playing golf at the suggestion of others. Until then, he had made fun of golf, wondering where the fun was in swinging a stick around. But he was told, "It's good for your health, and therefore it's good for the company." He practiced under the tutelage of a professional golfer and soon he was hooked. Before long, Mitarai "forced" the executives of his company to play golf as well, just as his friend Shuzo Imai had been "forced" to learn *nagauta* (traditional Japanese folk songs) by him when they were students. Mitarai had always been passionate about growing flowers and vegetables, but after he started playing golf, he began to say that "a small garden was nice, but a large garden would be grand."

Mitarai forced his executives to join the same country golf club, not only because he thought golf was fun and good for their health, but more importantly, because it allowed them to socialize with other executives away from work. He also judged a person's character based on their golf game, placing more importance on speed than skill. If a player was slow and lazy, he was considered indecisive. He always told them to play fast, even if they were bad at it, which, in terms of work, translated into asking them to make fast decisions, even if they failed.

If golf was Mitarai's "active" hobby, his "quiet" hobbies were *go* and gardening.

Although he took up golf in his fifties, he had started playing *go* when he was in elementary school. As an adult, he studied under the legendary *go* player Kaku Takagawa, who won the prestigious Hon'inbo title nine times. Mitarai was known to "recommend" the game to the executives and employees of his company, and even established a *go* club at the company.

Whether golf or *go*, Mitarai had a tendency to bring others into his circle.

Germany Fights Back

As discussed earlier, Mitarai brought numerous ideas into the company, particularly since the relocation to Shimomaruko until 1955. During this time, Canon experienced a rapid growth, marking what could be described as a golden age for the company. Sales skyrocketed, from 634 million yen in 1951 to 1.88 billion yen in 1955.

The products of this period were all variations of the S II model released in 1946. In February 1949, the company launched the improved Type II B, followed by the Type III in 1951 and the Type IV with a built-in flash-synchronization circuit in 1952. In 1953, the Serenar lens was re-branded as a Canon lens. At the same time, a photography contest was held and those who won the best prize were sent abroad. The launch of the IV Sb at the end of 1952 was the beginning of the heyday of high-end rangefinder cameras.

In 1954, while Canon and other Japanese camera companies were expanding their global market share, Germany fired a powerful shot, signaling that they were not about to surrender in the camera wars. That shot was the Leica M3.

"We groaned when we opened the cover, we groaned when we remove one of the parts, and we groaned when you cut off a part. No product has ever been that shocking. There was no way Canon could compete with that," said Satoshi Nemoto, who joined the company in 1951.

According to Hiroshi Suzukawa, "Canon had already done a pretty good job with lenses, so we had tried our best to make a solid mechanism until the IV Sb era. But when the M3 launched, we realized we were far behind in terms of advanced body functions, including the viewfinder system."

The situation was the same at Nippon Kogaku.

For the designers, who had been working for a year and a half on the development of a new Nikon model under the slogan "a camera that rivals Leica," it seemed as if the goal had been moved to an unattainable height. It was no longer possible to design a new camera model without thinking about the Leica M3. (Tatsuhiko Arakawa, *Akarui Kutsubako* <Bright Dark Box>.)

Nemoto says, "In retrospect, our capabilities at that time were limited." I wonder what the new employees saw at the manufacturing site at that time. In April 1953, exactly one year before the M3 shock, Kazuo Naito (born in 1930), a graduate of the Precision Engineering Department of the Faculty of Engineering at Niigata University, joined the company.

He knew that the precision machinery industry would surely grow because its products could be exported, but he was concerned whether the camera business would be large enough for him to feed his wife and children.

One day, Ryoichiro Yamagata, the head of the production department, sat down on Naito's desk and said, "Hey, do you want to make blades?" "Well, you can't use them the way you are now," Naito commented. "So, do you want to do it?" "Well, let me think about it for a few days." "I'll get someone else to do it then," Yamagata said. "No, that's OK. I'll do it," Naito said.

In those days, metal cutting was done by craftsmen who used whetstones to sharpen their blades. Each blade was unique. Sometimes while they were grinding, they would stop the lathe and chat. If something went wrong, they would stop the lathe and grind again. Therefore, the cutting time was not fixed and varied depending on the craftsman. The efficiency was extremely poor because the only requirement was that a certain number of pieces had to be sharpened each day. This was still the case between 1953 and 1955. Eventually, blades would be standardized and loaned out to customers, and when they were damaged, they would be replaced by new ones. Naito attempted to determine what blade number should be used to sharpen each part. Around the time he got close to that point, he was hospitalized with tuberculosis.

After this process, the VT, which was released in 1956, was Canon's answer to the Leica M3. For the first time, Canon produced their own original design, rather than merely imitating Leica's cameras. However, Canon had to release an "improved" version every few months. As Yamagata recalled, this was because "every mechanical change caused problems." For this reason, it was also referred to as the "behind" type because it ended up behind with everything in the product development race.

In April 1956, a mass-production prototype of the VT was exhibited at a camera exhibition in Chicago. One day around that time, Nemoto was summoned by Maeda, the managing director of the company. Everyone involved in the design of the VT was called in. Maeda produced a letter that had just arrived from Mitarai. It was written vertically. At that time, Nemoto and other young people had changed it to horizontal writing, which was a new style. Maeda read it out. "There have been many malfunctions with VT. I can only look up to the heavens in sorrow." Nemoto was speechless.

"I don't think I'll ever forget it. All of Canon's capabilities were in that camera. In the end, we could not overtake the M3. Later on, we made the VI and 7 models, which were better, but they still didn't surpass the M3. The production technology was completely different. The factory could not produce the cameras the way we designed them. This was what we were capable of. But while Leica's progress stopped there, Canon grew further with SLR cameras."

Appointed Chairman of the Industrial Association and Awarded the Okochi Prize

In 1953, Mitarai had visited Europe and the U.S. and held a debriefing session upon his return to Japan. Meanwhile Kazuo Tajima, the president of Chiyoda Kogaku Seiko, had conducted a market survey in the U.S. In response to the growing interest in Japanese products from abroad, there was growing momentum in Japan to increase exports. In December 1953, the Keidanren (Japan Business Federation) issued a "Request for the Promotion of Optical Machinery Exports" to the Japanese government.

In April 1954, the same month the Leica M3 was announced, the Japan Camera Industry Association (JCIA; currently the Camera & Imaging Products Association) was established and Mitarai became its first chairman. After serving for three years, he was elected again in 1969 and 1979.

In May 1954, the Japan Camera Inspection Institute (currently the Japan Camera Industry Institute) was established under the leadership of industry leaders such as Mitarai. Subsequently, it became a legal requirement for cameras to be inspected by this association prior to export.

The amount of the founding contribution made each member companies was a reflection of their strength at the time. Canon and Nippon Kogaku contributed 500,000 yen a piece, followed by Konishiroku, Mamiya, Chiyoda Kogaku, and Olympus, which contributed 300,000 yen each. The contributions of other companies ranged from 100,000 to 10,000 yen.

In November 1955, the JCIA established the Japan Camera Information and Service Center in New York to provide after-sales service, including the repair of exported cameras, as well as to handle complaints.

Based on his previous experiences in the U.S., Mitarai believed that competition among Japanese manufacturers was necessary, but that Japanese manufacturers should also work together to manufacture excellent products. "We must establish appropriate export standards and export high-quality products before complaints are made overseas." He was the driving force behind the establishment of the center in New York.

Despite the setback presented by the Leica M3, Canon continued to improve, and its production technology was recognized in 1957, the 20th anniversary of its founding, when it received the Okochi Memorial Production Prize.

The prize, named in honor of Masatoshi Okochi, a scientist and businessman who had served as director of RIKEN [Institute of Physical and Chemical Research], was awarded for (1) research related to production engineering, (2) inventions or devices related to production technology, and (3) achievements in the implementation of mass-production methods. Canon received the award for establishing a mass-production system for precision cameras, which had previously been considered impossible.

The process leading up to the award was as follows. First, in September 1956, the Committee on Industrial Efficiency and Production Management of the Japan Society of Mechanical Engineers decided to recommend Canon as a candidate for the Okochi Prize for fiscal year 1955, and the nomination was made official at the November board meeting. After that, the required documents were submitted to the Okochi Memorial Foundation, and in March 1957, three scholars from the foundation, including Masao Kuroda, a doctor of engineering, conducted an on-site examination of Canon factories. One week later, the award was officially decided.

According to the foundation's nomination letter, Canon's achievements were as follows: 1) practical application of materials for cameras in collaboration with material manufacturers; 2) successful use of pressed glass materials for photographic lenses, which was previously considered impossible; 3) full implementation of the limit gauging method; 4) practical application of automatic machining of metal and glass parts ahead of competitors; 5) practical application of a special plating method; and 6) improvement of productivity through reorganization of the company and adoption of a scientific process-control system.

Of these, 1) was a joint effort with Furukawa Electric, which was inspired by the fact that Sakichi Kishino, Mitarai's teacher at Saiki Junior High School, had joined Furukawa Electric, and 3) was a part of the modernization of production technology promoted by the technical officers who joined Canon after their time in the navy.

Pros and Cons of New Business

"Oh, you, 'that' one is good."

"Do you agree, Mr. President?"

"It's not just about the camera. Let's go with 'that' one."

Thus, Mitarai and Hiroshi Suzukawa, the head of the engineering team, decided on a specific direction for diversification, and Mitarai left in a hurry for the U.S. It was around 1955.

The company's cameras were selling well, but they were not must-have items for daily life. In addition, for Canon to grow, they needed to develop comprehensive technology, not just camera technology. "Canon can become a first-rate company only when it encompasses the fields of physics and chemistry, and I would like to make it so." While Mitarai was thinking this, Suzukawa told him that there was someone he really wanted him to meet before going to the U.S. Suzukawa had joined the company in 1948. Two years later became its technical director, and four years after that, at the age of 38, he became a director. Mitarai's bold selection became the talk of the industry.

Mitarai thought, "If Suzukawa says so, it must be important."

Under Suzukawa's leadership, young engineers were nurtured, as well as the leaders in each department, and a solid foundation for cameras was established. He was always thinking about the next step. He had always loved pictures and music and he was familiar with audio equipment. As he was increasing the sensitivity of his antenna to see if there was anything related to the family use, he had an opportunity to see something developed by Yasushi Hoshino, then a professor at the Tokyo Institute of Technology.

It was a sheet of paper with pictures and associated sounds recorded on it, which allowed visitors to enjoy the visual information (pictures) and the sound information at the same time. "A camera is a hardware product, but with this device, I could imagine a huge demand for the software (the "sheets") in addition to the hardware. It would be a relief from the frustration of watching Kodak call the camera a 'film burner' and then sit idly by while they pretended that the more cameras they sold, the more film they would sell. In addition, because the mechanical and optical engineers would be collaborating with the electrical engineers, new developments based on comprehensive technology would be possible," Suzukawa thought.

Mitarai's ambition as a manager and Suzukawa's ambition as an engineer were a good match. Around 1956, they formed a project team consisting of mechanical and electrical engineers and began work on a development plan. Since there were no electricians, they had to hire one.

Mitarai bet the company's fortune on this new technology, which was called the Synchroreader. Within the company, there was naturally some controversy over the company-wide effort to develop a totally new field.

Morimasa Kaneko, who joined the company in 1939 and was among those who evacuated Tokyo during the war, was also in charge of the materials section and worked hard to support Mitarai's idea of charting a new path. He was so eager to be part of something new that he eventually had to have an operation for a persistent stomachache caused by overwork.

In 1948, Yoshiya Agari, who joined the company at the same time as Suzukawa, was a member of the prototype team. It was his first experience working on a motor, and he had a very hard time because Professor Hoshino's demands were so precise that he had to make the impossible possible. Mitarai told him, "There will be criticism, but you must give it your all until it is done."

Shigeru Nishioka, who joined the company in 1947, was also a member of the prototype team. He had the feeling that things were not going well. He first contacted various electrical manufacturers regarding switches. One of them, Kataoka Electric (now Alps Alpine Co., Ltd.), was a small company, but they did their best to respond to Nishioka's various requests, so he regarded them as enthusiastic.

Ryuzaburo Kaku joined the company in April 1954 and he worked in the accounting department, where he and others who had worked at the company for several years would sometimes gather to discuss the new product.

Isamu Iwatsuru, like his fellow engineers, was pessimistic. "It's technically unsound, and it is foolish to work on something like that." Kaku was the only one in favor of the project. "I see," he said, "I suppose that's true from a technical point of view. However, the top management is trying to do something new, which is a good thing. First of all, we can buy land. The company is going to grow, so we should have enough land to expand. Besides, this will bring in electrical engineers. So, whether it succeeds or not is unimportant." When Iwatsuru heard Kaku frame the matter in such a "political" manner, he was furious.

Some people questioned what Mitarai was thinking. When Akira

Ohtomo, who was in charge of advertising and public relations at the time, asked Professor Hoshino about the patent, the professor became furious. Ohtomo felt that something was "not quite right" and mentioned the incident to Mitarai. However, there was an atmosphere within the company that if you didn't play some role in the Synchroreader project, you were not a valued employee." Some of the members of the development team half-jokingly stated, "Syn-kara chro-shite murea-der (We can't do it, struggling from the core)." In a situation where the majority of people at the company were moving toward the Synchroreader project, this joke did not act as a brake.

When Kaneko saw the finished prototype, he thought, "There is nothing like this in the world; it will definitely sell," while Agari thought, "In terms of precision, this is a wonderful thing that only Canon could have made."

In March 1958, the device was exhibited at the World Exposition in Brussels, Belgium, where it received a tremendous response. The experience bolstered Suzukawa's confidence. However, some of the positive reception was due to misunderstandings about the device's actual functionality. It was hailed as "the greatest invention since Gutenberg's printing press," in other words the typed text is directly converted into voice. People also thought that "sound comes out of a picture." Canon's stock price soared, from 171 yen at the beginning of the year to 284 yen on April 10.

Seiichi Takigawa (born in 1931), who joined the company at the same time as Kaku, was stopped by Mitarai at the company entrance one day toward the end of 1958. "Come over to my house tonight for ochazuke [rice with tea and pickles]," he said. Takigawa had met Mitarai several times as the editor of *Canon Life*, a magazine published in-house to commemorate the company's 20th anniversary.

When Takigawa arrived at the president's house that evening, he was treated to a proper dinner, rather than ochazuke, and Mitarai asked him to transfer to the newly created Synchroreader Section. Takigawa had submitted a proposal to create a regular company newsletter, which had been approved by the president, but he was beginning to get bored with it, so he gladly accepted the offer.

Mitarai had used the newsletter to declare, "We will bet the whole company's fortunes on the Synchroreader," and in September 1958, the company acquired 252,000 square meters of land in Toride, Ibaraki Prefecture, to build a factory to produce the devices. At that moment, plans to mass-produce the Canonet, a new camera product, were also underway within the company, and Saio Mitsui went to the Ministry of International Trade and Industry to seek approval to import the machinery needed for this purpose. When he was told, "You have a surplus of cameras, so we will not permit you to import this machine," he explained that it was actually for the Synchroreader, and the import permit was approved right away. Within the company, all you had to say was, "This is for the Synchroreader," and you could buy anything you wanted.

The Synchroreader was released in April 1959. Sales were dismal. It was heavy and expensive, and like a record player, you needed both the machine itself as well as sheets in order to play something. For the average person, sending a sheet as voice mail was useless. Canon even begged the bankers who financed the project to buy them, but they all remained in the warehouses, collecting dust. Canon's stock price plummeted.

Some people profited from the stock price spike at the time of the announcement, but the crash brought a flood of protest letters and phone calls to Canon's headquarters, and there were even reports of suicides precipitated by the heavy stock losses.

Michio Kimura, whose camera retail company had been selling Canon cameras since the days of the IV Sb, thought, "They will sell the land in Toride," while Eiji Hashimoto, President of Nihonbashi Camera Sales, thought, "Canon will finally go out of business."

The remaining products were transported to Toride, and the unused vacuum tubes and microphones were sold to shops in Akihabara, Tokyo's electronics district, driving down the market price of vacuum tubes. Fukutaro Tsuji, who was in charge of accounting, requested the presence of a tax inspector and smashed the products in front of him so that the products could be counted as damaged products. The motors that Agari and his colleagues had worked so hard on, once valued at 3,000 yen per piece, were now worthless.

Looking back on those days, Suzukawa said. "I led the charge to develop a new field for Canon, and as a result I caused trouble for everyone and was criticized for it. I was thinking only about the technology, but this failure led me to consider the social nature of the company and its products."

Thirteen years later, in 1972, at an internal roundtable discussion, Mitarai referred to this incident and said, "That was a big dream. Winding down the operation was a struggle. I had a really hard time with that." His voice on the recordings of that discussion reflects the seriousness of the circumstances.

When he decided to pull the plug on the Synchroreader, Mitarai called the department heads together. "This isn't anyone's fault. If anyone is to blame, it's me. Don't say anything about bad sales or poor technology."

As one would expect, Mitarai was not at ease before the annual shareholders meeting in February 1960. The Shukan Shincho magazine had covered the debacle with sarcasm. Furthermore, because they had not secured the patent rights, Ricoh was now selling a similar product at less than half the price. Mitarai was devasted by everything that had happened, but he had no intention of making excuses.

After his opening remarks, he spoke frankly.

"I was a fool. The company failed because it dabbled in an untested technology. The loss of earnings was also the result of the ship's captain failing to take the helm. I have failed as a manager, and I leave my fate in your hands. However, I did not line my own pockets by this. It all started from the idea that the company's technology must become more diversified."

Naturally, there were voices within the company asking who would take responsibility. Mitarai, however, did not hold anyone responsible, saying, "It was my decision," Mitarai said. "I was also the one who could say that I wouldn't do it when they advised me not to."

Meanwhile, the company decided to recall all the products but not to stop production as long as there were requests for magnetic sheets, following a policy of not causing any harm to the newly created distributors for the Synchroreaders. Mitarai was sick for a while, but only a few people in the company knew about it.

Canon had suffered a major blow. However, that pain would produce tangible and intangible assets that would later support the company's development.

The Year of the Security Treaty, and the Camera Industry in Turmoil

The Revision of the Japan – U.S. Security Treaty in 1960 (which was originally signed in 1951) became a source of controversy throughout Japan. On June 19, 1960, the treaty was ratified by the Japanese Diet, and opposition began to wane. Later that year, on August 22 something happened that signaled the beginning of a revolution in the camera industry.

This year is generally regarded as the start of the Ikeda Cabinet's high-growth policy, which wasye a turning point in the postwar economic history. It was also the year of the Dakko-chan doll boom, the spread of electric refrigerators and the idea of "three sacred treasures" (which states that every home should have a TV, refrigerator, and washing machine), the introduction of instant ramen noodles and instant coffee, and the publication of *Sei-seikatsu no Chie* (The Wisdom of a Sex Life) by Kokuken Sha. In addition, TV production ranked second only to the U.S., Sumitomo Bank began offering monthly installment financing for passenger cars, and Daiwa House Industry completed the first prefabricated housing prototype.

These are all taken from *Comprehensive Chronological Table of Modern Japanese History* (Iwanami Shoten) Also under the "Society" section on this chronology (on January 24, 1961) is the following line: "Canon launched the Canonet (popularization of EE <electric eye> cameras)." The product followed the general trends in which people appreciated convenience and sought enjoyment in life.

The *Shukan Bunshun* magazine at the time carried a five-page article titled "Down with the Canonet!" that included a collection of headlines from other publications such as "Sold out in just two hours," "The Canonet is too cheap! Are you trying to kill off other manufacturers?" "The 'high-end confectioner' is Canon, and the 'caramel' is Canonet."

The following is an account of the "revolution" as told by those involved. First, let's start with a rountable discussion held at Canon headquarters in 1968, seven years after the Canonet was launched.

Mitarai: "Two representatives from the Japan Camera Industry Association came to me and said, 'do you think it's all right for a fine restaurant like yours to offer the same kind of fare as a fast food shop? We are not happy about it. We want you to act like a fine restaurant.' So I replied, 'What are you talking about? Soon, Germany and the U.S. will climb over the levee and come flooding into Japan. But the wave of liberalization will not come if Japan has something like the Canonet. If you want, we can wait for you to make something similar and we can launch it all at the same time. What do you think?' Then, everyone looked at each other."

Hayashi (Executive Director): "For four or five months, we were attacked by everyone in the industry."

Maeda (Vice President): "At that time, I heard that other manufacturers went to the Industrial Machinery Section of MITI (the Ministry of International Trade and Industry), asking them to put pressure on Canon, but MITI said there was nothing they could do as long as we made products cheaply and sold them at a reasonable profit based on a rational production system, and that manufacturers should engage in friendly competition."

Mitarai: "Don't be fooled by the rhetoric about disrupting order and peace in the industry."

Maeda: "The Canonet grew the Japanese camera industry, and all our competitors modernized their production systems as result. Thanks to the Canonet, cameras have become more powerful and are now an export industry."

Mitarai: "Since the Canonet, the industry seems to be back on track."

Maeda: "At the time, there was a sense at the industrial association meetings that cameras were a declining industry and would continue to decline. That all changed with the Canonet."

Mitarai: "Our technology has also made great strides and helped improve mass production."

Hayashi: "Before that, there was the Populaire (Canon's first attempt at a mass-produced high-end cameras), which showed that mass production was at least possible. We proved it with the Canonet and sales increased by 50% every quarter."

Shortage of Goods Leads to Complaints at the Factory

Next was Takeshi Goshima, who played a central role in development and design. He was born in 1933, joined the company in 1956, and started working on the design of the Canonet in the fall of 1959. When it launched in August 1960, he was just 27 years old.

"I have loved tinkering with clocks and radios since I was a child — so much that I wanted to draw up blueprints and build them myself. I am so happy to see my designs come to fruition. No matter what my salary is, I am always hungry and eager to work. I can't help but want to design all kinds of new things.

"At that time, we had accumulated an inventory of turret-type 8-mm filming machines and needed to do something about it. Keizo Yamaji (who joined the company in 1951) was an expert in zoom lens design, and we worked together on the idea of attaching a zoom lens to an 8-mm camera. I designed the ammeter and used it to create an automatic exposure mechanism. When I showed it to Suzukawa, he thought it was a good idea, and when I told Maeda and Mitarai about it, they said, 'If you're going to do it, do it quickly.' I suggested the possibility of automatic exposure, but Suzukawa set the direction for the character and concept of the camera. Although people say that I designed the camera, I really only designed the technical aspects of the device.

"I think there was some debate within the company about the direction of the middle class models, but I didn't think much about it. My intention was to expand the field of power in the industry as much as possible.

"The problem with the Canonet was that it tended to break down quite often. This was partly due to design problems, but at the time, monthly production was a few thousand units at most. In contrast, production of the Canonet was 10,000 units, which was an order of magnitude higher. However, the technology of the time did not allow for high component precision. Moreover, while the company had not cared much about the cost of cameras up to then, they were very concerned about the cost of the Canonet.

"If the drawings from that time were used with today's production process, there would be no breakdowns, but that's not the way it should be. A good design isn't a good design unless it works well with the manufacturing capacity of the time. I was fully aware of this, but there were times when I became annoyed because I was bullied so much by everyone.

"I did most of the design work by myself with only an assistant, but when I went to the production site, people from various departments or divisions would come to me and say a lot of things. In short, they came to bully me. In the end, I turned defiant, saying that it will go nowhere if they continue messing around. 'You are only in charge of so many parts per person, but I designed them all, so please give me a break.' Of course, I will make changes. But I also went to my supervisors to persuade them to improve the accuracy of the parts. If you don't take some action, nothing will change. When I told them that the subcontractor making this mold was not good, they brushed me off, saying I am so insolent. But if you say it enough times, some people will realize the truth. That's how things gets better.

"As with anything, I think it's important to keep trying. As you do this, you will get to know each other better. I'm just trying to make things better. 'If you're going to say that much, we are going to do it, too,' they said. Eventually, I went to the subcontractor myself and gave them the order."

Understanding the process of a twenty-something designer realizing his design ideas while dealing with the older and more experienced workers on the site, many of whom had craftsman mentality, is very impressive.

So how did the factory handle the assembly of these cameras?

According to Kazuo Naito, "The Canonet was unlike anything we had produced before and it couldn't be assembled in a conventional assembly workplace. That is why Canon established the Canonet development start-up team. It was probably the first of its kind in Japan as well. We thought about how to make the process flow efficiently without causing any problems.

"Therefore, we took apart the prototype, placed the parts, took a picture of it from directly above, and assembled it in reverse. Before we first started the flow, we decided which parts were risky and measured their dimensions. That way, if a problem occurs after assembly, you will know which is at fault: the assembly method or the design.

Until then, when it came to pressed products, they were mainly pots and pans, and it was unthinkable to use press punched parts for the precision parts of cameras. The parts for high-end cameras were all machined. This was one of the reasons for the high cost. The Canonet was the first to use pressed parts."

There was also debate about the selling price of the camera. At a meeting of the New Products Committee, Masanori Seki insisted on a price in the 10,000 yen range, Maeda and Hayashi objected, saying it was too low, but ultimately Seki prevailed and the price was set at 18,800 yen.

Maeda had reservations about Canon entering the mid-range market, but after touring Europe with prototypes and receiving enthusiastic reviews, he became an active proponent. When he returned to Japan, he visited shutter manufacturers accompanied by Ryoichiro Yamagata and Goshima.

"We will buy at least 10,000 of these shutters per month," he told them. "In exchange, we would like you to lower the unit price as much as possible. Eventually, we will buy 20,000 to 30,000 per month."

Listening to him, Goshima was astonished. As a designer, he was convinced that the camera should be mass-produced, but he also wondered if it would actually sell. In any case, it was true that these were unprecedented figures, as no Japanese camera had ever sold so many units before.

At a camera show held at the Takashimaya Department store in Tokyo's Nihonbashi district, customers exiting the elevator flowed toward the Canon booth, prompting a Canon employee to yell, "You didn't come here to look at people's heads."

"The Canonet created a huge stir. It marked the beginning of the shift from buying one camera and having it last a lifetime to cameras being more of a disposable product," according to Michio Kimura, president of Camera no Kimura.

"I thought it would be okay if the price was 20% higher," said Eiji Hashimoto of Nihonbashi Camera, who later went to the factory in Shimomaruko to yell at the employees because they had no products to sell him.

Entering the U.S. Market with a Tragic Determination

Around the year 1960, Canon quickly rose to become a global brand. It began in 1955, after the M3 shock but before the Synchroreader disaster, and it was a period of great expansion that was marked by the launch of the Canonet.

Tomomasa Matsui, a former naval officer who had built airfields to fight against the U.S., and his five employees were now in a room in a building on Fifth Avenue in the middle of New York City. In July 1955, only the Consulate-General of Japan and Canon were displaying the Hinomaru (Japan's national flag). That same month, the contract with Jardine Matheson, the sole export agency, had expired.

However, Matsui and his team came to the U.S. with almost tragic determination. In March of the same year, only five units of the flagship model IV Sb were sold in the U.S., and in May, just 15 units were sold at a special discount price.

In fact, when they traveled around the U.S., they found that there were only one or two retail stores every 50 miles (80 km) in the Midwest. One time, they arrived at a store before it opened and waited out front, and the owner of the store was curious why they had come all the way from Asia. He asked them how many German scientists Canon had, and remarked, "The Japanese are very good at imitation and they have an artistic flair." They didn't know whether he was complimenting or disparaging them. Matsui would remove the screws from the camera and show the store owners what was inside, explaining the differences between the Canon camera and those made in Germany.

The company entered the European market in 1957, when Canon Europa was established in Geneva, Switzerland, as the sole distributor in Europe. At the time, West Germany was producing 200,000 cameras per month, 90% of which were exported, while Japan was producing only 70,000 units per month.

Canon's European operation was established when Mitarai and Maeda made an inspection tour of Europe and the U.S. It was a significant milestone for Mitarai, who had long dreamed of defeating Leica, to finally establish a foothold in Europe.

In July 1959, Keishi Fukuda (born in 1934, joined the company in 1956) moved to Geneva on his own. Retailers were under pressure from German camera manufacturers, making it difficult for them to also carry Japanese cameras. Import restrictions were strong in the U.K. and France, so Canon focused on Nordic countries, the Netherlands, and Switzerland, where German influence was not as strong. Fukuda's first job was sorting goods and preparing them for shipment, a job he held for three years.

The warehouse didn't have a heater and became very cold in winter. Even wearing heavy clothes didn't help much. There was a wine cellar nearby, where wine was delivered by wagon to be bottled. Some of the Swiss would steal that wine, heat it up, and give it to him to drink so he could finally warm himself up.

Hiroto Kagami (joined the company in 1954) was transferred to New York in 1959, the same year as Fukuda. The salary is $300 per take-home pay. The rent is $80. Seven dollars and thirty cents a day covers three meals, clothing, and other expenses. His friends would drop by his apartment and cook dinner for themselves, and he enjoyed occasional dinners at a Japanese restaurant. "It was the best when Mitarai came to visit and had a party."

A Japanese employee working at Fujifilm's New York office was similar, and since chicken necks were cheap, he bought them in large quantities. One day, the president of Fujifilm came to New York and he took him to the boarding house to show him how bad his living condition was. As soon as he entered, the president said, "Oh my, you are living in a nice place." In Japan at that time, the standard boarding houses for a bachelor were made of plywood, but in New York, even in the poorer neighborhoods, they were made of reinforced concrete.

Kagami bought the cheapest suit he could find for $30 in Times Square. It looked good but became shabby when exposed to the rain. He often went to the movies because they were cheap and air-conditioned, but when he left the theater, his trousers had baggy knees.

Germany in a Corner

The Brussels World's Fair, where the Synchroreader was exhibited, was held in March 1958, and 43 countries, including the U.S. and the U.S.S.R., participated. Canon and Nippon Kogaku won the Grand Prix in the photography category.

According to a report in the company newsletter written by Shigeo Suzuki, who was in charge of the project at that time, the whole of Germany was intensely hostile toward Japanese cameras. No Japanese cameras were sold in Germany, and German camera magazines refused to publish ads for Japanese products. However, for cameras in the same price range, Japanese quality was higher, and for cameras of the same quality, Japanese cameras were less expensive. Leica launched a price-cutting offensive as a countermeasure, but it was said that they had to lay off 1,500 employees, and it seemed that the Germans felt they were being "cornered."

Canon tried to exhibit at Photokina (see below) in September of that year, but the organizer refused, saying, "We cannot give a place to a Japanese camera manufacturer." In response, Canon registered for a booth under the name of a European distributor. It was a cramped area that is more of a hallway.

However, two years later, in 1960 (the year the Canonet was announced), Canon would achieve groundbreaking success in two major events.

One was the Canon Europa Sales Conference held in Tokyo for ten days in mid-April, which was attended by 54 distributors and retailers from 17 countries, an unprecedented feat for a single private company, not just for the camera industry but for other industries as well.

Although Canon had begun building a sales network in Europe and the U.S. four or five years earlier, few people in Japan recognized the courage it took to be Canon's distributor in Europe at that time. This can be understood, for example, by considering the difficulties involved when a foreign manufacturer attempted to enter the field of a traditional Japanese industry. If you became a distributor of Japanese cameras, you would be boycotted by German manufacturers. Under these circumstances, Mitarai decided it was best to select a company with more enthusiasm for selling Canon products rather than that with abundant money and employees. He also believed it was important to be "honest with your eyes even if you don't speak the same language."

Once they saw Canon's factory with their own eyes, attendees from other countries gained confidence in the company's products and developed a new appreciation of Japan. The fact that the standard of living in Japanese cities was higher than in many European cities also came as a big surprise. In his opening remarks at the conference, Mitarai used the phrase "Canon family," a phrase that has been used around the world since then.

Mitarai was always mindful to develop deep personal connections with the owner or president of a distributor. When he met them, he would greet them warmly, and when they parted ways, he would say "See you soon." Whenever he attended a party, he would soon be surrounded people eager to say hello to "Dr. Mitarai." This was an intangible but important force in the establishment of Canon's overseas branches.

The other event was Photokina (Cologne, West Germany) in September of that year. This can be thought of as a kind of camera industry Olympics, with the world's best cameras exhibited under one roof, competing for recognition as the best in the world. The attention and success of this event had a strong influence on the camera industry for years to come.

Canon was given a 200-square-meter area, an eye-catching location previously used by Kodak, which was proof that Canon's capabilities were starting to be recognized internationally.

Their first aim during the preparations for the event was to dispel the notion that Japanese cameras are imitations of German products. The day before the opening of the exhibition, Canon held a press conference and invited about 200 reporters to attend.

"For the past 20 years," Mitarai began, "we have conducted research and worked to develop the Japanese camera industry, but Germany is, after all, an advanced country, and we have great respect for them. Today, however, we compete on an equal footing. We are not, as some people think, making cheap or inferior products."

The most popular items on display were a 7-type camera with an $f/0.95$ lens, which captures more light than the human eye, and a super-telephoto 2000-mm lens.

On November 8, 1960, the *Mainichi Shimbun* newspaper reported on the world camera industry at that time as follows.

"Japanese cameras, which have been competing with German cameras dividing the world in two, are becoming 'the world's cameras.' In the U.S. market, Japanese cameras have an advantage over German cameras. The European market is still 50 – 50, but high-end products from Nikon and Canon are gaining market share faster than Germany's Leica and Contax. According to a survey by the Japan Machinery Center for Trade and Investment, the export value of the five major companies in the last six months was a combined 1.1 billion yen for Canon and Yashica, 770 million yen for Nippon Kogaku, and so on.

"In particular, the Model VII, with a lens that captures more light than the human eye ($f/0.95$), which Canon began marketing overseas at the end of September, has been greeted with astonishment in Germany and elsewhere.

"Japanese-made products are now making inroads into department stores and mail-order services, as well as the storefronts of camera shops in Germany, which has boasted of being the 'camera kingdom.'"

In other words, the consequences of the camera war between Germany and Japan were coming into focus.

Then, in 1961, Charles Percy finally bowed before Mitarai.

"Please let us sell Canon products for you."

Mitarai thought that "The enemy had fallen to the gates of war," and that "A bird in distress gets into your pocket." Ten years had passed since that time of "sorrow." He thought it had been a long time, but on the other hand, he was amazed that they have come this far in ten years. "All right, I'll embrace him," Mitarai thought to himself. Canon signed a five-year sales agreement with Bell & Howell.

By 1961, Japan had become one of the three largest camera-producing countries, along with the U.S. and Germany (see the table below, export value in parentheses).

	Still Cameras	Movie Cameras	Total(100 million yen)
Japan	194 (71)	78 (44)	272 (115)
West Germany	249 (146)	21 (10)	270 (156)
U.S.	188 (20)	177 (36)	365 (56)

Looking at Canon's growth, sales nearly quadrupled from 1955 to 1961, far exceeding the camera industry's growth as a whole. In the three years from 1959 to 1961, sales grew 2.5 times, profits grew 3.3 times, and capital investment grew more than 5 times (see the table below).

	Sales	Profit	Capital Expenditures(Unit: Million yen)
1959	2,862	224	130
1960	4,272	424	480
1961	7,126	733	680

The future looked bright.

In 1962, Canon Latin America was established in Panama, Central America.

Mitarai liked to surprise people from time to time. A Canonet factory was built on the land in Toride originally purchased to manufacture the Synchroreader, and a subsidiary called "Canon Inc." was established in December 1960 (the headquarters was still called Canon Camera). At the opening ceremony on January 5th of the following year, Mitarai and three executives from Tokyo boarded a large helicopter and flew to Toride with a banner reading "New Year's greetings from Canon" waving in the air. The three-hour drive by car took only 25 minutes by helicopter. This was the only way they could attend the opening ceremonies in Tokyo and Ibaraki on the same day, but he probably wanted to try something like this.

Standing on Top of the World

At the 8th Photokina in March 1963, a boat named Canon Maru floated down the Rhine River, where Canon officials and the employees of distributors from various countries stayed.

Mitarai, who gave a speech in German, used chopsticks as a conductor's baton to lead the 20 employees in singing the Canon company song. The song began with the words, "The eagle's banner flutters in the wind, as the glorious light shines on it," followed by the words, "With sincerity, we stand united in the times, with faith and love, our power is renewed. The flower of self-motivation blooms in the garden of self-governance, and self-awareness grows in the garden of cooperation. We vow "three selfs" at Canon, and we are here because of the three selfs." The singing voice was heard on the river. After that, each country sang their own songs, and the singing contest, scheduled to end at 10 p.m., lasted until 12 a.m., with even the ship's crew joining in the fun. The event ended with everyone singing "*Hotaru no Hikari*" (Glow of a Firefly) (sung to the tune of the Scottish folk song "Auld Lang Syne"), a great demonstration of the Canon family.

The centerpiece of the exhibit was an autofocus camera, something that had long been touted as a "dream camera." There is a good reason why it attracted so much attention. A few months before the announcement of this autofocus camera, a magazine had written that an autofocus camera would be as big as a small truck, and even if it were possible to build one, the functionality could not be achieved in a small camera.

"Before the opening of Photokina, Canon Camera held a special reception aboard the *Canon Maru*, on the Rhine River, and unveiled the world's first autofocus camera, much to the surprise of the assembled camera experts. "This camera is a sign of the direction of future cameras," said Carl Sandel, senior writer of the Swedish magazine *Photonator*." – March 15, United Press International (UPI) from Cologne

"The engineers at Canon have perfected the 'dream camera' or 'camera of the future.' This amazing camera can even automatically set the sensitivity of the film. To take a picture, you simply capture the subject in the viewfinder and press the shutter release button." – *Stern* (a weekly magazine with a circulation of 1.5 million in West Germany)

"Canon's AF cameras have already overtaken Germany's once leading position in photographic technology. After World War II, Japanese cameras broke the dominance of West German cameras in many countries, especially in terms of technology, perfecting the wide-angle 35 mm $f/1.5$ lens (in Germany it was only $f/2.8$) or the $f/0.95$ lens that captures more light than the human eye (both made by Canon)"– *Der Spiegel* (a weekly magazine for intellectuals, known for its sharp commentary, etc.)

When asked by a UPI reporter about autofocus cameras, Walter Hering, publisher of West Germany's leading camera magazine, said, "Japan has proven that it can create something new and wonderful, not just imitate or improve on our designs."

Immediately after Photokina, the *Herald Tribune*, an American business newspaper, wrote, "The image of 'made in Germany' as traditional technology and high quality is crumbling. The reasons for this are a lack of pride among workers, labor shortages, and frequent changes in workplaces."

Stern listed the Color Polaroid, Kodak Instamatic, and Canon AF camera as the three greatest inventions presented at Photokina.

Canon's in-house magazine published an article entitled "On Top of the World" about a roundtable discussion on the events of Photokina. In November of the same year, Canon moved its headquarters to Ginza, and in December the company issued European Depositary Receipts (EDRs).

For Japanese employees working outside of Japan, however, the situation was far from that of the "global" Canon.

After three years in the U.S., Hiroto Kagami was sent to Bell & Howell's Canadian office in Toronto to repair Canon products as well as train Bell employees how to perform repairs. Canon thought it had a partnership with Bell & Howell, but the Bell people thought it was a takeover of Canon. Different countries, different companies. Their ignorance of Japan was also difficult for Kagami. For example, when it snowed, they would say, "Hurry, come here a minute, this is snow." Or they would ask questions such as "Do they have elevators in Japan?" He felt alone and was inconsolable.

This discrepancy may have been a reflection of Canon's ambition to "stand on top of the world." It took more than 16 years from the debut of the "dream camera," which was hailed as one of the world's three greatest inventions, to be made into a commercial product and conquer the global market.

Chapter 5

Through the Depression

Chapter 5

Through the Depression

"If You Make the President Angry, You Win."

It was "common knowledge" on the union side that if they made Mitarai angry at the collective bargaining table, they would win.

GHQ, or General Headquarters, held absolute power in postwar Japan. Exploiting the acronym, an anti-occupation-forces slogan emerged, "Yankee Go Home Quickly." Building on this, Mitarai adopted the phrase "Go Home Quickly" as an expression of Mitarai-ism, sparking significant media attention. In addition, with the prospect that the same level of working hours as in Europe and the U.S. would soon become the norm in Japan, as well as for the health of his employees, Mitarai was the first in Japan to experiment with a five-day workweek. All of these efforts took place around 1960, at a time when the company was attracting attention for its unique products and achieving a number of successes at the annual Photokina exhibition.

As the Canonet's production grew, so too did the number of employees at Canon. The number of female temporary workers also increased rapidly, accounting for about half of the total number of employees. The union chairman at that time was Seiichi Takigawa, who had been treated to dinner at Mitarai's home before being asked to work on the Synchroreader project.

He was able to persuade the temporary workers, who were unwilling to listen to the president of the head office labor union, while he negotiated with management to establish a temporary worker promotion system, opening a path for them to become regular employees, thereby avoiding a situation in which there two unions.

Around the same time, a review of the wage structure was needed. In 1957, when Canon Europe was established in Geneva, conveyor belts were introduced to Canon for the first time, and mass production of high-end P-type machines began the following year. In other industries, Hitachi Zosen's Innoshima Works shipyard introduced flow work in shipbuilding in 1956, and Nissan Motor's Yokohama Plant used a transfer machine to serialize the machining process. This was the time when Japan began to innovate.

Because the use of machines improved productivity, the reward system, which was based on manual labor, no longer suited the reality. Just as Ryoichiro Yamagata and Kazuo Naito worked to standardize the cutting tools used by craftsmen, it is also a process of taking away their own personal tools that could be called their alter ego. However, new products were coming out one after another, and by the time the unit prices of parts needed for the calculation of rewards could be determined, the next product started flowing down the line. Therefore, in September 1960, a fixed wage system was introduced.

Takigawa was also involved in the negotiations as chairman of the union. He became the head of the Personnel Section in 1962, where he was responsible for implementing the new wage system. However, there were various problems, and he and Mitarai often disagreed.

"You're hard-headed, you don't know anything, you only know about Japan," Mitarai told him.

One day, Takigawa received orders from Mitarai to go abroad to study the labor situation and conduct a fact-finding survey. The mission was to determine how to incorporate a Western-style job-based wage system into the Japanese lifetime employment system, or in other words, how to reflect Mitarai's long-standing insistence on a meritocracy without regard to academic background in terms of employee wages. This became the basis for the subsequent wage system at Canon.

When Michitsura Ishihara, the managing director, participated in the negotiations with the union, things did not go well on the union side. He was very patient and never showed anger on his round face, but wages did not rise. Eventually, the union would say, "Well, next time." However, when Mitarai thought that the union had not understood what he said and they made remarks that didn't make sense, he got angry. Instead of expressing his opinions out loud, he became angry, and refused to back down and pay more. People around him might be upset that they wouldn't be able to pay as much as he promised, but he didn't care about such things. The union often demanded, "We want to talk with the president."

"The president's personality had a positive effect on the company. Every employee had the impression that the president was an honest person, and there was no sense of cunning in his image to his employees," according to Takigawa.

This impression was not limited to Takigawa and his colleagues or the older employees. Kiyoshi Uehara, who had joined the company mid-career in 1962 and now based in Singapore, had the impression as a union representative that Mitarai "always seemed to take our demands seriously and did not dismiss them cunningly."

In the early 1950s, when Takigawa, Kaku, and the others joined the company, Canon was known for its high wages, which was the main reason that Takigawa decided to work there, and he was not alone. Even Canon's factory in Shimomaruko was said to be exceptional. The company's bonuses were above national standards for a trichotomy system. There were between 1,000 and 1,500 employees, and the company created a family-like atmosphere by organizing monthly birthday parties, annual family reunions, Bon Dance festivals, and other events. Under these circumstances, it was nearly impossible for the few workers who wanted to strike to convince everyone else to join them. One of Mitarai's greatest boasts was that Canon never had a strike since its founding.

The GHQ Movement and the Five-Day Workweek System

In April 1952, the Treaty of Peace with Japan and the Japan–U.S. Security Treaty came into effect, and in the same month, the General Headquarters for the Allied Powers (GHQ) was abolished. Seven years later, in 1959, Mitarai started the Go Home Quickly (GHQ) movement.

Mitarai described his thinking as follows: "A person who has a healthy and happy family is a good employee. Some men play *mahjong* (a Chinese table game) or go for a drink after work. When he comes home late every night, his wife loses respect for him and they fight. That is not a good way to do good work. At the drinking parties after work, employees are only wasting the company's money. They should have dinner with their beloved wives and children as much as possible."

Tadashi Nakamura, who joined the company in 1949, recalled a conversation with his wife once when he came home late.

"The president said 'GHQ,' didn't he?" "Don't be silly, my work doesn't allow me to leave early." "You were probably drinking somewhere," she complained. "No, that's not what he meant. He meant that we should leave as soon as we finished work."

Whether or not his wife was convinced by this, she said, "My husband comes home late, but the president tells him to go home early. He (Mitarai) is a good man." In other words, Mitarai was a "sensible man." Among the wives of his employees, the number of "fans" who looked forward to hearing Mitarai's stories at family meetings increased.

In 1960, a five-day summer vacation was implemented, and a five-year plan to shorten working hours began in 1963. Mitarai explained his motivation at the beginning of 1962 when he said, "I have been traveling abroad since 1950, and people always tell me that Japan is a country with cheap labor and long working hours. I want to show that this is not the case." He made this statement without first consulting the other company executives.

The labor–management council discussed the issue, sent out a questionnaire to union members asking what kind of time reduction they would like, and then shortened Saturdays to half-days during July, August, and September of that year as a trial. In the fall, the union requested "five-day work week, even if the daily working hours are longer" and in July 1966, a five-day work week was instituted. Soon, Matsushita Electric Industrial Co. followed suit.

The Nikkeiren (Japan Federation of Employers' Associations) scolded Mitarai, saying, "What a load of nonsense!" Mitarai also heard criticism such as, "His idealism is good, but he is too forward-thinking, imitating foreign countries and getting ahead of everyone else." Mitarai himself told the then secretary-general, "I may have been a little premature." However, the idea behind the five-day work week system was clearly stated in his New Year's greetings in 1964.

"I am convinced that corporate management must be based on ideals or dreams, and I have been working with you all to this day with these ideals in mind.

Looking back on last year, first of all, we took steps toward the long-dreamed-of five-day work week system. This was a major revolution in the Japanese labor world as a whole. However, we did not take the lead simply out of a sense of vanity.

Perhaps other Japanese companies will follow our lead, one after another. Fortunately, the first year went well. I am hopeful that we will manage to do well again this year. If we fail to do so, I believe it would be a great tragedy for all of Japan's industries. People will surely say, 'Look at Canon, they tried but failed, and we can't just sit back and shorten our work hours.' And the general workforce will say that 'Since even Canon couldn't do it, we can only dream about it.' We all have a huge responsibility to fulfill. Let us fulfill this responsibility one way or another.

When Canon employees went out on Saturdays with their families, they became objects of wonder and envy, with some people asking, "Oh, how come your husband is here with you?" But there were also times when people were suspicious. "He says he doesn't have to work today, but I think he was fired from his job."

"I Know How Suicide Victims Feel."

Thus, Canon seemed to have developed in a good way, both inside and outside the company. However, in 1963, when Canon attracted the world's attention with its AF cameras, negative signs were beginning to emerge, such as the problem of "dumping" of Japanese cameras overseas. And in 1964, every camera manufacturer in Japan was frantically competing against each other to expand their sales. Although they had increased production in anticipation of the 1964 Tokyo Olympics, sales were not as strong as expected, and inventories were overstocked.

As a result, manufacturers engaged in a variety of new sales tactics designed to undercut the competition, including pushing inventory to dealers, prize giveaways, invitational sales, rebate competitions, and price discounting, which resulted in a noticeable decline in profit margins for each company across the industry. In the first half of 1961, Canon, Minolta, Nippon Kogaku, and Olympus had combined sales of 7.9 billion yen with a net income of 360 million yen, whereas in the first half of 1965, their sales and net income were 21.6 billion yen and 630 million yen, respectively, a dramatic decline in profitability (according to Japan Camera Inspection Institute (ed.), *Japanese Cameras around the World*).

In 1954, when Canon's IV Sb was flourishing, the factory cost ratio was 45% and gross profit was 55%, which was a time when "people at Canon couldn't stop smiling." In 1959 and 1960, performance leveled off, and by 1965, the cost ratio had increased to 72%.

Against this backdrop, Mitarai proposed at a meeting of the Japan Camera Industry Association board of directors that each company reduce production, and in April 1965, a cartel was formed to deal with the recession. This was the first recession countermeasure ever taken in the camera industry.

Kazuo Mizukoshi (born in 1926), who joined the company in 1950 and was then the manager of the Engineering Design Section of the Production Engineering Department, was sad to see the cancellation of a planned equipment order.

From 1964 to 1965, regular events such as birthday parties, family reunions, coming-of-age celebrations, and the party celebrating the anniversary of the company's founding were canceled. In March 1965, the head office was moved from the Fukihara Building in Ginza back to the factory in Shimomaruko. They had been in Ginza for only 16 months. Some ridiculed the company, saying, "If money becomes tight, they'll move their headquarters," and they were also criticized for their "inconsistency" However, Mitarai remained unconcerned, saying, "A wise man changes his mind, a fool never."

In his New Year's address in 1965, Mitarai took responsibility for his leadership, saying, "I ask you to hold out for development of the Grand Canon. It was I who created the optimistic mood" However, there was a story circulating within the company that he had expressed a desire to quit. Four or five years later, we finally learned what Mitarai was feeling at that time.

"I don't mean to gloat, but when I am in pain, I can never get myself to snore peacefully in bed at night. At the time, I thought to myself, 'I see that suicide is a last resort when people are in pain, and I understand to some extent how people who attempt suicide feel.'"

"When Japan lost the war, I felt like I was in the depths of grief. In those days, experts said that, considering the long history of Japan, losing once or twice was no big deal and that this would eventually become the basis for the next great leap forward. The previous hardships taught us lessons in many ways, and I came to feel that we could make even greater strides in the future if we could grow out of the suffering." (1968 Intra-Community Symposium)

"Remember Pearl Harbor, so that we will not forget the recession of 1964 and 1965. We will deal with the situation in a normal manner so that the seriousness of the situation will not be repeated." (New Year's Greetings for 1969)

"The year 1965 was a crisis for our company. An optimistic mood prevailed in the company, but the warehouse was in a pitiful state, with inventory piling up and hardly anything leaving the warehouse. However, it is a great memory, how everyone worked together to rebuild the company. (New Year's greetings for 1970)

A Newborn Child to Be Enrolled in School Right Away?

However, during this period from 1964 to 1965, there were new developments in fields other than cameras that would go on to be successes in their own right.

AF cameras became a hot topic in 1963, although, in July of that year, Hiroshi Ito, then deputy director of Tokki Seisakusho (Special Machinery Works), was in Moscow to participate in a scientific machinery trade fair. A telegram reading "Kodomo umareta" (The child was born) was to be sent from Japan if the prototype of a transistor-based desktop calculator that Ito had been helping to develop in secret for some time worked well. One day, the long-awaited telegram arrived, but it read "Shiken ni goukaku" (Passed the exam) but there was no sender.

Because he had two daughters and was dealing with the issue of their education, he thought the message might have been about their school entrance examinations. He sent a letter to home, asking why they had sent such a telegram, but in the end, he did not understand the meaning of the telegram until he returned to Japan.

In fact, during Ito's stay in Moscow, work on the prototype should have progressed to the point where it could perform the four arithmetic operations (i.e., addition, subtraction, multiplication, and division), and if that could not be achieved, then the project would likely be canceled. However, it was even more successful than expected, and the person in charge was so excited that he sent the aforementioned telegram, signifying that not only had the "child" been born but had grown up and passed its "entrance examination" as well.

This desktop calculator was the result of one of Canon's various attempts to expand beyond the camera field, while keeping in mind the terrible failure of the Synchroreader.

162

Up to that point, Canon had produced high- and mid-range cameras, and 8-mm movie camera as well as X-ray machines, and in October 1961, had entered into a business partnership with the American company DocuMat to produce microfilm cameras and launched a microsystem to duplicate checks. Also in 1961, Canon created its first long-term plan, which was the first step in its efforts to diversify.

As part of its diversification efforts, the company established Tokki Seisakusho in September 1962 as an unprecedented experiment. The new facility would be home to an experimental group of 200 employees. Their mission was to conduct R&D with the aim of commercializing products other than cameras. The facility has development, production, and sales departments within it, and it aims to turn profit as an independent unit. Ryuzaburo Kaku, the head of the Planning Office (director, Masanori Seki), who drew up the long-term plan, proposed the establishment of a company-wide business division system, but his proposal was rejected.

The electrical engineers who had worked on the Synchroreader were assigned to the new team, and they came to be known within the company as the "remnants" of the Synchroreader team. Around that time, an agency that handled microsystems asked if there were any other office machines available from Canon. Ito, who had previously worked in lens design, had always wanted a new type of calculator because the relay calculators they used for lens calculations were unusually loud and prone to break down, and the number board spun around, causing the user to develop astigmatism. Even Kaku, who worked in accounting, was put off by how noisy the calculators were.

At the time, the desktop calculator ANITA by a British manufacturer was already on the market, but it merely replaced part of the mechanism with electricity, and the transistor technology was not fully utilized.

Ito decided to take the plunge into calculator development when he became deputy director. He began researching the ANITA patents, among other things, but soon three questions emerged.

(1) Should we use a full-key system for entering numbers? In other words, should it be an ANITA type device, with keys from 0 to 9 for the number of digits that can be calculated, or should it be a ten-key system?

(2) Thousands of transistors and diodes are needed, but when assembled, they are too big to fit on a table, so can we make them smaller?

(3) To date, we have always displayed the results using a drum engraved with numbers that is rotated by gears, but how can we display the numbers that are calculated electronically?

As their research efforts progressed, the volume of transistors and diodes that Canon ordered increased sharply, and the electronics manufacturers that supplied them became suspicious. Sometimes the team would hide their true purpose by saying they were for special medical and optical devices.

The Calculator Wars Begin

The result was reflected in the telegram mentioned earlier, and Ito wanted to exhibit the calculator at a business show in May 1964. Maeda, who was managing director at the time, was concerned about repeating the Synchroreader disaster and wondered whether to exhibit the calculator. Sensing this, Ito asked Mitarai to take a look at the prototype before his trip to Japan. Mitarai was so pleased with the prototype that he took off for foreign countries, but he was said, "No way. You shouldn't do that. You'll lose out to the electronics manufacturers very quickly." Accordingly, Mitarai sent Maeda a telegram telling him to "call it off." One month before the show, a meeting was held to decide whether or not to exhibit the calculator.

Meanwhile, Seki, the head of the planning office, and Kaku, the section manager, were also thinking about persuading Maeda to move forward with the project. But Seki's father died around that time, and the date of the funeral coincided with the meeting. The day before the meeting, Kaku called Seki and told him, "I am sorry, but I will not be able to attend your father's funeral because it is an important meeting," to which Seki replied, "Okay, you can make the big pitch."

Tomomasa Matsui, who had become the managing director and head of the personnel department, was Seki and Kaku's former boss and had also introduced Seki to his wife. When he heard about the decision, he chastised Kaku, saying, "Is it true that you're not going to the funeral? Isn't he your direct subordinate?" Kaku replied, "I have a feeling that this project will change the fate of Canon. I will go to the meeting if Mr. Seki's says it's OK." Matsui, was a compassionate man but replied angrily, "You can go to a meeting anytime you want. But Mr. Seki's father will have only one funeral. Let's go to the funeral, both of us." Kaku replied that he would like to have one more night to think about it, and after having a premonition, he chose not to attend the funeral after all.

As expected, the meeting did not go smoothly. Ito wanted to get permission to proceed with the project. The young engineers, including the "remnants" of the Synchroreaders, had been working hard to be of service to the company, and if they succeeded, it would be the beginning of a turnaround for the loss-making Tokki Seisakusho team. Maeda, however, didn't see it that way. "You have studied hard and produced a very good product," he said, "but let's stop with the prototype."

Ito expressed his conviction as an engineer that their creation was superior to conventional calculators, that there was nothing else like it in the world today, and that even if Canon did not release one, another company surely would. "Even if we make two or three hundred units and don't sell them all, we will only lose 20 million yen, so please let us do it." He continued on for an hour. Finally, Maeda had nothing left to say. Maeda asked Takaaki Yamamoto, the manager in charge of sales at Tokki Seisakusho, if he thought it would sell, and Ito was relieved to hear Yamamoto reply, "I think it will." And thus it was decided that the prototype would be mass-produced and exhibited at the show.

In May 1964, the Canola 130 was announced, and around the same time, Sharp announced the Compet CS-10A. Shortly before that, Sony had announced a similar model in New York, but it remained in a glass case. The Canola 130 was a ten-key calculator with a thirteen-digit display and cost 360,000 yen, while the Sharp was a full-key calculator with a ten-digit display and cost 535,000 yen. Generally, Sharp is regarded as the pioneer of calculators (which I wrote about in my book *Sharp Pioneering New Electronics*), but the Canola 130 was far superior to the Compet CS-10A, with less than half the power consumption, two-thirds the weight, a simple ten-key interface, and a much lower price. This is the reason why Kaku says, "Canon was the first company to invent the calculator."

Sharp's Compet CS-10A was released just after Canon announced the Canola 130. Meanwhile, Canon had to quickly learn soldering and other processes. "If a camera company makes a calculator and it fails, it's a disgrace to the precision industry, so let's spend the money to make a good one," said Hiroshi Ito. Once the Canola 130 went on sale in the fall, it overwhelmed the Compet CS-10A. Sharp responded in the following year by launching a competing model, the CS-20A, which had a ten-key interface and was sold for 379,000 yen. That same year, Casio also launched a product for 380,000 yen, but Canon was the price leader at this point.

The way in which the Synchroreader had been withdrawn from the market was actually a positive factor in the creation of a sales network for the Canola 130. According to Seiichi Takigawa, this was because all the dealers at that time had come together to support the Canola 130.

Despite all the drama, the Canola 130 was a success and helped to keep Canon stable during the 1965 recession.

The Wall of Xerox, the World Giant

"From now on, we need to aim for the Hannover Messe."

Those who were listening could not believe their ears. Although they were about to attend Photokina, a trade fair for cameras, Mitarai was talking about a trade fair for office machines, which was also held in Germany. Satoshi Nemoto (who joined the company in 1951), the head of the technical department, didn't know what to say when his subordinates asked him, "Does that mean that we have had enough of cameras? We're going to Photokina, not Hannover!"

This was at a time when the office equipment division was just beginning to sprout, and Mitarai was determined to expand beyond the camera field.

The story goes back to 1961, several years earlier. To conclude a sales agreement with Bell & Howell, Mitarai went to the United States accompanied by Hiroshi Suzukawa, Director and General Manager of the Technical Department, and Keizo Yamaji (born in 1927, joined Canon in 1951), who was known for his zoom lens design. The three unexpectedly agreed that the company should create a division specializing in something other than cameras.

In February 1962, Yamaji traveled to the U.S. on a fact-finding mission to learn about the technology being used in the electronics industry. He visited Eastman Kodak, IBM's Watson Research Center, and the Massachusetts Institute of Technology to observe their cutting-edge technology, and was inspired by the R&D efforts of optical equipment manufacturers and research institutes in the field of office equipment. In September of that year, Yamaji was appointed manager of the newly established Product Research Section of the Engineering Department. In fact, because Nemoto had been in charge of creating the company's diversification plan when he was the Planning Office manager, this was an unexpected beginning to the realization of the plan.

Seven members, including Yamaji himself, began research and trial production of microfilm, video cassette recorders, autofocus cameras, cameras with built-in strobes, and photocopy machines, but only one member, Hiroshi Tanaka, who joined the company mid-career from Oriental Shashin Kogyo (currently Oriental Photo Corporation), was in charge of photocopiers. It was impossible for one person to cover everything, including the photoconductor, developer, and other mechanisms, and he needed more people. However, Yamaji did not have to worry. Likely at the behest of Mitarai and Suzukawa, Seiichi Takigawa, who was the head of the personnel section, told Yamaji, "We will give you all the personnel you need, regardless of the economic situation," and he did not restrict the budget.

The challenge was how to overcome the problem of the 500 patents held by the "world giant" Xerox. Arthur D. Little, a well-known research firm based in Boston, Massachusetts, wrote in a report at the time, "In the 1960s and 1970s, there will be no technological development that will pose a threat to Xerox, and even if there were, it will be subpar. Xerox is amortizing its machines through a rental system, so when rivals appear, Xerox will offer amortized machines at low prices, and rivals will be quickly eliminated."

What is written in the report was correct, and to that extent, any effort to challenge the wall that is Xerox was reckless. However, in April 1968, five years after development started, the Canon NP System was presented at the Keidanren Kaikan (Japan Business Federation Hall) in Otemachi, Tokyo, and then in May at Hannover Messe, where it attracted the attention of Xerox officials and others.

NP had two meanings: "new process" and "no pollution." Until then, the photosensitive plates of plain paper copiers (PPCs) were made with selenium, a heavy metal, and they were exposed and could be touched by hands. In the NP system, however, the surface of the photosensitive plate was covered with an insulating film, and its three-layer structure differed from the conventional two-layer structure.

Specifically, there was a conductive layer that conducted electricity at the bottom and a light-sensitive photoconductive layer over it, and another film on top of that. Therefore, there was no contact with selenium, no selenium powder, and no selenium dissolved in the developing solution. To obtain a clearer image with the three-layer structure, a new three-step method was devised: 1) conventional charging, 2) exposure and static elimination, and 3) full exposure. This was different from the conventional two-step method of 1) charging and 2) exposure. Because of the uniqueness of this new method, Yamaji, Tanaka, and Giichi Marushima (patent-related) received the Commendation for Science and Technology.

In October 1970, the NP-1100 was launched, followed two years later by the liquid-dry NP-L7. This was the world's first PPC that did not use the thermal dry development method typified by Xerox.

In the thermal dry method, powder is fixed to the paper by heat. The liquid-dry method was simpler, less expensive, and required less space.

However, the development of a liquid-dry toner (developer) was a difficult task to achieve. The size of the powder particles was several tens of micrometers, while the liquid particles were only a few micrometers, so the liquid toner produced sharper images. Canon's patent for this technology would earn the company over 3 billions of yen in licensing fees each year (at the time of interview).

Canon differentiated itself from Xerox in its approach to sales as well, with its unique "Total Guarantee Method." The sales system for copiers was either a Xerox-style rental or a direct purchase. In the rental system, the customer's upfront costs were lower. However, with rental machines, customers would likely demand an upgrade when new products are released. Canon therefore decided to earn its profits from copies rather than from the equipment itself, and adopted an arrangement that fell somewhere between renting and selling. The customer would buy the machine but Canon would take care of all after-sales services, including the supply of consumables.

The initial environmental tests were conducted in the bathing room of the Shimomaruko Plant, testing the paper feed in an environment with close to 100% humidity. They continuously boiled water to keep the room full of steam, and tested the machine, but it failed due to condensation. In the next test, they warmed the machine up on a stove first and then brought it into the bathing room, where it was functioned as intended.

In 1962, Xerox became the first company to enter the PPC market in Japan (in a joint partnership with Fuji Photo Film, presently Fujifilm). This was followed by Canon in 1970, Konishiroku and IBM Japan the following year. then Ricoh, Minolta, Mita Kogyo, Toshiba, Sharp, Copier, Sumitomo 3M, Tokyo Koku Keiki [Tokyo Aircraft Instrument], Olympus, Matsushita Electric, Kyocera, and Sanyo Electric. In all, sixteen companies are engaged in fierce competition.

Too Much Bonuses, and Employees to Give Something Back?

Canon celebrated its 30th anniversary in 1967, the year before the announcement of the NP System photocopying technology. How did Mitarai view the company at that time?

The following is Mitarai's New Year's greeting at the Tamagawa Plant that year.

"I am confident that we will be able to lay the foundation for the company's prosperity on its 30th anniversary, as expected. Last year, exports accounted for 60% of our total sales, while domestic sales accounted for 40%, finally achieving the goal we have been talking about for some time. We will work to strengthen our three bases: Geneva in Europe, New York in the U.S., and Panama in Latin America. And to be more specific about how Canon will change on the occasion of its 30th anniversary, I would like to surpass 20 billion yen in annual sales by maximizing the potential of 'cameras in the right hand, business machines in the left' "

The following is from Mitarai's speech to new employees at the initiation ceremony of the same year.

"Competition among free countries will be fierce. Our weapon is the accumulation of technologies. The world will change drastically in the next five to ten years. There will surely come a time when our company's technology will be put to use amidst these changes. There are many things we have yet to announce. There will surely be something that will astonish the world. Your seniors are finally creating world-class technologies, and they have achieved some of them. From now on, I would like you to study languages."

The following is from Mitarai's speech to new employees at the 1968 initiation ceremony.

"Our company has something unrivaled. I am convinced that if we fully demonstrate this strength, we will rise to the top spot in the industry. I just returned from Panama four or five days ago, and I thought we won't be able to continue our business in the future by simply dealing within the narrow domestic market of Japan. I keenly felt that we must demonstrate our strength in the export market."

As always, family members were invited to the ceremony and a luncheon was held afterward. In his speech before the luncheon, Mitarai said the following.

"I would like to take this year's new recruits to Hawaii on the *Canon Maru*. What do you think?" (Wild applause) "Sorry, it's my April Fool's joke." (A roar of laughter)

"But I have such a dream. I wish we could all visit our overseas branches together."

After this, they toasted with glasses of beer against the backdrop of classical music playing in the hall. Then suddenly, the rhythms of the Canon Ondo could be heard. After the master of ceremonies explained what the Canon Ondo was, Mitarai led the executives in dancing, and the audience gave a big round of applause and called for an encore.

In July of that year, Mitarai, Maeda, the vice president, and Hayashi, the managing director, held a roundtable discussion, and an article on the event was published in the company newsletter (some of what was discussed in the roundtable was introduced earlier in the Canonet section of Chapter 4). The discussion focused on the prospect of achieving the long-awaited goal of 20 billion yen in annual sales, and reflecting on the company's history leading up to that point.

Maeda began to speak in a conventional manner, saying, "If we achieve the second-half targets, we will be able to reach the target of 20 billion yen for the year." But Mitarai interrupted him, asking in a very strong tone, "Wasn't it 20 billion yen for just the second half of the year?" The tone of his voice conveyed the feeling that something terrible had happened. "Oh, I see…" Mitarai continued, "I said 'for the year' because it wouldn't be realistic if I said 20 billion for half the year, but I still feel that we should aim for 20 billion in half a year," and then he burst out laughing. Whether or not it was intended as a joke, it can be said that Mitarai was never satisfied with the state of the company, no matter how pleased the other executives might have been.

The following is from Mitarai's New Year's greeting for 1969.

"The world can be an interesting and painful place. One day, I don't recall exactly when, but an employee representative came to my office and said, 'From what I hear, our bonuses are among the top ten in the nation. Is that all right? We'd like to give a little bit of it back as it's going to be a cause for concern.' After some back and forth, I told him, 'I appreciate your concern, but there is nothing to worry about. But if you think it's too much, why don't you donate some of that money to people with physical or mental disabilities?' That's when I woke up from a dream. This *is my* dream." (At this point, laughter erupted from the audience, and some people groaned for a while.) "I would like to discuss with you how to turn this dream into reality. I would rather have you understand. I want to make this happen. I would like to achieve this by the company's thirty-fifth anniversary. Now, I would like to state how this can be done."

He then touched on such issues as training overseas personnel to increase exports, changing the company name, labor-saving campaigns, personnel evaluations that reward hard work, and encouraging employees to propose improvements. He concluded his speech with the words, "Let's all do our best to bring prosperity to the company" and received a big round of applause.

Mitarai's jokes about going to Hawaii and his opinion about the high bonuses reflect his confidence and dreams after surviving the 1965 recession. Looking at Canon's specific activities during this period, the company announced the NP System photocopying technology in 1968 and changed its name from Canon Camera Co., Inc. to Canon Inc. in 1969, impressing upon people both inside and outside the company that it grown beyond being a mere camera manufacturer, with its camera business and office equipment business each accounting for roughly 50% of its total sales.

In May 1970, Mitarai chaired the Third International Conference of the Camera Industry held at the Kyoto International Conference Center. This was called the Tripartite Conference and was born from the idea of creating an international cooperative body for the photography industries of the three major camera-producing nations: the United States, Germany, and Japan. The first meeting was held in Cologne, Germany in 1968, and the second in New York in 1969.

The conference in Kyoto was a success, with then Minister of International Trade and Industry Kiichi Miyazawa attending and delivering a congratulatory speech. Soon thereafter the Japan Camera Industry Association held a leadership position in the industry worldwide.

In 1970, Canon's annual sales exceeded 40 billion yen, and the following year, in 1971, the company introduced the F-1, a high-end system camera.

When the new camera was exhibited at Photokina, a foreign journalist who had written in Popular Photography, "I don't know of another example of so much buzz focused on a single camera," told a Canon representative, "The F-1 is the first camera since the Leica M3 to excite me this much." The F-1 was a tangible rebuttal to the widely held view that Canon had dropped out of the high-end market since the Canonet, and that Nikon was the only true high-end camera manufacturer in the world. The F-1 was also a response by the company's young employees, who opposed Mitarai's call to "aim for the Hannover Messe" and felt that the company was focusing too much on office machinery and not enough on cameras.

At this Photokina, Mitarai became not only the first Japanese, but also the first non-German, to receive the Photokina Merit Award from the Photokina Committee.

In the spring of 1971, he was awarded the Order of the Sacred Treasure, 2nd class by the emperor, in recognition of his outstanding contributions to the nation.

In 1972, Canon exported its copier technology to the Saxon Company (January) and the Adlefgraf Martigraf (May) in the United States, impressing both domestic and foreign markets with Canon's technical capabilities. In 1973, another drama with Bell & Howell ensued, and the curtain finally came down.

From Nurturer to Creator

"As you all know, there is a difference between a 'birth parent' and a 'foster parent.' A birth parent gives birth to the child and raises them to adulthood. A foster parent takes in a child and raises them as if they were their own flesh and blood. The camera, for example, is our beloved child, and it has been cared for to this day by Bell & Howell as its foster parent. Fortunately, the child has grown up well and is loved by everyone. After discussions between the two parties, it has been decided that it would be better for the child to be taken care of by its creator. And so from now on, Canon will be selling our child directly to the public. However, we are very grateful for the love and affection shown by the foster parents who raised our child for more than 10 years. Now that it has returned to its parents, you can rest assured that we will raise it to be a truly great product."

Mr. Mitarai made these comments on March 12, 1973, at a party at the Plaza Hotel in New York. In attendance were Masao Sawaki, the Japanese Ambassador, and his wife; Suzukawa, senior managing director; Ito, director; Seiichi Takigawa, president of Canon USA; Chairman Frey of Bell & Howell (Percy had left the company in 1966 to become a U.S. Senator); Wagner, vice president; and other industry representatives and members of the press. At this event, it was announced that Canon and Bell & Howell ended their sales agreement that lasted eleven years.

When companies decide to end a business arrangement, it is possible to get into litigation issues, but the Japanese ambassador described the gentlemanly way in which the two parties parted, saying, "It is a milestone in the history of corporate alliances for leading companies in Japan and the U.S. to have a good bond and a good parting."

In Toronto, Canada, Mitarai remarked, "Toronto men are tough and really manly, and the women are very beautiful and kind. I think this is the charm of Toronto," drawing laughter and applause from the audience.

However, the drama leading up to this point that had taken place over the last two years involved three roles: the Bell side, which did not want to terminate the agreement; Maeda, then the vice president of the company, who wanted to revise the terms of the alliance in Canon's favor because the company did not yet have the ability to conduct direct sales in the U.S.; and Mitarai, who wanted to establish a direct sales system in the U.S. as soon as possible.

In February 1970, Takigawa, the personnel manager, was asked by Mitarai to go to the U.S. He was surprised at the suddenness of the request, not to mention the fact that he didn't speak English. In May, Mitarai again asked him, saying, "We're screwed. You have to go."

Takigawa wondered what he should do. The idea was for Canon USA to sell products on its own, but many among the management team were asking, "What if we break off relations with Bell & Howell and then we can't sell anything after that?" Maeda, who had worked in the sales field for a long time before becoming vice president, knew the horror of losing sales, so it was natural that he opposed the shift to direct sales. However, Mitarai told him to go, saying that he would eventually persuade the board of directors to approve the change. First, Takigawa decided to investigate whether it would even be possible to break with Bell & Howell and, if so, how long it would take to set up Canon's own direct sales channel. One month later, Takigawa returned from the U.S. and reported to Mitarai.

"If you entrust everything to me, I can end the partnership with Bell & Howell and establish our own sales channel. But if I have to get permission from Tokyo at every step, I can't do it." Takigawa made a further demand: "Once we cut ties with Bell & Howell, we'll need to move quickly. We're going to need a sizeable staff and I would like to appoint people as I see fit. If you allow me to do so, I am sure we will succeed."

Mitarai nodded in agreement, and on October 1 of that year, Takigawa was officially appointed president of Canon USA.

However, the board did not agree with Mitarai and Takigawa's plan. But

Takigawa was determined, saying, "Once I'm appointed, I can end the deal with Bell & Howell, no matter what Tokyo says."

After being transferred to the U.S., Takigawa immediately consulted with a lawyer and, after careful consideration, sent an official notice of termination to Bell & Howell in June of 1971. Because the contract was signed in the name of the president of Canon USA, there was no legal problem. However, at that time, the global headquarters in Tokyo was in the process of drafting a revised contract that called for the purchase of more products, which Takigawa was aware of, but the termination notice had to be sent two years in advance.

Bell & Howell was surprised. They were skeptical about the true meaning of the "Takigawa Document" because they had received the official termination notice from Canon USA, a subsidiary of Canon, while they were negotiating a renewal with Tokyo. Bell & Howell wanted to continue the contract. Although Canon products accounted for just 10%–15% of their total sales, they did not have their own still cameras to sell, and Canon products were one of the mainstays of the company's photography division.

Three months later, in September, Mitarai visited the U.S. Negotiations between Tokyo and Bell & Howell were still ongoing. Bell & Howell, eager to meet with Mitarai, invited him and Takigawa to the executive cafeteria on the seventh floor of the head office. The Bell side said, "The year after next is the time to renew the contract, but we are sure you will continue to work with us. The terms of the contract will be as you request." However, Mitarai did not say yes or no. But in his heart, he knew it was good-bye. When they talked about golf, he would smile, but when it came to the contract, he would say, "I haven't decided yet." Takigawa, who was standing beside him, thought, "This must be the worst lunch of the president's life." Based on Mitarai's attitude, the Bell & Howell team started to think that the "Takigawa document" was true.

However, Canon's headquarters had not yet reached a conclusion. Later that year, the issue was formally considered at a board meeting but no consensus was reached. Takigawa said he would resign as president of Canon USA if even one person objected. At the next day's board meeting, Maeda, who believed they should renew their deal with Bell & Howell, backed Takigawa, saying, "If you think this is the right decision, I support you," and the decision to dissolve the partnership with Bell & Howell was made official. One year after Canon started direct sales in the U.S., Bell's photography division collapsed.

Products for Persons with Physical Disabilities

In February of 1973, when direct sales in the U.S. began, a new business division called the Audiovisual Aid Division was established under Mitarai's direction, a division that was prepared to lose money.

This was a time when Japan was in the midst of the "Remodeling the Japanese Archipelago" boom under the prime minister Kakuei Tanaka, and Canon's sales were growing so rapidly that the company's executives were beginning to think that 100 billion in sales, once only a distant dream, was now possible.

In fact, sales records were being rewritten year after year: sales surpassed 20 billion yen in 1968, 30 billion yen in 1969, 40 billion yen in 1970, and 47 billion yen in 1971. However, Mitarai said, "Businesses can't possibly do that well. It is impossible for sales to grow by 20% – 30% every year, and even if they did, there would always be a reaction. In every age, there are good times and bad times. It is at times like this that we must brace ourselves up, and I suggest that we all think about giving something back to society at this time." Employees came up with a variety of ideas, including a fund for international students from abroad, an institute to think about the future of humanity, and donations to universities.

However, Mitarai was dissatisfied with all of the proposals. It would be not worthy of Canon, whose motto was to deliver products to the world based on its unique technology, to do things that anyone can do.

As Mitarai pondered whether there was anything that only Canon could do, he remembered a blind girl he saw in a laboratory at Stanford University several years earlier who, as part of a study, was using a special device to read not Braille but ordinary printed text with ease.

"I wonder what happened to that study afterwards."

Mitarai traveled to California to meet with Dr. John G. Linvill, dean of the School of Electrical Engineering at Stanford University, in order to see the latest research in electronics. Canon had just released the Canola 130 calculator (1964) and Mitarai was interested in integrated circuits (ICs) and large-scale integrations (LSIs). At that time, many of Dr. Linvill's students were working as engineers at semiconductor manufacturers such as Intel and National Semiconductor. Thus, he can be considered one of the fathers of the U.S. semiconductor industry.

The doctor showed Mitarai a device he had developed for his daughter that scanned text and caused tiny pins to vibrate, allowing the user to "read" the scanned letters by touching the pins.

"My daughter Candy lost her sight when she was three, and my wife had to translate her school textbooks into Braille for her, which took a lot of time. So we were conducting research to see if there might be a way for her to read directly from the text."

(Note: In many places in the U.S., there are no special school for handicapped children, and they attend classes like other children in regular schools).

In the fall of 1971, Dr. Linvill completed development of the product. Subsequently, Stanford University established a company called Telesensory Systems and a factory was built on the university campus to manufacture the product. Mitarai decided that Canon would import the product for the Japanese market and Maeda and Suzukawa were sent to meet with Dr. Linvill.

Although there was no point in importing a product that would quickly be imitated by other companies, Suzukawa was convinced that "this is a legitimate product," and Maeda returned to Japan with the opinion that "Even if it doesn't sell well, it's something the world needs, so we should do it." The General Planning Office immediately decided to investigate how to accept them.

When Saburo Nagata, who was in the General Planning Office, visited organizations for people with blindness, everyone knew about the Optacon and wanted one, but they said no one was willing to import it. The reason for this was the characteristics of Optacon itself, which stands for "optical-to-tactile converter," meaning that the device converts optical input into tactile input. The principle of the device is for characters captured by the camera to be converted into vibrations of pins, and for the shape of the characters to be read by touching the pins with a finger.

The camera has a total of 144 semiconductor photodetectors (i.e., silicon retinas) laid out in six rows and 24 columns, covering an area of 3.6 mm × 1.8 mm. This grid functions just like the retina of an eye.

When the device scans a page of text and light is reflected from the surface of the paper, the camera emits an electrical signal corresponding to the intensity of the light. Then, the 144 pins of the tactile disc vibrate up and down in correspondence with the shape of the letter, allowing the shape of the letter to be felt by the user's fingertips. In the case of the letter O, the finger perceives a vertical oval line with a hole in the center. The camera weighs only 39 grams, and the tactile disc and batteries weigh 1.8 kilograms, including the leather case, making it portable.

The pins of the tactile sensing board vibrate subtly at a frequency of around 230 Hz. In other words, they can move about 230 times per second. Because there are so many delicate moving parts, after-sales service in the event of a malfunction would be difficult. Also, because they are imported, an inventory of replacement parts must also be maintained. In addition to selling the machines, trainers are needed to teach users how to read using the Optacon. Moreover, because the Optacon was originally developed for English speakers, it would need to be modified to read and recreate the nearly 2,000 complex Japanese characters used in daily life. For these reasons, no one was willing to import them.

Nagata said, "Blind people want it. However, it would be very costly to make this product work in Japan. I am not confident that Canon will be able to handle it." However, Mitarai does not like to hear "We can't do it." He scolded Nagata, "What do you mean you can't do it? If there is a demand for it, then why don't you make it work."

Mitarai asked Nagata to head up the project but Nagata declined. He said, "I think these issues would be best handled by someone who has experience dealing with these kinds of issues, perhaps someone who has worked at the Ministry of Health and Welfare."

Mitarai was livid. "Would you turn your back on those in need? I didn't think anyone at Canon could be that heartless." Nagata, who was in a panic, explained, "I'm not saying I don't want to do it, I'm just think there must be someone else who is better qualified." But Mitarai wouldn't take no for an answer, and in February 1974, a new business division was started with Saburo

Nagata as the department head, one female clerk, and one service personnel.

Nagata continued to voice his concerns after he was assigned to the project, telling Mitarai, "If we do this, much of the work will need to be taken care of by someone outside the company. Just because we do this does not mean that the world will appreciate it. Even if we say we are doing this for the blind, people will say 'Canon is using blind people for publicity,' not 'Look at what a great company Canon is.'"

Mitarai replied, "There is such a thing as 'hidden virtue.' Goodness is something we do in hiding."

As Nagata said, Canon alone could not have achieved this diffusion, and in 1975, the year after the division's establishment, the Japan Optacon Committee was formed, chaired by Yoshishige Kasai, former Vice-Minister of Health and Welfare.

By 1982, there were 8,490 units in use worldwide: 5,300 in the U.S. and Canada, 640 in Italy, 430 in the U.K., 300 each in West Germany and Sweden, 190 in the Netherlands, and 254 units in Japan, including 100 in welfare facilities and 65 units owned by individuals. A number of companies purchased units for employee use, including Ozeki Shuzo, Musashino Bank, Machida Municipal Hospital, Kaneta Shirts, and Nishinippon Telex, and Naha City Library made the device available to local residents.

Canon sold each unit of Optacon for about 1.3 million yen, including the import costs, but would lose close to 100 million yen on the devices every year.

Canon also produced and sold Communicator, a small device worn on the wrist that enables people with a speech impairment to communicate. This was jointly developed by Dr. Uden and Dr. Mielo of the Netherlands and Canon, who came up with the idea when they saw Canon's Palmtronic calculator, which has a printing mechanism. They asked Canon Amsterdam if they could print letters instead of numbers.

It was not until 1977, though, that a small portable tape writer was commercialized. The most difficult thing for Nagata was that no semiconductor manufacturer was willing to produce the LSIs for the Communicator because of the extremely small production volume of 200 units per year. The minimum production lot for LSIs was said to be 100,000 units, but was usually closer to one million units. After checking with various companies, Hitachi agreed to produce 5,000 units.

However, it was not practical to make only two or three hundred Communicators each year, so the company decided to make 3,000 units and store them in the warehouse. When Nagata said "3,000 units" at the plant, he was asked if he meant monthly or daily production. When he replied, "One run would be enough for five years," they asked if he was joking.

Mitarai also instructed them to make a device that would not break when dropped, since it would be used by people with physical disabilities. As the user presses the alphabet keys, the device prints the resulting words on a strip of paper, allowing them to freely express themselves to others. Although the Communicator was sold for about 70,000 yen, it was much cheaper than similar products on the market, ranging from about 1,000 to 2,000 dollars. The Swedish Ministry of Health purchased many units for use at factories and facilities around the world where people with speech impairments worked. In Scandinavian countries such as Sweden and Denmark, the products were certified as prosthetic devices for the people with physical disabilities and were subsequently provided by the government.

When Nagata went to Canon Amsterdam to work on the communicator project, an "incident" occurred that he would never forget.

While he was in a business meeting, the receptionist told him that he had a visitor. When he came outside to see who it was, he found a young man covered in snow, huddled in a crouching position. The young man, who had cerebral palsy, had traveled from Paris by himself to buy a Communicator. His clothes were dripping wet, so Nagata decided he would sit down on a wooden chair next to the front door and talk with him. But the receptionist did not hesitate to show the young man to the best room with the finest carpet in the building. She told Nagata with pride, "Canon has become a full-fledged company."

Nagata didn't understand what she meant by this. When he asked Ems Magnus, the PR manager, about it, he was told that, "A company would not be trusted in Europe unless it was one where people with physical disabilities are proud to come and ask for help." When Nagata reported this to Mitarai upon his return to Japan, Mitarai responded, "That's how it should be," which made Nagata feel extremely embarrassed.

In 1982, this business division began handling a new product, the "Crib-O-Gram Type G2A" a device for screening hearing in newborns. Whereas the Optacon and Communicator were designed to assist people with disabilities, the new product was used to check for a potential disability. Like the Optacon, the Crib-o-Gram was developed at Stanford University and manufactured by Telesensory Systems.

Nagata remarked, "We are both importing and exporting Chairman Mitarai's ideas."

First Failure to Pay a Dividend since the Company's Founding

As mentioned earlier, it had been 23 years since Mitarai's first visit to the U.S. and 36 years since the company was founded when the direct sales system in the U.S. was finally realized. However, four months later, in November 1973, the oil crisis hit Japan, and the effects of the crisis hit the Fukushima Plant, which was just about to be expanded, especially hard.

In 1970, the company purchased 80,000 square meters of land in an industrial park to meet the growing demand for cameras. After constructing two buildings, a third one with a floor space of 10,000 square meters had been planned. It was the first time a factory of this scale had been built since Canon's founding. The foundation had been laid and the steel frame had been delivered. Shigeru Nishioka, the plant manager, was on his way to visit a client in Aizu, Fukushima Prefecture when Tokyo called his office.

When he returned to the factory later that day and returned the call, he was told that the construction project had been canceled. However, construction was supposed to begin the next day and the construction crew had already been hired. Nishioka traveled back to Tokyo. Mitarai and the other executives were all gloomy, saying that the Japanese economy was ruined. They said if the situation was not handled properly, the company could be forced to lay off workers for the first time since Canon's founding, and building a new plant was out of the question.

But Nishioka could not simply say, "Yes, I see," and leave. Not only were the construction workers standing by ready to work, but also if the steel frames were left out in the open they would rust. It would not be enough to simply apply a rust inhibitor. They would have to repeat the process every six months, and the expense of doing so would be a considerable burden.

"At the very least, let me erect the steel frame, put up the roof and walls, and…." But before he could finish saying, "I won't do anything for the interior," Mitarai, who had a frightening look on his face, asked, "What are you talking about?" It was clear that it would be a great loss to let the steel frame rust, and it would be a waste of money to preserve it until the time came to build it, but he knew that once Mitarai made a decision, he would not back down.

Nishioka returned to Fukushima dejected. He was taking a walk around the site when his secretary rushed out and told him that Mitarai had called. It was uncommon to receive a phone call directly from the president. He thought, "He's going to fire me." With trepidation, he called the president back. "Ah, Nishioka-kun, I see your point. Proceed with the construction according to your plan," Mitarai said. Nishioka's shoulders suddenly relaxed and he felt as if he had been brought back from the brink of despair.

Later, the Fukushima Plant was able to respond to the demands of the Canon USA, whose sales was skyrocketing since the start of the direct sales, and increase production swiftly, because the exterior of the third building had already been built.

At the beginning of the following year, 1974, Mitarai asked his employees what Canon should do in these "Very uncertain times, which could be called a national crisis."

"I would like to say that it is in times like these that we should demonstrate the Canon corporate culture that we have constantly cultivated. We have the spirit of self-motivation, self-awareness, and salf-governance, which is the foundation of everything we do. In times like these, we should do everything through self-motivation. It is precisely in times like these that we should be aware of the situation and try not to act rashly or blindly. We must protect our companies by ourselves no matter how uncertain these times are. Just because we are in a recession does not mean that the government will protect our company. The same is true in the lives of individual families. When you are in trouble at home, your relatives are not going to extend a special helping hand. In the end, you have to take care of yourself. Let us all pool our wisdom and cooperate with each other to develop a bright future.

He concluded by saying that the way forward is "internationalization" and that we must earn foreign currency through exports, given that oil had doubled in price.

"Don't say, 'I'm in trouble.' We have limitless wisdom and courage. Let us do what we can with the *san-ji* (three self's) spirit"

In August of that year, Mitarai appointed Maeda as president and himself as chairman. He was seventy-three years old.

Suzukawa, the managing director, became vice president, and both Mitarai and Maeda had the authority to act as representatives of the company. Tomomasa Matsui, Ryoichiro Yamagata, Hiroshi Ito, Ryuzaburo Kaku, and Keizo Yamaji became executive directors. Four new director positions were also created. At the inauguration of the new management team, Mitarai appealed for unity under the new president and clearly stated his role as chairman, as follows:

"I myself have more than 30 years of experience, so I would like to give various advice to the president and all other operations from the highest place and from the side, so that there will be no need to worry about the future. From now on, as chairman of the board of directors, I will preside over the company's policy decisions and focus on personnel and management of the board of directors. On the external front, the chairman will also be responsible for dealing with issues related to shareholders, stocks, and so on.

"I have been studying and thinking about the system of having both a chairman and a president, but I believe that this system will not make sense unless there is harmony between the two. In the worst case, it could lead to a divided system. Fortunately, in the case of our company, President Maeda has been my closest advisor and has complemented me in many ways. We are able to communicate with each other without saying a word.

"People often tell me, and I myself think, that Canon's only true assets are its human resources. One of the major tasks I have been engaged in for a long time is to nurture our human resources. When I assumed the position of chairman, people said to me, 'You have nurtured a fine group of people. When I looked at the lineup of people, they were all very impressive,' and I was both flattered and happy at the same time.

"In any case, the only way to run a company is for everyone to work together to move forward. Business is all about people. From now on, the authority for corporate administration rests with the president, and it is necessary for everyone to support and cooperate with the president."

Mitarai also emphasized that there is nothing more miserable than being the acquired company in a merger or acquisition, and that Canon must go its own way and avoid being taken care of by others.

At the time, the oil crisis triggered a shift in Japan's economic policy that suppressed demand, and a recessionary mood was felt throughout the country.

The biggest reason for the decline in Canon's business performance at this time was calculators. Along with Sharp, Canon had pioneered the calculator market, but the company was not an electronics manufacturer and was therefore unable to respond quickly to the shift from office use to personal use as transistors were replaced by ICs and LSIs, which became smaller and smaller.

Furthermore, as calculators flooded the market and price competition intensified, Canon released a defective product and suffered a devastating blow. The company had imported an LED display from a joint venture in the U.S., but it stopped working after it was installed in the final product and put on the market. Without a clear understanding of the cause of the problem, the company accumulated a mountain of returned goods, which caused losses estimated at one to one and a half billion yen.

Comparing the second half of 1974 with the first half of 1975, sales of calculators decreased from 9.3 billion yen to 6.35 billion yen (down 32%), cameras from 18.98 billion yen to 18.76 billion yen (down 1%), and optical and micro products from 3.66 billion yen to 3.46 billion yen (down 5%). Only copiers showed growth, from 4.11 billion yen to 5.21 billion yen (up 27%). Total sales dropped 6%, 36.05 billion yen to 33.79 billion yen (down 6%), and profit after tax was 323 million yen, resulting in a loss of 172 million yen.

However, there were no furloughs or layoffs. Toshizo Tanaka, who joined the company in 1964, was in the Accounting section of the Accounting Department at the time, but was surprised that upper management reflected on what needed to be considered, rather than trying to hide the causes of the company's deteriorating performance. Tanaka recalled that there was an air of pessimism within the company, as if "the bad times would continue for a while."

The company did not pay dividends during this period, the first time since the company was listed on the Tokyo Stock Exchange in 1949. In fact, they were prevented from doing so because the convertible bond contracts issued in 1969 prohibited the company from drawing down reserves to pay dividends.

However, in the second half of the year, business performance quickly recovered, with camera sales up 19% from the previous period, calculator sales up 29%, and office equipment sales up 52%. Although optical and micro products were down 14%, total sales increased by 22% to 41.27 billion yen, the highest since the company's founding.

Chapter 6

The "Premier Company" Plan and the AE-1 Revolution

The "Premier Company" Plan and the AE-1 Revolution

Appointment of Ryuzaburo Kaku as President

Not being able to pay a dividend in 1975 after assuming the position of president came as a great shock to Takeo Maeda. One day, he gathered some people together and asked for their opinions on the company's restructuring plan. Among them was Ryuzaburo Kaku, who had previously served as director and general manager of the accounting and administrative department and had been appointed to managing director upon Maeda's appointment as president. He said, "If you reflect on the history of the company, you will understand. Let's come up with an initiative to become a truly excellent company. To achieve this, we must establish a divisional system." Kaku proposed a restructuring plan, and Maeda agreed. The president announced the "Premier Company" Plan in his New Year's address at the beginning of the following year, 1976.

However, in June of the following year, Maeda died of cancer, just three years after becoming president. Two days later, Mitarai called Kaku and asked if he would be interested in leading the company. Kaku himself had no intention of doing so. He thought it suited him to stay at a lower position and be able to say whatever he wanted. He had often come into conflict with Maeda and was frequently scolded by Mitarai. Even though Mitarai would be furious when it happened, after a day or two he would admit, "Yes, you're right. Let's go with that."

If it had been a normal company, he would have been fired long ago. Kaku thought that he was always forgiven because it was Mitarai, but he still wanted to swim freely for a while longer. So he said, "Since you are in good health, why don't you take over as president again?" But Mitarai replied immediately, "I have no intention of doing that." He was proud of the fact that his ideas had been incorporated into the company's policies up to that point. Finally, Kaku relented. "If you insist, I will do it," he said.

During the week leading up to the official announcement, reporters from *The Nikkei* newspaper visited them at their homes every morning and evening. One night, Mitarai called Kaku's house and said, "I have been pretending I am not home, but it's almost 11:00 p.m. and they are still outside. What should I do?" Kaku replied, "Why don't you go out the back door and come in from the front?"

This year, in the general trend toward streamlining management after the oil crisis, there were changes toward younger generations in the top management of many major companies across Japan. One example of such changes was the selection of Toshihiko Yamashita (born in 1919) as president, from the 25th position in Matsushita's executive hierarchy, which was widely reported in the media as "Yamashita's leap."

The number of changes in leadership among companies listed on the Tokyo Stock Exchange reached more than 150, an all-time high, with the Meiji-born generations retiring and the Taisho- and Showa-born generations ascending to top management. The average age of the new presidents was 59.5 years, which was 7.3 years younger than the outgoing presidents (Heibonsha's *Sekai Daihyakka Nenkan* (World Encyclopedia Yearbook), 1978 edition). Kaku was born in 1926 and had just turned 51 years old. The ascendance of such a young president attracted a lot of attention in the media, but within Canon, it was taken as a natural development.

Ever since the *mahjong* argument at his job interview, Kaku had been one of the people Mitarai had been eyeing as a successor. He was a member of the 1954 group that had joined the company at a time when the company was promoting high efficiency and high wages in order to attract more human resources with the aim of growing and improving the company, and Mitarai had always paid attention to Kaku's words and actions, believing that he was right in his policy.

It was also Kaku who had squarely argued the advantages of the divisional system, in response to Mitarai's insistence that such a system would lead to sectionalism. Although their views differed, Mitarai knew they were both sincere in their desire for the company's development. Kaku's "Premier Company" plan was also a continuation of Mitarai's own line of thinking, which was to strive to make Canon a world-class company.

Kaku's father, Toshio, was born in 1890, making him 11 years older than Mitarai. He was a nationalist who admired Shumei Okawa, and during World War II had promoted the spirit of hakko ichiu (the whole world under one roof). Ryuzaburo grew up under his influence. During the war, Toshio had lived in China with his wife and his aunt, and when he returned to Japan after the war, all he had with him was a brush and ink for calligraphy, while his wife had a trunk with some clothes.

Ryuzaburo had graduated from Qingdao Junior High School and entered the Fifth High School in Kumamoto Prefecture, and when he heard that his father had returned from China to his brother's house in Nakatsu, Oita Prefecture after the war, he went to see his father. His father said, "I'm going to wash off the dirt (bad memories) of my Chinese life." He went from Nakatsu to Hosenji Temple, and then to Sujiyu, and spent all the money he had received from the government (1,000 yen) when he returned to Japan. Ryuzaburo was anxious about what he was going to do with the rest of his life, but his father did not seem to mind in the least. He then went to work at a relative's drapery shop in Nakatsu, where he wore haori hakama (Japanese formal attire for men) for ten years.

Ryuzaburo had two older brothers, and his father lived with his second brother in Takatsuki, Osaka Prefecture, spending his time writing and reading books. One year, he announced that he would stop writing, including New Year's cards, and would only read books. In March of that year, 1961, he died of intestinal torsion.

Before the war, Ryuzaburo moved from job to job and had little money to spare. He would run out of money in the middle of each month and have to ask for an advance on his pay. Whenever friends or acquaintances came to ask him for loans, he would even borrow money from his company to lend them, so he was always poor. As if it were a virtue, he said, "I feel like I've been walking toward it my whole life." He recalled that his mother was always busy entertaining guests on Sundays, and that she was "a victim of my father's life."

When Kaku graduated from Kyushu University with a degree in economics in 1954, the economy was in a recession and it was difficult to find a job. His father often sought employment opportunities for the children of acquaintances without being asked, so Ryuzaburo asked his father for help.

"What a pathetic man you are. I didn't bring you up that way," his father said. "Nowadays, we need connections to get in," Ryuzaburo replied. "Don't be silly, I never did any job hunting. You know the story of Zhuge Liang Kongming? Liu Bei came to meet him, showing a special courtesy, but he turned him down. A man must have that kind of mindset," his father said. "I know it's a story from the *Legend of the Three Kingdoms*," Ryuzaburo said, "but that was a long time ago. Such things are not acceptable in today's harsh world." "No, it's the same," his father replied. "If you are a really talented person, people will come to you. A man should have this kind of mindset."

Ryuzaburo was stunned. He realized he didn't really understand his father, but at the same time, he thought he was a great man. "I understand. I was wrong to ask you to do this."

He searched for employment opportunities at the school's academic affairs section and submitted applications to Sumitomo Bank and Marubeni. At Sumitomo Bank, he was to be interviewed by President Hotta, while at Marubeni, his eldest brother was to take the first examination, but due to an unfortunate scheduling conflict, he had no choice but to turn down Sumitomo and take the Marubeni and Canon examinations.

There is a kind of chance encounter in life that is hard to comprehend with human knowledge. One day, Ryuzaburo's aunt, who was living in China with his parents, came to Tokyo to visit her aunt in Odawara, Kanagawa Prefecture. The president of a certain company had taken her to his villa because she had looked after him when he was in junior high school. Just after Ryuzaburo had returned to Nakatsu to look for a job, he heard that his aunt came back to Nakatsu. His mother had always described the woman who lived in Odawara as "Kaneda's older sister" and Ryuzaburo had heard of her name. She was the one who took good care of Mitarai when he lived at the Kaneda home in Saiki, Oita. (See Chapter 1). The president's company was called Canon, a name Ryuzaburo had never heard before. According to a magazine, it was a start-up company with a white chalk beautiful building in Shimomaruko and it had a unique management style. He asked his aunt to write a letter on his behalf to the woman in Odawara. She replied, saying that although the examination was difficult and there was no guarantee that he would get in, he would be allowed to apply.

During his interview, Kaku mentioned that he played mahjong. Mitarai, who disliked the game, was furious and scolded him. There were about a hundred applicants, so Kaku was certain he would not get the job and began preparing to apply to Seibu Gas and Oita Bank. To his surprise, he received a letter from Canon Inc., offering him a job and he accepted. He was happy because it was the place he most wanted to work. He was one of sixteen university graduates hired that year.

After joining the company, he was assigned to the accounting department. The manager was Tomomasa Matsui and the section chief was Masanori Seki. He was at a loss because he had never used an abacus and knew nothing about bookkeeping or cost accounting. However, considering the terrible part-time job he had had after the war (after graduating from high school), temporarily giving up on his university education to become a substitute teacher, sleeping in a construction company's field shed, and selling candles in the countryside, he was grateful to have a job and a steady income.

The female employees looked at him puzzled after they had completed three or four pages while he had completed only one. The high school graduate who had joined the company two years earlier sarcastically remarked, "You work like that and your salary is still 1,000 yen higher than mine." He took the work home with him in order to meet his quota because he didn't want to be ridiculed over not being able to perform such a trivial job.

Kaku had always been a sports enthusiast, and in junior high school he was a keen shot putter. He would practice in the yard until dark, and when he was in good shape, his record would sometimes increase by five centimeters a day. One year, his record increased by one meter. His mother made him a sandbag so that he could do some weightlifting. Those experiences came back to him when he became a businessman.

"I'll do it as if I'm going to challenge myself to set a new record."

In those days, work started at eight o'clock. Because "cheating" is not allowed in sports, he kept his pencils sharpened and waited until precisely 8:00 a.m. and would then work until 12:00 on the dot. These four hours of work were a series of monotonous calculations, and while he used to pause often to drink tea when someone came over to speak to him, after he began this "challenge" he will be completely focused during the morning hours, speaking no words. The afternoon went by in a blur as well. He never worked overtime. After six months, he was able to do twice or three times as much work as the colleagues who are ranked abacus users.

Through this approach, the new businessman learned something about "efficiency." At first, the vertical and horizontal lines didn't match, and after doing it a few times, it would be difficult to tell which line was correct. Then, after another two or three times, the lines would be perfectly aligned, and the number of errors was greatly reduced. "When I looked around at my seniors coworkers, I saw that they always did the calculations twice, once vertically and once horizontally. If you did it once and got the last one right, you didn't need to do the calculation twice. This alone would reduce the number of calculations by a factor of two. In some cases, one out of several cards would not match, and only then did the calculation need to be done twice. Finally, I was able to reduce the total calculation time by about 30% or 40%."

He had started using electronic calculators and found that if he divided a large digit by a small digit, the machine took longer to calculate the answer because of how the machine worked. However, if he did the opposite, he would get the answer faster. Moreover, if he operated the machine with his left hand and wrote with his right hand, he could work even faster. Most of his coworkers took a break after each calculation, but not him. By putting all of the things he had figured out into practice, he was able to overtake his senior coworkers.

"You could turn an unpleasant job into an enjoyable one by making it into a sport. And that was not all. When the time came, we could go home and do whatever we wanted." To his surprise, his boss appreciated the way he worked. Whenever the boss came into the room, he saw that Kaku was working diligently, with his eyes wide open. He was a competent man who did more than his fair share of the work. Kaku himself was no longer afraid of the workload. He thought, "If it comes, it comes," and he didn't mind when, in later years in overseas offices, he had to work all night issuing American Depositary Receipts (ADRs) and European Depository Receipts (EDRs). (This is a good example of turning a negative into a positive. If Kaku had been a good at using an abacus, he might not have had to think about how to improve his efficiency, and he might not have been given an important job in the company later on.)

But despite this, he was able to fit in and work well with others. During lunch breaks, when he wanted to play, he played with everyone to the fullest.

When he had working in accounting for about five years, it was time to conduct a company-wide job analysis, and Kaku was selected from the accounting department to be a member of the job analysis team, which consisted of about ten people.

First, they asked the person in charge to describe the work in their section. What kind of work was done at the beginning of the month? What about mid-month? What was the nature of the temporary work? This was investigated for each person. They would identify what was necessary and what was not, what could be integrated and what could be eliminated, and then used this information to improve the workflow. Furthermore, they would measure the weight of responsibility and authority of each job. Each person wrote a report on such matters and submitted it to a university professor in order to get their opinion on the matter. Kaku learned a lot from this process.

"It is necessary to look at things not from a single perspective, but from all sides. It is also important to be able to express this in a three-dimensional way. Just by reading it, it should come to life in a three-dimensional way. In this way, the company's system of work was drilled into my head."

By performing this job analysis, Kaku came to believe that the company was still an immature camera manufacturer, and that there was much room for improvement.

Sales Surpass 100 Billion Yen for the First Time

What kind of plan did Kaku propose to make Canon a truly premier company?

At the beginning of 1976, Canon achieved a new record of 41.211 billion yen in total sales for the second half of the fiscal year 1975 (ending in December). President Maeda told his employees that "Canon warehouses around the world have sold almost all of their products and are empty, but many are still short." In a tape-recorded message for Japanese employees working overseas, he first announced the sales record (as described above) and the export sales, which exceeded 26 billion yen in the same period. He then added, "I am extremely thrilled to report that in just six months we have recovered from the disastrous performance of the first half of last year, when we could not pay out any dividends, and I would like to extend to you my best wishes for the New Year and express my sincerest gratitude and excitement for what is to come."

In 1975, the number of corporate bankruptcies and total liabilities had reached a postwar high for the second year in a row, and layoffs were widespread. Many companies in various industries went bankrupt and the total liabilities were 5.09 billion yen.

Of course, Canon had also managed to downsize its workforce as other companies did, but not by laying off any employees. Instead they hired fewer new recruits and didn't replace workers who had retired, reexamined their capital investments, and cut costs where possible, even down to the lights in the corridors.

For the first time since 1951, no male university graduates were hired, and although 117 women were hired, 75 were assigned to the Fukushima Plant, while only 42 were assigned to the head office as supplemental staff. The company's cost-cutting attitude is evident in a company newsletter from 1975. The quality of the paper was poor and the number of pages was the fewest it had ever been. Canon's business performance could always be determined by looking at the quality and number of pages in the company newsletter.

Maeda's goal at this time was to make Canon a top Japanese company in the three years from 1976 to 1978 and a top global company in the three years after that. To achieve this goal, he established the Canon System Review Committees for Development, Production, and Sales in an attempt to learn from the best companies in the world.

In the 1976 fiscal year, sales increased 35% over the previous year, surpassing 100 billion for the first time, while management profit increased 250%, setting a new company record. In his New Year's address for 1977, Maeda said, "Based on this achievement, I would like to make this the year we achieve our goal of becoming a top company in Japan."

However, as mentioned earlier, in June 1977, Maeda passed away and Kaku took over as president.

The following year, in 1978, the company implemented a divisional structure (company consisting of autonomous divisions) under Kaku's "Premier Company" plan.

In his New Year's address for 1979, President Kaku reviewed the three-year plan, and said, "although the business structure improved rapidly, I must say that we still have a long way to go" to reach his goal, and listed four priority measures.

1. In order to produce products backed by advanced technology, we will go back to the basics of "Canon with Technology" and establish a "Canon with Technology" for the future. We will establish a Future Technology Center to conduct research, perform evaluations, and plan for trends in product and production technologies in Japan and overseas. Hiroshi Suzukawa and Hiroshi Ito will be the directors of the center.

2. We must strengthen our overseas strategy. Canon has 5,000 employees overseas, and in the first year of our initiative to become a top global company, the export-related divisions will be integrated to form a new Overseas Business Division headed by General Manager Yoshiaki Otake (born in 1930, joined the company in 1953).

3. We will reinforce the divisional structure.

4. We will invest further in human resource development and training. We will promote educational activities so that each employee, who bears the responsibility of helping us achieve our goals, will enhance their abilities by developing their creativity and deepening their insights.

A Great Concept Created in a 2DK

The following year marked the beginning of the 1980s. Kaku set the goal of becoming a one-trillion-yen company by the end of the decade. The company's sales in 1979 were 187.5 billion yen. The year 1980 was the second year of the Global Premier Company initiative, and although no new policies were set, the company announced that it would allocate 33 billion yen for capital investment, three times its capitalization of 11 billion yen.

Although this may have been seen as "a very risky gamble," the company was "willing to take some risks in order to build the foundation for a breakthrough," said Kaku. It was therefore inevitable that achieving debt-free management, which was one goal of the "Premier Company" plan, would take longer than initially hoped.

The year 1981 was the sixth and final year of the "Premier Company" plan, and it was time for the finishing touches. In five years, sales had tripled and management profit increased 13-fold. In addition, several measures were taken to solidify the foundation for the one-trillion-yen plan set forth the previous year, and capital investment amounted to 100 billion yen over two years, including the previous year.

However, the company was urging its employees to recognize that the combination of external factors such as the strong yen, and internal factors such as amortization burden due to large-scale capital investment, interest burden, as well as the fact that all new product launches would be concentrated in the first half of the year, would "force us to prepare for unprecedented profit pressures."

It should be noted that the company was not only expanding its product fields horizontally but also diversifying vertically through vertical integration of its products, while reflecting on its late entry into some areas.

One of these areas was the production of semiconductors, with general-purpose ICs and LSIs to be procured externally, while proprietary products were to be produced in-house. In addition, the company established a component business for high-precision, micromachined elements such as display elements, optical elements, and circuit elements, which are produced using laser technology. In addition, to further strengthen the concept of "selling our own products by ourselves," they expanded their sales channels both domestically and internationally.

Kaku also listed the human qualities that support a truly premier company and called those that lived up to them "premier corporate workers." He says, "In addition to knowledge and ability in the workplace, each employee should improve their own character, be courteous, and develop a good personality. Only in this way will a truly premier company be realized. When passing visitors in the hallway, no one even makes eye contact with them. A company cannot truly be called an premier company unless its employees are at least willing to exchange nods with strangers."

The Shimomaruko Plant had laid the groundwork for Canon's postwar rise from a small local factory to a global company, and Mitarai had long dreamed of constructing a magnificent head office building there. In May of 1981, the administrative department of the head office was consolidated in a high-rise building in Shinjuku, as a temporary lodging until the new building could be constructed. In the same month, the development center for components was relocated to Hiratsuka, Kanagawa Prefecture (on a 31,000-square-meter site), and the Ami Plant was constructed in a factory park 40 minutes by car from the Toride factory in Ibaraki Prefecture. The company decided to shift production of calculators, office computers, fax machines, and word processors to this plant. In July, a plant for copier toner and other consumables opened in Iga Ueno, Mie Prefecture.

In August, in accordance with Mitarai's policy, Canon Sales (president: Seiichi Takigawa, capital: 672 million yen, 2,800 employees) and Canon

Electronics (president: Yoshiyuki Hayashi, capital: 500 million yen, 1,650 employees) were listed separately on the Second Section of the Tokyo Stock Exchange.

In 1981, net sales were 282 billion yen (up 17% over the previous year), operating income was 26 billion yen (up 1% over the previous year), and net income was 15.8 billion yen (up 7% over the previous year), while the capital adequacy ratio increased from 31% to 51.8%.

By product category, sales were 559.5 billion yen (52%) for cameras, 436.9 billion yen (41%) for office equipment, and 76 billion yen (7%) for optical equipment and other products combined. By region, Europe accounted for 30% of sales, North America and Japan for 29% each, and other territories for 12%.

In his New Year's address in 1982, Kaku described the corporate environment surrounding Canon as follows. "The boundaries between industries will be broken down on a global scale, and we will enter a period of warfare in which strong companies will survive and weak companies will be eliminated, and fierce competition will begin in earnest with Japanese electronics manufacturers and western giants in addition to traditional competitors." He continued, "this new Sengoku Era (referring to the warring states period of Japanese history) will be an age of opportunity in which companies with the right capabilities can make great strides." He stated that the company had become a small feudal lord in the last six years but that he believed it could grow into a large feudal lord, depending on future developments, and the Second Premier Company Plan would be implemented over the next five years.

The three pillars of the Premier Company Plan were the Canon Development System, the Canon Production System, and the Canon Sales System.

Among these, the Canon Production System (CPS) achieved a cost reduction of 63.6 billion yen over six years. The CPS Promotion Office tabulated the targets and results for each plant and related personnel by classifying waste into nine categories: work in progress, defects, facilities, costs, management, design 1, design 2, human resources, and operations. The first year's total was 3.5 billion yen, the second year 6.3 billion yen, and the third year 9.8 billion yen, but from the fourth year, the figures increased markedly to 13.5 billion yen, 15.2 billion yen, and 15.3 billion yen, respectively. In some years, the accounting department at the head office saved 800 million yen just by reviewing interest rates.

The Premier Company Plan was a far-reaching plan, yet meticulous in its implementation.

After becoming President, Kaku was interviewed by various newspapers and magazines. In the July 15, 1977 issue of *Toshi Keizai* (Investment Economy) magazine, he said of the Premier Company Plan, "It may sound like a rosy plan, but if we don't do this, we will end up in poverty, and it is a plan borne out of a rather tragic determination." To fully explain what Kaku meant by "end up in poverty," we would need to approach it analytically, but that is beyond the scope of this book. Kaku was aware that this was the course that had to be taken. It was this awareness that had given rise to the meticulousness seen in the CPS.

Later in the interview, Kaku stated, "There is a lot of talk about the total quality control (TQC) and other methods for streamlining factory operations, but my feeling is that efficiency will always improve. If you work hard and make improvements, it will happen. That is the idea that forms the basis of the Canon system. Efficiency can be improved even in how calculations are performed. Thus, if this idea is incorporated into the production process, you will get excellent productivity. I think that the three years I spent working on cost accounting when I first joined the company were very useful for me."

After becoming president, Kaku talked about "invisible profits" in the August 6, 1977 issue of Shukan Diamond (Weekly Diamond) magazine. According to the article, when he was living in a 2DK (two bedroom, dining room, kitchen) apartment, cleaning was very difficult. There were books piled up in one room and tools in the other. To clean the rooms, he would first take the books out and empty the room, then move the books and tools to another room. Although the room was small, it required a lot of work. If there is enough room, cleaning is easy. Even in a factory, building a new factory and making it neat and tidy, rather than just packing it in because there is space, will generate invisible profits.

He noted that some corporate structures cannot be represented by balance sheets alone. "In human terms, it can only be said how many employees there are, and their abilities cannot be assessed in monetary terms," he said, reflecting his mindset as an accountant.

In other words, the seemingly rosy and ambitious vision of the Premier Company Plan was rooted in his very human experience of living in a 2DK apartment and being ridiculed for using the abacus with just one finger. No matter how good an idea is, it won't be able to move people unless it has at its core the human nature of ordinary people.

The Labor Cost Increase Is Not 4.5 Billion Yen, but 9 Billion Yen

During the period when Takeo Maeda, who succeeded Mitarai, was developing his vision of the Premier Company Plan, Canon produced a "revolutionary" new product, which was inspired in part by the oil crisis.

In the midst of the oil crisis of 1973, Kazuo Naito (born in 1930, joined the company in 1953) thought, "This is the chance God has given me." The reason he thought it was a good chance can be explained by his "bitter" experience.

In October 1963, Naito became the head of the Engineering Section of the Production Control Department at the Shimomaruko Plant, and it was during this time that he was "bullied" for trying to automate part of the camera assembly process. He did not insist on automation just to satisfy his need for "fun" as an engineer; he thought it was necessary to thoroughly automate the assembly process in order to reduce costs because there were many people working on it. But he was told, "Even if we use machines, we can't produce anything good. It's a waste of money," and to his great disappointment, his department's budget was cut by one million yen at the next budget meeting.

The Canonet had been launched two years earlier and was now in its heyday. Breaking its own production volume rule, the company set new monthly production records of 10,000, 20,000, and 40,000 units. In terms of manufacturing, automatic machine tools and automatic surface treatment equipment were introduced, while in assembly, the workers' tasks were simplified and the manual labor became more efficient, through process analysis and the adoption of conveyer systems. As a result, it became possible to supply large quantities of products of consistent quality at a much lower price, which was one of the innovations in the camera industry (Kazuo Naito, "Issues in the 1980s in the Precision Industry Centering on Cameras," in the *Journal of the Japan Society of Mechanical Engineers,* No. 734).

Subsequently, the quality of Canon's manufacturing methods improved, and the company diversified its products and expanded its scale of production.

In 1969, the year the company changed its name from Canon Camera to Canon Inc., a company-wide labor-saving rationalization plan was initiated, the first phase (1969–1972) of which consisted of reducing the use of spot labor by increasing automation as well as the rationalization of individual machines.

However, automation can create its own problems. For example, if the cutting blade was flawed or if there are bad parts, the output would not be good. Sometimes the company buys an expensive machine and it breaks down for two or three months. If upper management notices that and asks, "What's going on?" there may not be a good response. This results in a deficit on paper. By contrast, when the same process is done manually, problems can somehow be covered up, and if efficiency improves and profits increase even by a little, the workers will be praised for their good work. Therefore, it is safer to extend conventional techniques than to take risks by mechanizing the work.

The first plan called for an investment of 3.8 billion yen over the four years from 1969 to 1972 to save labor costs equivalent to 1,600 people, but when the time came to implement the plan, the budget could not be fully spent. In fact, less than half of the budget (1.6 billion yen) was actually used, and labor costs equivalent to just 800 people were saved. Moreover, at the time, it was a widely held belief among industry and academia that not only should the camera assembly process not be automated but was in fact impossible to do so in the first place.

This was partly due to the structure of the camera itself, with its complex mechanism consisting of many precision parts, and partly because the production volume of 30,000 to 40,000 units per month was not enough to justify the introduction of automated equipment. In addition (and this is an important point), there was a certain "pride" or "sense of superiority" in the fact that the Japanese, with their dexterity, were capable of making high-end cameras having elaborate and complex structures. (Production engineers such as Naito did not believe that "manual dexterity" was the only factor that made high-end cameras possible.)

However, the fall of 1973, when the second phase of the plan began, was marked by the oil crisis. In the following year, wages were set to increase by about 30%, and Canon calculated that almost 1.5 billion yen per year would be added to the cost of labor in the production division.

Naito visited each factory with the figures and asked, "Where do you get the money for this?"

However, with a projected 4.5 billion yen in labor costs over the next three years, everyone thought they could get by if they worked as efficiently as possible.

However, no one was aware that behind this 4.5 billion yen were some hidden figures.

Although the first year would cost 1.5 billion yen, the second year would double that amount to 3 billion yen, and the third year would triple it to 4.5 billion yen, for a total of 9 billion yen over three years. Hearing this, a factory manager groaned, and Naito thought to himself, "I've got it."

The "Battle Argument" and the Challenge to the "Myths"

Meanwhile, sales of the FTb, a major SLR camera model that had been on the market for almost a decade, were sluggish, and the company needed to do something to address the situation. However, the price of raw materials had risen due to the oil crisis, making it difficult to cut costs, and the demand for cameras as a whole was poor. In addition, most manufacturers were producing products that had changed very little, and in the end, they were only able to make minor cost-cutting improvements.

At the same time, "external pressure" was beginning to mount on Japan, the country that had dethroned West Germany. Rollei of West Germany had built a plant in Singapore to assemble the Rollei 35, its famous compact camera, and Canon built a plant in Taiwan (in 1970) to cope with the "external pressure." In Japan, the twin realities of soaring wages and labor shortages made this a natural course of action.

Everyone was aware of the danger to the Japanese camera industry if China began making good products using cheap labor. It was believed that cameras had to be hand-assembled and therefore it was impossible to compete with low wages.

There were no new ideas for camera features that might attract mass popularity, and the only way forward was to reduce costs through the use of plastic molds and automation. Naito and the other production engineers presented a thorough rationalization plan to the development department. He thought he had he done his most thorough work to date, but the response from the design team was, "It's only this much cheaper?"

Naito was annoyed. "It's not right to say 'only.' Despite the large increase in wages, we have made the utmost effort to bring the costs down to this level. If you insist, why don't you convert everything to electronic?"

"We can't do that."

"Then why not have the calculator designers do it?"

"No, it will be more expensive to go electronic. We already estimated that."

"That's why you guys are so behind the times. You know that the costs go down over time. Sure, they are expensive now, but they will be on the market for years to come. If you apply the cost curve, you'll see that they will definitely become cheaper."

The person in charge of design at the time was Torakiyo Yamanaka, who joined the company in 1956 and had been a dedicated camera developer ever since. Yamanaka was also annoyed at being called "outdated," but it was fair to say that his sense of crisis was even greater than Naito's. Six years earlier, in 1967, Canon's sales ratio of cameras, excluding 8-mm filming equipment, was 61.5%, but had continued to decline, reaching 37% in 1973, which put a lot of pressure on Yamanaka as the person responsible for development.

It is fair to say that the technology level of the five major manufacturers of the time (Canon, Nippon Kogaku, Minolta, Asahikogaku, and Olympus) was at about the same, but Canon was a little different. They had hired a lot of electrical engineers for the Synchroreader project and, later, to design calculators.

Yamanaka narrowed down his basic development objectives to two: (1) lower cost and (2) automatic exposure (AE). Given that 8-mm and mid-range SLRs had already adopted AE, it was expected that this trend would extend to high-end SLRs as well, but most in the industry remained skeptical. However, Yamanaka thought that if the AE system were more reliable, professionals would come to prefer it over conventional cameras.

Nevertheless, it was a bold decision. Even though the company was slowly losing money over the FTb (released in March 1971), it had been one of the major backbones that supported Canon, and was the source of its livelihood. If the company made the expensive investment to switch to a new model and it failed, the entire company would be severely affected. In the U.S., Canon had just started selling the FTb.

However, Naito was surprised when he saw the blueprints.

"I didn't realize they'd become so electronic."

Overcoming Dichotomy

So how to set the price? At that time, manual cameras priced at between 60,000 and 70,000 yen accounted for 65% of the market, while AE cameras, which had begun to appear around 1971, were priced at over 100,000 yen.

In terms of functionality, AE, in which the shutter speed or aperture value is set in advance and the shutter speed or aperture is automatically determined according to the movement and brightness of the subject, is much easier to operate compared with using an exposure meter and performing the necessary operations each time a picture is taken. It was predicted that AE would become the norm in the future and also that heavy cameras would be unpopular with users.

So, what functions should be included? For the purpose of their research, the evaluation was divided into five levels: absolutely necessary; necessary in comparison with other companies' products; better to have; only if cost permits; and not necessary. The results were as follows: (1) shutter speed priority, (2) compact and lightweight, (3) automatic setting of shutter speed and aperture when using a strobe, (4) automatic film winding when a winder is attached, and (5) a price of 80,000 yen (at that time, the Canon EF with similar functions was 101,500 yen with an $f/1.4$ lens). The challenge was to strike the right balance between advanced functionality and low cost. To this end, the company sought to combine development design with production technology, something that had rarely been done at Canon up to that point. Because both parties were well aware of the crisis, they had no choice but to abandon their sense of territoriality.

To achieve the cost target, both the number of parts and the time required to assemble them needed to be reduced. Accordingly, the following targets were set.

(1) Implement electronic control of camera functions in order to achieve the functional requirements while reducing the number of mechanical parts in order to achieve cost reductions.

(2) Introduce automated assembly and improve the accuracy of components in order to make the assembly process non-adjustable.

(3) Use more plastic parts in order to reduce the time required to process parts while reducing the overall weight of the product.

However, it would be too risky to try to achieve all three targets from the beginning. Therefore, the development of the camera as a whole was carried out using existing and improved technologies, while the parts were divided into five major units (viewfinder, shutter, mirror actuator, auto-exposure, and auto-iris) as well as 25 subunits. Development groups were formed for each unit and each group was responsible for developing new technologies. At the same time, target costs were set for each unit.

The use of electronics does not necessarily mean that conventional mechanical parts are replaced with electronic ones. The main electronic component was a CPU (central processing unit) that was designed to make instructional decisions based on information such as the set shutter speed, film sensitivity, brightness of the lens used, and brightness of the subject. In addition, ultra-large-scale integration (ULSIs) and ICs were used.

In the past, electronic components were incorporated into the gaps between the mechanical parts of the camera body and wired together. Although this reduced the number of mechanical parts, the total number of parts tended to remain the same. In addition, electronic parts were more vulnerable to changes in the external environment, and faulty wiring could cause the camera to malfunction. To overcome these disadvantages, the electronic components were eventually integrated into a single flexible substrate.

Each unit had its own independent function, and each unit was checked for function and accuracy. The couplings between units as well as those between units and the body were also made to be non-adjustable.

In addition, the top and bottom lids were now made of plastic. The complicated shape of the top lid, which was conventionally made of metal, required a large number of processing steps. By using industrial plastic, the number of processing steps could be reduced to just five, compared with the 15 steps required for metal processing. At the same time, the development of multi-layered metal coating technology for plastics had made it possible to replace metal in terms of strength, elasticity, appearance beauty, and feel, and to reduce product weight by a factor of two compared with metal. (According to Torakiyo Yamanaka's article, "Case Study of VE Introduction in the Development of the Canon AE-1," published in the December 1978 issue of *Kojo Kanri* (Factory Management) magazine).

Thus, the number of components in the FTb was reduced from around 1,000 to about 650 in the AE-1.

Canon Electronics, a subsidiary of Canon Inc. established in 1954, manufactured the main mechanical parts for shutters. Meanwhile, the camera business was beginning to lose money due to the declining demand for cameras, as evidenced by the slowdown in the FTb market. Naito had dared to ask the company to automate its facilities, a project that would cost between 400 and 500 million yen. Canon Electronics also needed work, but was afraid to make a large capital investment in facilities. Naito did not have any other outsourcers in mind, but he adopted a semi-coercive stance, saying, "If you don't automate the facilities, we will outsource the production to other companies." In the end, Canon Electronics completely overhauled its facilities to facilitate the production of the AE-1.

Automation was implemented to reduce costs, but for automated assembly to be possible, the accuracy of the parts themselves needed to be high. If the accuracy was poor, the assembly process would immediately stop. Therefore, great efforts were made to improve the accuracy of the parts, and the quality of the camera as a whole was enhanced, resulting in a very low defect rate. Although most products were usually commercialized with a safety factor of 120%, the AE-1 achieved a safety factor of 200%. The test was repeated like "knocking on a stone bridge before crossing it" (a Japanese idiomatic expression to describe the state of being excessively cautious).

Finally, in April of 1976, the AE-1 was put on the market at a price of 82,000 yen with an $f/1.4$ lens. "The most contentious issue was the price. There was talk of parallel sales with the FTb, but it was decided to make the switch once and for all. It had been about ten years since Canon had started selling directly to the public, so they were able to push new products through that channel. It was good timing," said Kikuji Kikuchi, who went on to become the manager of the Osaka branch at Canon Sales. Other manufacturers were amazed at how low the price was.

"Are you going to crush us?"

The AE-1 became the spark that ignited the worldwide demand for SLR cameras, especially in the U.S. market. Other companies increased their production volume and were able to produce the same cameras at substantially lower prices. This revitalized the industry, which had been stagnant, and unleashed latent demand. Any fears that the Japanese camera industry might be replaced by cameras from underdeveloped countries with low wages had been dispelled. The AE-1 was the best-selling model on the market, and a record 4.5 million units were produced over the next five plus years.

"It's Canon, so we could do it. The pioneering spirit is instilled in our young people, and our corporate culture allows us to do bold things freely. In the electronics industry, you need fresh minds in their early twenties, and these young people did a great job. Canon would spend the money as long as the objective was clear and the process was correct. This has been true since the days of President Mitarai. Even if we fail, we are not scolded much," Torakiyo Yamanaka said. "But when we do succeed, we don't get much praise either," he added with a laugh.

The AE-1 "helped to instill the concept of profit in the production engineers," said Naito. Until then, when they installed equipment, they did not consider how many years it would last. When products changed and manufacturing equipment was retired, what had been calculated to be profitable during the planning stage became unprofitable. This was a big blow to the calculator business.

After the oil crisis, efforts were made to understand the connection between development and sales in order to determine how much net profit could actually be generated by the equipment. "We asked the sales people what we were going to do, but we needed to sell the product for a few years in order to achieve profitability, so we asked the development people if they could design a product that could be automated accordingly." For Naito, the most valuable lesson he learned from his experience with the AE-1 was that inter-organizational ties needed to be strengthened, not between the heads of organizations but rather between the people who were actually engaged in solving the problems.

In the third labor-saving rationalization plan, which commenced with the launch of the AE-1 (through 1978), the outcomes surpassed expectations for the first time. Originally the plan was to invest 4.5 billion yen to streamline labor costs equivalent to 900 workers, yielding a net income of 6.2 billion yen.

As a result, the investment was adjusted to 5 billion yen, leading to savings in labor costs equivalent to 1,000 workers and generating a net income of 7 billion yen.

When Mitarai saw the English-language film of the AE-1 manufacturing process, he was overjoyed. "This is what I have been telling you to automate. It finally bore fruit," he told Naito. The AE-1 revolution was a wholly internal reform movement at Canon. As a result, it caused a huge ripple effect outside the company. The AE-1 revolution showed that one cannot change the outside world without internal reform.

However, the year after the AE-1 revolution, Konishiroku launched the Jaspin Konica, an autofocus camera, which was a huge hit. (Before that, the Piccari Konica, launched in 1975, had also been a hit.) Along with similar models from Fujifilm, the market was soon flooded with autofocus cameras made by film manufacturers. Camera manufacturers followed suit, determined not to be left behind, but they were unable to break the dominance of Konishiroku and Fujifilm. Canon, on the other hand, was no longer in the same position it had been in the past, when it once held 30% of the mid-range market thanks to the Canonet, and was always in second or third place.

The AF35M Autoboy, launched in 1979, was Canon's attempt to regain ground on the mid-range market. The most notable feature of this camera was the absence of a film-winding lever anywhere on the camera. The focus was automatic, and the built-in flash popped out, just as in other models, but once the shutter release button was pressed, the film would wind up automatically. It was truly a "single-press" camera. Mitarai had asked the engineers to automate the focusing function from the user's point of view.

The price was set at 44,800 yen, the same as similar products from Konica, Fujica, and Minolta, and although it was launched just over a year after the

Jaspin Konica, it quickly took the top position in the market.

The idea for this fully automatic model came from a group of designers led by Torakiyo Yamanaka. Everyone on the design team was around 30 years old. As we will see later, the Autoboy became huge hit overseas as well, and Yamanaka called its success a "triumph of planning."

Mitarai Receives the Mainichi Keizaijin Award

In December 1980, one year after the launch of the Autoboy, Mitarai received the second-ever Keizaijin Award (Businessperson of the Year Award), sponsored by the Mainichi Shimbun newspaper, together with Tsunezo Makino, chairman of Makino Milling Machine (chairman of the selection committee: Professor Emeritus Kazuo Okochi, University of Tokyo.)

The award is presented to business people who have contributed to the development of the industry and, through their products and services, improved people's lives. In Mitarai's case, the award was given in recognition of his role in making Japanese cameras world-class, his development of X-ray cameras and medical equipment, and his leadership role in the Japanese camera industry. One of the first recipients of the award was Katsutaro Kataoka, president of Alps Electric (formerly Kataoka Electric), which had manufactured the switches for the Synchroreaders when it was still a small company.

Chapter 7

Within the International Community

Chapter 7
Within the International Community

Mitarai's Overseas Awards

When the Autoboy was launched in 1979 (four years after the implementation of the Premier Company Plan) and export sales topped 100 billion yen for the first time, Mitarai was overwhelmed with emotion.

He recalled his first trip to the U.S., when his ambitious and painstaking work was met with the rejection and he was told that "Made in Japan" wouldn't sell. He remembered returning to Japan with a deep sense of humiliation and thinking to himself, "Someday, I will erase this stigma and take control of the market with my own hands." He had achieved his once seemingly impossible goal of "defeating Leica," and Japanese cameras were now competing with each other for the world's top position in the global market.

After World War II, the promotion of exports was one of the most important national policies, and this was in line with Mitarai's belief that the only way for resource-poor Japan to survive was to become a technology-driven country.

Then, as the company's dependence on overseas demand for cameras increased, overseas expansion became inevitable, and in the early stages of this expansion, it adopted a distributor system. In doing so, the company emphasized human relationships with store owners and company presidents, and here, too, it strove to realize a "new familialist" approach. Later, in response to Canon's development, market expansion, and the diversification of its product mix, the company shifted to a direct sales system in which the company "raised its own children."

They have never forgotten our company creed of "making the world's best products and contributing to the improvement of culture," Mitarai reflected, and to this end they have always insisted on "no complaints and no trouble." He also recalled that he once gathered the managers of related divisions and instructed them to establish a quality assurance system.

"You must not give in to the sales side of the business. They want to avoid spending too much time and effort on quality control for the sake of the immediate future. However, doing so will damage the brand, and in the long run, we will lose the market. Therefore, you must take charge of quality control. I'll protect you so you don't ever have to make any lousy compromises."

This kind of thinking has now become common sense. "When we had a problem with a product, I yelled at our employees in a fit of rage, but I knew it was the right thing to do."

Mitarai received international honors in 1980 and 1981.

One was the 1980 International Man of the Year Award from the Photographic Manufacturers and Dealers Association in the U.S. The commemorative plaque reads (in English), "In honor of Dr. Takeshi Mitarai for his significant contributions to the development of the world's photographic industry and the recognition that photography is a universal language."

In 1981, he was inducted into the Hall of Fame at the 57th Photo Marketing Association International Convention and Trade Show. The award was established in 1968 and is presented to individuals who have made significant contributions to the photographic industry. At the ceremony, Mitarai was honored for his activities as the three-time Chairman of the Japan Camera Industry Association (JCIA), as well as his contributions to the development of the camera industry around the world.

This chapter traces Canon's development overseas.

The Netherlands

From the sky, the coastline of the Netherlands is a beautiful green lattice of tightly plotted reclaimed land. In Amsterdam, the streets are lined with dense rows of townhouses characterized by their white window frames, and the abundance of goods for sale in the outdoor markets is the very richness of life in this country.

Keishi Fukuda, who once warmed himself with heated wine during his days in Geneva, was transferred to Canon Amsterdam in 1974 as its vice president and became president in 1979.

In 1974, Canon's products were cameras (FTb) and calculators. The camera division had already won its war with Germany, leaving only Japanese companies to battle for supremacy. The competition remained fierce, and no one was able to get an advantage until the AE-1 launched in 1976 and then Canon suddenly overwhelmed the competition. Sales exceeded expectations, and it was difficult to fill all the orders. Soon the number of dealers doubled from 500 to 1,000.

The Autoboy, launched in 1979, quickly made up for the poor performance of the previous mid-range models, selling so well that there was an extreme shortage of the product.

According to a survey by Dataquest, a research company based in California, Canon ranked first in Europe in terms of the number of newly installed PPCs in 1980 with 41,400 units, followed by Rank Xerox (Xerox's sales company in Europe) with 35,000 units, Minolta with 32,000 units, Nashua with 30,000 units, Sharp with 24,000 units, Ubix (Konishi roku) with 17,000 units, Calle Infotech with 16,500 units, Toshiba with 16,000 units, and so on.

Nashua and Calle Infotec were original equipment manufacturers (OEM) of Ricoh (sold under the brand name of the company from which they are purchased), so when the two were are combined, it effectively put Ricoh in the first place, but the day would be coming soon when Canon would overtake this one. Canon's aim was to enter the field of high-end equipment, where Xerox had a near monopoly, but it needed highly knowledgeable salespeople to do so. "It costs money to headhunt talented people, it takes time to train them, and even if they are trained, they will be headhunted. It is very difficult to compete with Xerox in the same field," says Fukuda.

Cameras accounted for more than 50% of sales, copiers 30%, calculators 12% to 13%, and the rest is micro-related. Canon Amsterdam has 60 Japanese staff members, including President Fukuda, and 130 local employees, and I interviewed three local managers.

J.R. Doorn, the accountant, joined Canon Amsterdam when the branch was established. He attributes Canon's development to "Good products, a market policy of making them number one, and the hard work of the young staff." At first, he could not understand why Japanese people worked so hard, from early in the morning until late at night, but when he started to participate in meetings where the Japanese staff took time to decide policies, he understood. They work as a group to create policies, whereas in Europe, there is a clear division of responsibility and individuals handle things on their own. However, he found that such an approach was not acceptable in a Japanese company, so he decided to exchange opinions with other departments.

One memorable incident happened to Doorn when Canon Amsterdam was still small and Yoshiaki Otake was president. As the organization expanded, Doorn delegated some of his authority to one of his subordinates, but the subordinate did not fulfill his responsibilities, so Doorn wanted to fire him. However, Ohtake simply reassigned the man to a different department, saying, "That was because of our poor management, but he is a member of the Canon family." This, he says, renewed Dooren's thinking about the Canon family.

J.C. Linden saw a copier at the Canon trade show in Amsterdam in 1973, which led him to join the company, where he was put in charge of copier service. "Canon tries to maintain good contact with its customers, and that attitude is very important. Large companies such as Xerox and IBM didn't pay much attention to such things because they held a large share of the market, but they seem to have changed their approach since the Japanese companies came on the scene." When I mentioned Doorn's views about the Canon family, Linden said, "When someone makes a mistake, there is an atmosphere in which everyone covers for each other, rather than blaming each other. Canon does indeed have a family organization."

E. Magnus is in charge of public relations. She has been with the company since its Geneva days and has had the most contact with Mitarai among the local staff. She said, "What is most impressive about Dr. Mitarai is his personal connection with the agency staff. In particular, he deeply values our relationship with those companies who were willing to handle Canon cameras more than 20 years ago when Japanese cameras were not as popular as they are today, and these people also have a good impression of the Chairman. At a Hannover Messe dinner in 1969, a calculator distributor used the term "Canon family," which was very strange to us Europeans. However, once we learned about the relationship between the Chairman and the distributors, we understood the Canon family better, and it came to be understood and accepted among us. He has an excellent personality, but on the other hand, he gets upset and angry when things don't go his way. However, he has created a good interpersonal atmosphere among businessmen working in a fiercely competitive field. I hope that he will continue to travel to Europe and meet as many people as possible." (Interpreter, computer manager Naoki Nambu)

Fukuda was 25 years old when he was sent to Geneva to work for a general agency, but before leaving Japan, he was told by Mitarai, "Take care of yourself and absorb everything you can. In the future, Canon will have the opportunity to sell our products by ourselves, so you should develop a lot of strength before then."

France

The Champs-Élysées boulevard leading to the Arc de Triomphe in Paris was crowded with people on the weekend. There were stores on both sides of the street with signs advertising products from Canon, Sony, and other Japanese companies. Colored leaves cover the bank of the Seine River, and the antique bookstores are attracting the tourists.

Canon France was established in 1972, and Yoshiaki Otake (born in 1930, joined the company in 1953) became president in December 1979. There were ten Japanese staff, including Ryozo Hirako, the vice president.

For cameras, Canon has the the top market share in SLRs, mid-range (e.g., Autoboy), and 8-mm cameras. Olympus and Minolta were tied for second place (the U.S. firm Nielsen conducts market research and publishes a report every two months on retail cameras sales).

Xerox was the leader in copiers. Canon was ahead of Nashua, Minolta, and Sharp in terms of sales and installed base, and was closing in on Xerox's lead.

The local staff, numbering less than 1,000 in the office equipment division and 150 in the camera division, were not bad workers, but they were not good at working together as a group toward a single goal. Traditionally, there is a strong centralized management system, which is good when someone like Napoleon or de Gaulle is at the top and giving orders. But there is not much hope for them to take initiatives.

Unlike in Japan, reassignment is difficult. A person in a certain post has entered into a contract with the company for that post, and if the company unilaterally reassigns the person, it is considered a breach of the contract by the company. If the company is sued by the labor court, it cannot transfer or appoint a replacement until the matter is resolved. In general, labor issues play a very important role in the management of companies in France.

French companies tend to have a large head office structure because power is concentrated in the center of the country and local regions are given detailed instructions. In this respect, Canon France is oriented toward "small government."

United Kingdom

In a corner of Piccadilly Circus, the heart of downtown London, there are neon advertisements for major Japanese companies such as Canon. Pigeons and visitors from the country flock around the fountain in Trafalgar Square, the famous double-decker buses run on the streets, and people drive old black Austins, a symbol the British people's perseverance.

Canon Business Machines (UK) was established in Croydon, a suburb about an hour's drive from London, in 1975, and its President, Yukio Yamashita (born in 1939, joined the company in 1962), was appointed in August 1980 after spending some time at Canon Amsterdam. The company had been continuously in the red, and for the first six months after his arrival, he analyzed the business situation in order to identify the problem and propose remedies. According to Yamashita, Europeans in general, rather than the British, do not question orders from the top management. Because they are connected only with their direct superiors at work, they do not have the opportunity to think about the company as a whole and do not work based on consensus as we do in Japan. Naturally, they simply carry out the work they are assigned.

To change this, the company adopted the profit center concept. The organization was split into two divisions: copiers and calculators. The copier division, which accounted for 80% of sales, was operated under a regional branch system, and each branch was independently financed. Challenging "common wisdom" that a council system was impossible for British people as they tend to be assertive and stubborn, the company established a management committee to build consensus among local managers and communicate company policy to the lower levels of the company. The British were reluctant to delegate authority to subordinates, and for more than a year after his arrival, Yamashita had to sign even the smallest withdrawal voucher.

Rank Xerox was headquartered in London and boasted a 50% market share, while Canon was still at 10%. More than a dozen companies, mostly Japanese, were mixed in the market. Canon's overly large organization had long been a weakness, but this was about to be turned into an advantage.

When I was shown around the office, I found myself in a room with the door open, where a Japanese man was shouting with so much force in fluent English at several stout Englishmen. He was Yasuyuki Matsuda, a general manager in the copier division, who had previously worked at Canon Amsterdam and had been assigned to the UK branch in April 1981.

The copier division had 270 employees spread across five regions. Minolta,

Sharp, and Ricoh had a dozen to twenty employees, mainly Japanese, and as they sell only through distributors (no direct sales), they are able to generate profits quickly without large organizational structures such as branches. Minolta launched an excellent small model in 1981 and captured the second largest market share after Xerox, while Canon, according to Matsuda, was "miserably kicked around."

However, Canon was able to leverage its size and sell to national accounts, including large corporations like British Petroleum (BP) and government agencies. Other Japanese companies do not have branches in the region, so they ask their distributors to make such arrangements. However, the distributors are small companies, and given that the buying price for national accounts is so low and copy fees are also low, they are unable to handle the request. Only companies such as Xerox, Nashua, Calais, and Océ were able to do so, and Japanese companies could not even touch them. Canon, which had 100 service personnel nationwide, began to make inroads into this market in 1981.

"However, it is not enough just to have a network of branches. You have to have total control of the managers and be able to say, 'Do it!' with just one phone call," Matsuda remarked. "Other Japanese companies would incur losses if they wanted to do this, but Canon has done it well enough so far," he said with a laugh.

Yamashita asserts, "We are confident in our quality, and Canon has the most development capability." Matsuda then added, "Sales volume doubled in 1981 compared with 1980, and will double again in 1982. Rank Xerox's sales are ten times that of Canon. Although our annual sales have come very close to Xerox's, their copy charges are enormous. I can tell you, though, things have shifted a lot in the industry, but the general public doesn't know that. If Canon becomes number one in sales in 1982, and if the winds blow hard against Japan around 1983, we Japanese are thinking of going back to Japan," he said.

P.M. Benham, manager of the shipping department, was featured in the trade press after he managed to save 25% on shipping costs. The company had five warehouses in the U.K., but he was able to consolidate them into a single location.

Masayuki Miyazaki, a former designer, was in charge of selling mask aligners, a type of equipment used to make semiconductors. Although growth was slower than in Japan and the U.S., the U.K. was making a concerted effort to nurture its semiconductor industry, and it had a promising market for the future. In the fall of 1981, the Dutch government established a semiconductor project, and two universities placed orders with Canon for mask aligners.

In anticipation of the future, foreign semiconductor manufacturers such as National Semiconductor, Motorola, and NEC have begun building factories in the UK, which is expected to become a large market when they begin operations. According to Miyazaki, American-made semiconductor-baking equipment has been overwhelmed by Canon's products and has lost momentum, and a manufacturer in Munich, Germany, is offering products that are inferior to Canon's.

USA-Challenge to the Wall

During my flight over the North Atlantic from Europe to the U.S., the cabin was filled with a diverse range of passengers, just like New York, which is a "melting pot" of different ethnicities. When Canon first opened its New York branch, only the embassy and Canon offices were decorated with the Japanese flag, but now Japanese restaurants and ramen shops are popular among the locals.

The headquarters of Canon USA is located in Lake Success, a suburb of New York City. The president since 1997, Fujio Mitarai (born in 1935, joined the company in 1961), is the third son of Takeshi Mitarai's older brother Nobuo. He has been working in the U.S. since 1966. When Takigawa became president in 1970 and started direct sales, Fujio was the head of the General Affairs Section, and from 1973 he was the head of the Camera Sales Department.

At that time, in the U.S. Kodak had a lot of success with a compact, "instant" camera, and it was common knowledge that SLR cameras were for semi-professional use. When Canon started direct sales in the U.S., Nikon, Minolta, and Olympus had already established a good track record, and Canon was no match for them. When Fujio visited Japan, retailers would take good care of him when he mentioned he was from Canon, but in the U.S., they would not. This was the first thing that astonished him.

Retailers would only carry Nikon cameras if they were Nikon dealers in the franchise system, but retailers also rise and fall, and not all first-rate stores yesterday are first-rate stores today. Takigawa and his colleagues adopted an open system for Canon after a heated debate. This will provide more opportunities. However, at that time Canon could not hire top-notch salesmen. The only people who applied for the job were second-rate people from first-rate companies. So, Canon aimed for top-class salesmen from third-rate companies. It was the first time for them to handle such an excellent product as Canon's, and the strategy worked.

Canon, a latecomer, had to do something different to break through.

Nevertheless, the sales representatives' enthusiastic visits to retailers were not enough to make any headway against the other more established Japanese manufacturers. So what could be done? Shouldn't the Canon brand be marketed directly to each and every consumer, beyond the control of individual retailers? However, even here, there was a "common belief" involved. The "common belief" was that mass advertising and mass sales like Kodak's were only acceptable for instant cameras, and that it would be absurd to do so for high-end SLR cameras.

But then, has an SLR manufacturer ever invested the same amount of time, energy, and money in reaching out to consumers as Kodak did? While we were having heated debate over whether we should do it or not, the AE-1 came from Japan and challenged the "common wisdom" of the industry. The company's need to somehow break through the barriers of its predecessors led them to create the AE-1. "This is it. This is Canon's answer to the common belief that SLR cameras are expensive and difficult to operate. It's not expensive. It's easy to operate."

Takigawa made the bold decision to invest 1.5 million dollars (about 350 million yen) to advertise the AE-1 on television.

The strategy worked beautifully, and the AE-1 flew off store shelves and quickly ran out of stock. As Fujio Mitarai later characterized the situation, it used to be that people who bought SLR cameras were the same kind of people who drove luxury cars. However, with the decline in the value of money due to inflation and the rise in incomes, students were now able to earn two to three hundred dollars even with part-time jobs.

In addition, the boom coincided with the unprecedented expansion of the U.S. economy from 1975 to 1979. As in Japan, the boom led to rapid growth in the SLR camera market, and in 1979, 1980, and 1981, Canon, a latecomer to the market, held the top market share position. This success was due to "the shift from selling through retailers in the existing market to creating a new market by appealing directly to the masse," according to Fujio Mitarai.

Surprisingly, Canon tried to do the same with copiers. Here, too, the dominance of Xerox continued for a long time. At the time, most workers had to go to their company's copy center, which had one or more large high-speed machines, to make copies. This was time-consuming and inconvenient, especially when secretaries were absent and queues formed. In some cases, manuscripts were left behind and corporate secrets were leaked. Thus, there was an unmet demand for small, easy-to-use copy machines in individual offices.

When small Japanese copiers entered the market, the demand for these smaller machines grew rapidly. However, copiers were not a mass-market product like cameras, so there were concerns. Nevertheless, in February 1980, the company decided to conduct a thorough experiment and began advertising on television, which proved to be successful. Sales doubled in 1980, and by the fall of 1981, they had increased by 60% over the previous year. According to a survey by Dataquest, Canon overtook Xerox to become the top company in terms of number of new installations.

There is a story about Fujio Mitarai. He had come to the U.S. branch office and was in the president's office. He surprised then president Saio Mitsui by answering the telephone as soon as it rang. Even after that, he was infamous for picking up the phone as soon as it rang. This was his way of learning English, but the company received a lot of complaints that the man who always answered the phone could not speak English.

When Fujio took over as president of Canon USA, he was concerned about how to win the hearts and minds of his employees and how to ensure that the will of management was communicated all the way down to the lowest levels.

He scheduled a regular management meeting for the first Monday morning of each month. There was a large conference table in the president's office, and in one corner of the room, directly behind the president's desk, stood a 70 – 80 cm tall statue of Kannon, the Buddhist Goddess of Mercy, looking down at the desk. The statue was brought from Japan by Tomomasa Matsui, the first manager of the New York branch, and it is the only object from that period that remained until Fujio took over as president.

In American companies, work was generally separated by division, with the president usually talking to the vice president in charge of cameras, then to the vice president in charge of copiers. And a department head doesn't care or listen to other departments. Fujio, however, did not follow this practice. For the past four years, he has continued to have the heads of each department, as well as those in charge of accounting and human resources, attend his meetings.

Then, in January of each year, the branch managers and managers from all over the U.S. gathered in New York for a joint management meeting to discuss the three-year plan. About 100 people attended the meeting in total, and revisions were made to the schedule for the following year, based on the difference in performance between the previous year and the present year. The meeting begins with Fujio's New Year's address and presentation of management policy, followed by a report on the past three years' results by the head of the accounting department, a personnel policy by the head of the human resources department, and a statement of management policy for each department based on the overall plan by the vice president, who is the head of each department. Seventy of the one hundred attendee were American employees, and each attendee returned to their assigned area and informed their subordinate managers about what was discussed at the meeting, and the vice president at the head office informed the middle-level staff, who in turn informed their subordinates.

In other words, long-term thinking, horizontal connections (teamwork), and the transmission of the top management's thinking to those below were realized. "Let's try it in the U.S. It's a Sisyphusian effort, it doesn't easily take root. But I was determined, so I said 'do it anyway,' and finally we did it," Mitarai recalled. The American staff have become accustomed to this. For them, holistic, long-term thinking is the top management's job, and each of them works as a specialist, with the know-how and knowledge they possess belonging only to themselves it is their own strength, and they are not willing to share it with others. But "I am trying to challenge that 'wall' of preconception," Mitarai said.

For the 25th anniversary of the founding of Canon USA, Canon sent 30 employees to Japan, from warehouse workers to managers, regardless of their level; those who had been with the company for seven years or more were eligible. In the U.S., such awards are usually given in order from the top, so the Canon ceremony was well received and served to deepen the understanding that Canon is both global-minded and family-oriented at the same time.

A major priority is to avoid laying off employees, which Mitarai believes would result in the collapse of familialism itself.

Sales skyrocketed from $96 million in 1975 to $707 million in 1981, nearly doubling every year. By product, cameras accounted for 55%, office equipment 40%, and optical equipment (e.g., mask aligners) 5%.

Excluding banks and trading companies, Canon ranks ninth among the top Japanese manufacturers in terms of sales in 1975 to 1981, followed by Toyota, Nissan, Honda, Matsushita, Sony, Fuji Heavy Industries, Toyo Kogyo, Sanyo Electric, Canon, and Sharp. Canon is the only company on this list that is not an automobile or electronics manufacturer.

During the three-year plan from 1978 to 1980, the company became a first-rate Japanese company operating in the United States, approaching the status of a 'Premier Company.' And in the 1980s, he hopes Canon to become a 'Premier Company' in comparison with American corporations, by repeating the three-year plan three times.

The first three-year plan for the 1980's contained five objectives: (1) achieve annual sales of $1 billion, (2) achieve a pre-tax profit of 6% or more, (3) maintain a sound financial structure (asset turnover of four months or less), (4) review the business management system to accommodate a billion-dollar company status, and (5) review the wage and benefits system. Mitarai said, "There are no short cuts in business management. It is important to complete common-sense things persistently, solidly and thoroughly."

Hiroto Kagami, who was once told "Harry...this is snow" while working at Bell & Howell in Canada, was transferred to Canon USA in 1971 and is now one of the vice presidents (head of the service department), which has more than 200 service personnel. The amount of parts supplied to all over the U.S. alone is enormous. There are nine training rooms on the ground floor of the headquarters building, where the service staff of 600 to 700 office equipment distributors in the U.S. are trained every day. Ninety percent of the instructors are American, and there are other training centers in Chicago, Los Angeles, Atlanta, and Dallas.

David F. E. Farr, the director of human resources, was a University of Cambridge graduate who came to the U.S. after working for the tobacco company British American Tobacco. When he was offered a transfer to Australia, he thought about changing jobs and was later introduced to Canon by his lawyer. After doing his own research on Canon, he decided that it was a promising company with good management indicators and a sound policy based on meritocracy.

American management is primarily focused on serving shareholders, with one superstar deciding management policies. What surprised Farr when he joined Canon was that the relevant department staff, both Japanese and American, would spend considerable time discussing a single issue, and once a policy was decided upon, the organization would move in that direction, which was something Farr had "never expected."

Farr noted that Japan differs from Europe and the U.S. in that it places more importance on the goals of the organizations than on the goals of the individuals, and he listed the family, school, community, company, industry, and nation as such "organizations." (In other words, he sees everything from the family to the state as a series of concentric circles representing human organizations.)

(Interpreter, Kenichi Mori)

Canada

To understand the grandeur of Niagara Falls, which is located on the border of the U.S. and Canada, one must experience the scale, sound, and spray of water at the same time. The view is awesome in its natural beauty. In contrast, the buildings in nearby Toronto are lit up at night to protect them from thieves.

Canon Canada, located in Mississauga, Ontario, was founded in 1972 with 200 employees, 17 of whom were Japanese. Cameras and copiers each accounted for 38% of sales, calculators for 15%, and the remainder is microcomputers and so on. According to customs statistics published in 1980, Canon's cameras accounted for 38% of the market share, followed by 14% at Minolta. Canon's photocopiers accounted for 36% of the market share, and although it was unable to match Xerox in terms of the total number of photocopiers installed, it topped the list in 1980 and 1981 in terms of number of new photocopiers installed.

Canon boasted an outstanding market share of 50% in the calculator business, which was due in large part to Canon's early entry into the Canadian market. Canon Canada began operations in 1973, but two years later, in 1975, the Foreign Investment Review Act (FIRA) was passed, strictly regulating investment by foreign companies. The law dictates the number of Canadians that must be employed for every foreign worker, and companies that do not comply must undergo a FIRA review aimed at protecting the domestic industry. For this reason, calculator manufacturers other than Canon were not allowed to sell directly in Canada, and Canon was the only company that could do so, according to Azuhiko Takano, vice president of finance.

Sales in Canada increased twenty-eight fold in the eight years from 1973 to 1980, growing at an average annual rate of 40%. As a result, the administrative department could not keep up, and the Japanese staff worked late every day.

Donald A. Phillips, a service manager who worked above Mamoru Maeda at Bell & Howell in Canada, was vice president of Canon Canada until the fall of 1981, and his room was decorated with a picture of Takeshi Mitarai.

Phillips believes "with great passion" in the idea of the Canon family and thinks it is universal. "I believe that people do not follow the balance sheet of a company, but rather the ideals of its top management," he said. When he first met Takeshi Mitarai in 1965, he knew he was dealing with the man who had started the company that was producing the industry's leading cameras. "He is a wise man, an astute observer, and good at finding what is unique in each person," he said.

(Interpreter, Mamoru Maeda)

Chicago

Driving along Chicago's lakefront road along Lake Michigan is pleasant, and the view of the skyscrapers at night is magnificent, befitting the country's second largest city. Unfortunately, the day I visited Chicago, it was raining and the top of the 443-meter-high Sears Tower was completely shrouded in fog.

The Chicago branch was established in 1971 by Takashi Fujimura (who joined Canon USA in 1963) and two others. At the time, Bell & Howell still held the rights to sell cameras, so they were competing with Sharp to sell pre-pocket-type calculators that cost 10,000 yen per digit. Fujimura started by renting an office and installing a telephone, desk, and curtains. The only Japanese companies operating in the region other than banks and trading companies were Sony and Honda. At the time, Nikon cameras were famous, and there was also a well-known American towel company called Cannon. Fujimura, however, still felt as if he was working for Canon in Japan. When he attempted to purchase office equipment, he was told he had to pay for it up front, and since he didn't know anything about credit cards, he had to come up with the cash. He worked on Saturdays and Sundays, and other Japanese employees had items stolen from their apartments while they were away.

The branch manager at the time of the interview was Junichi Tominaga (joined the company in 1964, later transferred to Germany), and there were about 140 employees, including 17 Japanese. The service area was slightly different for cameras and copiers, but covered between 12 and 15 states including the Dakotas, Minnesota, Wisconsin, Ohio, and Texas. Sixty-five percent of sales were cameras and 25% were copiers, and "the market was so big that you didn't feel the limits," and there were often shortages of products. The area had many large chain stores such as Kmart, J.C. Penney, Venture, Target, and Walmart, and sales were said to vary by several million dollars depending on whether these stores carried the products or not (sales in 1980 were $111,800,000).

The image that the local staff had of Takeshi Mitarai could be summed up as "a great man" and "a great gentleman." They all knew that his background was unique and respected him for having been a doctor. However, they are also familiar with his sense of humor that made him easy to feel comfortable with. In 1980, on the 25th anniversary of Canon USA, a special allowance was given to the employees. While the gift was unexpected, the staff were even more surprised by how much they received.

Atlanta

Atlanta is the capital of the state of Georgia in the southeastern U.S. It is the home of Coca-Cola, and Atlanta's massive airport has a subway system that allows passengers to easily move between concourses.

The Atlanta branch was established in 1979, with service areas in ten states, including Virginia, Tennessee, Florida, and Georgia, and 75 employees, including 10 Japanese.

Sales nearly doubled from $39 million in 1979 to $77 million in 1981. Cameras accounted for more than half of the sales, photocopiers were in the 30% range, and calculators around 15%, while photocopiers were still growing at a remarkable rate of more than 40%.

The branch manager, Shigeru Hayashi (joined the company in 1969), was in charge of cameras. Minolta was the first Japanese camera company to open a branch in Atlanta. Around 1978, when Canon opened its office here, Minolta was strong, but the AE-1 and Autoboy (branded as "Sure Shot" in the U.S.) were growing at a "breakneck pace" and soon overtook Minolta at that time.

The branch manager, Katsumi Takizawa, was in charge of copiers. The number of distributors had increased from 20 or 30 to 140, and they were competing with Minolta and Sharp. Takizawa was not afraid of Xerox. He was more concerned about the competition between Canon's own product lines.

The Atlanta branch once ran an advertisement that said, "Atlanta is famous for Coca-Cola, the airport, and Canon" alongside advertisements for Coca-Cola and other companies.

Los Angeles

The sunset sky over Los Angeles was breathtaking. Disneyland was bustling with people from all over the world, and Little Tokyo was crowded with Japanese.

The Los Angeles branch was established in 1973 in suburban Costa Mesa. The service area covered eleven western states (including California, Arizona, Nevada, Oregon and so on) and Alaska. The company had 85 employees, 20 of whom were Japanese, and half of these were service personnel. The branch manager, Toshizo Tanaka (joined the company in 1964), was appointed in June 1979. Although camera sales have not exploded at retail stores, the partnership with the large chain store Sears has boosted sales. Camera sales used to account for 65%–70% of total sales, but the growth of copiers has been remarkable, and as a result, the percentage of cameras is approaching 55%, the same level as in Japan.

The Los Angeles branch was unique in that sales of mask aligners (semiconductor baking equipment) reached around $1 million each month thanks to its proximity to Silicon Valley, home to a number of U.S. semiconductor manufacturers.

Tanaka had a hard time with certain cultural differences. During interviews, American job candidates would tell him how many words they could type in a minute, but when he asked them to demonstrate, they couldn't do it. They boasted of their accounting skills, but in reality, they had only performed some supportive work for a month or so. He said if you were to believe them when they said they could do something, you would fail.

In addition to New York, Chicago, Atlanta, and Los Angeles, Canon USA also has branches in Dallas, Washington D.C., San Francisco, and Honolulu.

Latin America

The company's expansion into Latin America began with the designation of a sole distributor in 1962, followed by the establishment of Canon Latin America, Inc. in Panama in 1967.

The company had 18 Japanese and 60 local employees, and Kin'ya Uchida (who joined the company in 1963) became president in April 1979. Canon Brazil (São Paulo), Canon Latin America de México (Mexico), and Canon Venezuela (Caracas) are among its subsidiaries. At the time, Canon was the only company that had made inroads into the local markets for cameras, copiers, and calculators, although Ricoh entered the market for copiers in 1981.

Finding a good distributor in Latin America is very difficult. It requires not only financial resources but also political relationships (i.e., establishing personal connections with government officials). Because of strict import regulations, political influence was required to obtain a license. Furthermore, political and economic trends fluctuate wildly, making it an unstable market where one must be on one's guard at all times. The gap between the rich and the poor is wide, and cameras are bought mainly by landowners, successful merchants, and bureaucrats, while the high-end F-1 and A series, including AE-1, AE-1 Program, and A-1 became status symbols for the rich.

Brazil, Argentina, and Mexico together accounted for about 75% of sales in the Latin American market, and the economic trends in these three countries have had a significant impact on sales. However, Canon's sales growth was remarkable, rising from $2 million in 1969 (cameras and calculators) to $10 million in 1974 (cameras, calculators, copiers, and microphones), and in 1980, sales exceeded $30 million.

Australia

From Los Angeles, I traveled to Australia via Honolulu. When I arrived in Sydney in November 1981, the city was in the midst of a cleaning workers' strike, and in the tourist areas downtown, garbage was piled up in plastic bags, many of which were torn and emitting a foul odor. However, the view from the hotel over Sydney Harbor, with its countless floating yachts framed by the blue the skies and sea, was striking.

In Australia, agency sales began in 1952, and in 1973, a joint venture, Repco Canon, was established, which later became Canon Copier Australia. Canon Australia was established in 1979, and Shuichi Ando (who joined the company in 1953) was appointed as president in September 1980.

The company has a head office and branch office in Melbourne, as well as branches in Sydney, Adelaide, and Canberra, where copiers are sold directly, while in Brisbane products are sold through a distributor. The company has 350 employees, of which more than 60% are service staff, including service personnel and training center personnel.

Canon's share of the photocopier market is 17% – 18% according to customs statistics. Xerox began selling photocopiers in Australia in 1961 and dominated until 1970. Based on its success during that time, it remains strong in high-end machines, and the company advertises confidently, "For twenty-five years, every manufacturer has tried to imitate us."

The rest of Canon's sales are from cameras, calculators, and microcomputers, but because Australia is a largely agricultural country, televisions and cameras are considered luxury items by farmers, and wholesale prices are taxed at 30% (the highest rate in the developed world). Furthermore, because the cities are scattered over a vast area, distribution costs such as telexes, telephones, and transportation costs are twice as high as usual, resulting in a very high end price. For example, the price of the development and printing for a photo is double that in Japan (I went to a stationery store to buy a notebook, but the price was also double that in Japan).

As a result, there is a peculiarity not found in other regions. Even when products are advertised, many people buy cameras only when traveling abroad. Nevertheless, the share of Sure Shot (Autoboy) cameras is "unusually" high at 34%.

The Canola calculator was launched just as Australia began switching to a decimal system, and because it sold faster than a similar machine from Sharp, it was adopted by all government agencies and soon boasted a market share of over 30% in the first half of 1981. However, it is uncertain to what extent they will be able to compete in the office and desktop computer market.

There are twelve Japanese employees, including Ando. The Australian staff believe that it is management who thinks, and they should just do what they are told, so the salesmen take a vacation when they achieve their monthly goals. Even relocating an office would be done on a Saturday or Sunday in Japan, but in Australia, it would take a month. Therefore, it was necessary to change the speed of work.

Australia is rich in natural resources, and there is no sense of urgency in daily life. The greatest pleasure is to have a villa on the shore of Sydney Harbor and spend time on a yacht. Only a small percentage of students go on to university, so there are no exam reference books in bookstores and no management books. In other words, it is not a competitive society.

Sixteen or seventeen years earlier, Shuichi Ando accompanied Mitarai on a trip to visit distributors in several countries. They went to have dinner at the invitation of the president of a distributor in Athens, Greece, and Aristotle Onassis was sitting behind Mitarai's table. The president told Mitarai that Onassis was there, but Mitarai did not turn around. Ando joked, "Onassis buys a lot of ships from Japan, so we have to show respect," but Mitarai told the president of the distributor, "You are more important to me than Onassis. You are our benefactor and we look forward to your continued support." The president was very impressed by this.

When Ando was transferred to Australia, Mitarai gave him the following advice: "be careful of people who try to take advantage of you; be careful with alcohol because you never know who might be watching; and don't stay up late at night and come to work late the next day."

Singapore

Walking around the city of Singapore, where the average annual temperature is 27°C, the white sign on the bus reflects the bright light of the scorching sun. Then the red letters of "CANON" caught my eye. When I went out at night, I felt the sweltering heat enveloping my body, and it reminded me of Japan.

In addition to the Taiwan plant in 1969, the company expanded into Asia by establishing the Hong Kong Branch in 1971 and Canon Singapore in 1980, with Hiroshi Saito (joined the company in 1958), the former Hong Kong Branch manager, as president and, at the same time, establishing Hong Kong Trading and transferring the operations of the Hong Kong Branch.

The service area covered Afghanistan, Pakistan, India, Sri Lanka, Nepal, Bangladesh, Burma, Thailand, Malaysia, Singapore, Indonesia, Cambodia, Laos, Vietnam, Hong Kong, and Taiwan.

Of these, Hong Kong and Singapore were unique in Asia because they are duty-free areas, which make them appealing to tourists. Indonesia was a large market for cameras and copiers. India did not hold much foreign currency, so it was difficult to legally import cameras, but there was domestic demand, and there was a special route for Chinese companies to handle them.

When Saito visited Japan External Trade Organization (JETRO) in New Delhi about ten years earlier, the station chief had employed three locals as typists. When a typed letter arrived, it was stamped with a "true-copy" seal, meaning that the director had already checked it. With a photocopier, such hassles are quickly solved, and without foreign currency restrictions, India would be a promising market for photocopiers, they said. However, it would be better to bring rice than a camera to India and Bangladesh. When I arrived at the airport, I was swarmed by barefooted beggars. At the time, the company was planning to place representatives in Jakarta, Manila, Bangkok, Taichung, and so on.

Canon Singapore had been a British-owned company called Guthrie

Berhad until December 1980, when Canon took over its office and 70 local employees. In the British style of management, the numbers on the balance sheet were good enough, and the top management rarely interacted with the employees. During Guthrie's time, the restrooms were segregated for executives and other employees. If it were a factory in Japan, it would be normal for the factory manager to wear the same uniform as the factory workers and share meals with them on site, but British factory managers would always wear a suit, so it would be easy to tell that they were different from the workers. In other words, they do not discuss management issues with their employees, but instead let each employee concentrate on their own individual tasks, maintaining a clear divide between the top and the bottom. Saito had to transition the company from the British style of management to the Canon style.

He said that the work performance had improved since he started paying bonuses twice a year, the same amount as Guthrie in June, and again in December, instead of just once a year during Guthrie's time. Saito also started giving employees birthday cards, which were a nice surprise given that such an act of kindness would have been unthinkable under the previous regime.

However, when I spoke with four Japanese employees after interviewing Saito, some said, "The local employees are loyal to their bosses but they are not interested in other things, and we are trying to change that little by little. However, I'm not sure whether they should become more Japanese or we should become more British." This is a universal problem that Japanese managers face when they try to manage overseas branches in a Japanese way. But this might be a transitional phenomenon as Japanese business people become more westernized in an increasingly global society.

(In the afterword of this book, the author shares his personal views on what kind of problems Japanese-style management may face in different cultures, and what kind of public and private problems Japanese employees may face in local markets.)

The above is a case study of a sales company, but I also visited factories in Germany, the U.S., and Taiwan to see what the situation was like at overseas production plants and what problems they were facing.

Germany – generous or laid-back?

Back to Europe again.

Walking through the Frankfurt Airport in West Germany, I was surprised to see pornography stores operating openly. On the way from the airport to Giessen, 80 kilometers north of Frankfurt, we drove at 150 kph on the famous Autobahn freeway, while viewing the Flemish forests and meadows.

Mitarai himself had gone out of his way to acquire the land in Giessen, the home of Leica, which is something Mitarai could never forget. On the drive to the registration office, Mitarai passed by Leica's headquarters. The company, which once dominated the global camera market and made the Japanese camera industry tremble, was now just a shadow of its former self.

In the car, Mitarai was almost moved to tears.

In 1972, the photocopier manufacturing company Phisotech was established in Giessen, and in 1974, the company was acquired by Canon and renamed Canon Giessen, with President Tsuneo Enome (born in 1932, joined the company in 1956) taking over in July of 1979.

The three main activities that Enome undertook were (1) visible management, (2) improvement of work efficiency, and (3) ordering parts in Germany.

For this reason, the layout of the site was made as linear as possible, and the office partitions were removed. Enome recalled, "When we went to one of the managers to ask about a certain issue, we were told that another manager was the one in charge of the problem, so we had to go to a different room and open the door again. This was wasteful, so we decided to use only movable partitions." He noted that there was little resistance from the local employees to this change, but for some reason they didn't want to be seen doing their work and preferred working in a corner of the building. They also said that without a private room, they could not conduct personnel evaluations or scold their subordinates, but Enome had never seen them scolding their subordinates.

When he gave them a Japanese example of work efficiency, they said, "This is not Japan." So he introduced an efficiency-based pay system that displays the production schedule and actual results every two hours in the factory, while setting a standard man-hour rate and giving additional pay if fewer man-hours are worked, which proved to be a very effective strategy.

He also made the decision to order parts from German suppliers because the same parts would take four months to arrive from Japan. However, he was aware that the German way of conducting business was slow and cautious, and the company might not be able to respond promptly to sudden changes in the product design. In contrast, the Japanese way of working involves staying up all night to meet deadlines, which is not the norm in Germany.

In the previous decade, Japanese industries had outperformed European ones, which Enome attributed to differences in attitudes towards labor. However, he worried that "the work ethic of Japanese youth will eventually become westernized."

In West Germany, strikes were a rare occurrence. The country had the lowest number of working days lost due to strikes per year, even lower than Italy, the U,S., the U.K., France, and Japan, in that order. The reason for this is the "management participation" approach, where workers have a say in management policy-making before resorting to strikes.

(There was an episode that highlighted the importance of protecting workers' rights. The local employees of a Japanese affiliated company went on strike, and in order to avoid inconveniencing customers, the Japanese technicians worked on the weekends. Unfortunately, the situation was taken to court and the company was forced to pay the workers the wages they would have earned if they had worked during that time.)

In July of 1981, Kunihiro Nagata (joined the company in 1970) was transferred there as a controller (not a department head position). Despite not being a department head, he was responsible for overseeing the budget and accounting sections, and he noticed a distinct difference in labor awareness between Japan and Germany. To better understand this, he engaged in daily discussions with the German employees. After being transferred to Germany, Nagata stayed at the Goethe Institute, where he spent two months in an immersive language training program to learn German. However, the language barrier continued to pose a challenge for him.

Without a clear plan and theme, moving forward can be challenging for many individuals. Nagata was frustrated that many discussions seemed to focus solely on logistics rather than ways to continue making improvements, as is typically done in Japan. (Enome noted that it was extremely difficult to implement employee-initiated improvement measures.)

It seems that some workers lack a clear perspective for the future work. Even if certain tasks must be completed today in order to start working on other tasks the following week, they leave as soon as their shift ends, without finishing the tasks. The section manager in charge sometimes leaves before everyone else.

The Germans enjoy high quality of life, as they prioritized their health and family harmony. (They sometimes take a day off from work for minor ailments such as toothaches.) They don't work like the Japanese, who rarely take vacations and often work on holidays. Does this mean they are "generous," or they are "laid back"?

In addition, Nagata remarked that Germans tend to be stubborn. Nagata noticed that even when pointing out a simple error in a calculation, many of his German employees were reluctant to admit it and often insisted that they were "absolutely not wrong." Even when Nagata showed them the correct calculation, they would still refuse to acknowledge their mistake and maintain that "it did not look that way when I did it."

Despite everything, Nagata maintains that Germany is an outstanding country. Even in smaller places such as Giessen, the essentials of life are readily available. While not flashy or trendy, every item is thoughtfully chosen. If Canon's management style were to succeed in such a place, it would be quite an accomplishment. Maybe we need to approach the issue from a different angle. Nagata secretly hopes that by adopting German-like ideas, we can engage them in meaningful discussions.

Kurt Hansen (factory manager) was working for Pelican Lumoprint, a German copier manufacturer, when his company entered into a cross-licensing agreement with Canon, and he became interested in the NP (New Process) Electrophotographic System as an engineer. He joined Canon Giessen in January 1981.

Since 1980, Canon's Tokyo headquarters has hosted the Tokyo Seminar, an annual training program for employees from overseas offices. Hansen traveled from Giessen to participate in the program and had a renewed appreciation in Japan's technological innovation and international competitiveness. He was also impressed by the concentration exhibited by female assembly workers at the Toride Plant. He was also amazed by the Canon production system, which had saved the company tens of billions of yen.

I inquired about the availability of German publications on Japanese management methods, to which he presented me with a book titled Japanische Organizations-prinzipien (Japanese Organizational Principles). This book was most likely the earliest publication on the subject. He mentioned that he had provided a copy of the book to every department manager at his factory for training purposes. The author, Peter Engel, could have served as the personnel manager at Ford Cologne. (Interpreter, Hiroshi Iizuka = Assistant Controller)

United States – The Quality Mindset Difference

Canon Business Machines (CMB) is located four or five minutes by car from the Los Angeles branch of Canon USA. The work to establish the company began by using a rented warehouse as an office.

In 1969, Michihiko Senoo (born in 1941, joined the company in 1963) was assigned to Canon USA to conduct technical research. Three Japanese engineers were chatting about their dream of doing something interesting and building a factory and eventually a research institute, when President Takigawa said, "All right, let's do it." At the time, the printing paper for the Canon Pocketronic calculator manufactured in Japan was supplied by 3M, while the LSIs were supplied by Texas Instruments (TI). Both items were imported from the U.S. and assembled in Japan, and then exported back to the U.S.

Senoo traveled to Los Angeles on his own to search for suitable land. The rationale was straightforward. Due to the high costs of land and labor in New York, the west coast was perceived to be a more affordable option. Upon finding a potential parts manufacturer, they leased a warehouse at the L.A. branch and posted a job advertisement in the newspaper in December 1973. Takigawa and Senoo interviewed prospective employees.

Senoo thought, "Japanese people are now coming to the U.S. to interview Americans," but in reality, I was shaking inside and wondering, "What am I supposed to ask them?"

Takigawa stumbled upon a 33,000-square-meter plot of land for sale near the branch office. This was just before he was leaving for Japan. The following day, Tokyo sent a telex to Takigawa, informing him that Mitarai had given his permission to purchase the land. An American employee expressed his surprise, saying, "I didn't know that a Japanese company could make decisions so quickly. Canon is indeed proactive." Canon was able to acquire the land for $2.50 and $1.90 per square foot, and it was less than 300 million yen in total.

In October 1974, with a monthly production plan of 3,000 units of product components, the company started with 30 female assembly workers and 10 clerical workers, but half of them had never done this kind of work before and didn't even know which direction to turn a screw. Some of them worked for half a day and quit after lunch. They were trained how to solder for a week, but they built up a mountain of defective products.

The following year, when Mitarai visited the U.S., he held a party to celebrate the opening of the new company, at which time he remarked, "We have to start a copier business." There were 280 employees (200 assembly workers and 80 clerical workers), including 16 Japanese. The plant manager, Kenzo Seki (born in 1936, joined in 1961), was appointed in September 1978. The computer business was still in the red, and no one was sure how to connect it to future development. However, the company also had a development function and did not receive assistance from the Tokyo headquarters.

The copier division was responsible for importing the toner in concentrated form from Japan, mixing and bottling it, and then producing the photosensitive drums.

A major obstacle to producing high-quality products is the considerable gap in the idea of quality or the "quality mindset," between the Japanese managers and the local employees. Many of the local employees were immigrants with little formal education, and many did not speak English. Sixty to seventy percent were Mexican, so many instructional documents had to be prepared in both English and Spanish. When Seki addressed everyone, he first spoke in English and then read the Spanish translation.

To encourage a strong work ethic, there were monthly awards for the best employees and best proposals, from which the best employees and best proposals for the year were chosen. There were also awards for the most proposals and perfect attendance. Recipients of the monthly awards were given a camera, while the annual awards included a cash prize. When Seki walked around the factory, he would talk to each employee he saw, and he would also review each person's wages himself.

When they had a company picnic in the park as a kind of teambuilding event, the employees tended to form groups according to their home countries. When they decided to play baseball, many of the Mexican and Black employees did not know how to play according to the rules because they hadn't had the opportunity to play baseball before. Later, the company formed a softball team and Seki played third base. The team won one game and lost ten games against other local company teams. Employee turnover is high, so the company decided to pay for only half the cost of their uniforms. Although Seki tried to spend as little money as possible, the employees would sometimes come to him, saying, "We will pay this much, so please help us with this." On the day before

Thanksgiving, the lunch break was extended and a party was held for all employees, both in the factory and in the office.

As mentioned earlier, this plant started from the "dream" of Takigawa, Senoo, and others, and Seki believes that this plant will be a base for Canon to build more plants in the U.S., which will require the training of human resources and the accumulation of technical know-how. In addition to selling products to Canon USA, he thought that the company should have the ability to develop its own market. CBM will not be able to do so unless it has its own technologies, not just those imported from Tokyo. They would like to have something to base their business on, and for this purpose, Seki was considering how to make the most of the existing development function.

Taiwan – Catching up with Japan

Looking at Taiwan from an airplane, one can see high mountains and well-cultivated land. Looking down from the window of an inn in Taichung at the streets during commuting hours, it was not uncommon to see motorcycles with two, sometimes even four, passengers on them. At night, the sight of food stalls piled high with all kinds of delicacies lining the main streets and people hanging out around them was spectacular, and one could feel the somewhat casual energy of the Taiwanese people.

Canon Taiwan, officially known as Canon Inc., Taiwan, was founded in 1971. At that time, the conveyor belt for the assembly line was brought into the factory by water buffalo, and it recorded its first profit in its fifth year of operation. When I visited the factory in November 1981, the production of the Canonet camera was ending. Now the main products in the factory were Autoboy and motors for audio equipments. Located in the Taichung Processing

Zone, the factory is required to export all of its products.

Mr. Enome of Giessen, Germany, was in charge of training workers during the start-up period of the project, and here, too, there was a problem with the "quality mindset" mentioned by Mr. Seki of CBM in Los Angeles. It was difficult to convince the local employees that the slightest misalignment of the skin stretched over the camera body or dust in the viewfinder was a problem that needed to be corrected.

Shoji Aoki, who joined Canon in 1952, was appointed as president of Canon Taiwan at the beginning of 1978. That year was used as a preparation period for the introduction of the Canon Production System (CPS), and the system was implemented in 1979. However, it was difficult to achieve the production targets due to the lack of confidence among the local employees, who believed they could not perform the work as well as the Japanese workers. The employee turnover rate was one factor (5% per month, compared with less than 1% in Japan). For this reason, Aoki decided that the factory's productivity should not be dependent on who actually performed the work.

In 1980, the company proposed improvements to TCPS (Taiwan Canon Production System) and set a goal of nine improvement proposals per person per year, but the actual number of proposals was 13. And in 1981, the goal was set at 15, but 19 proposals had already been received through the first three quarters of the year. The improvement proposal committee chairperson sent a letter to the 200 employees who had not submitted any suggestions, and 170 employees responded to the letter. Each proposal was rewarded with a cash prize, and a Canonet or SLR camera was given based on the cumulative score evaluation to the person with the highest evaluation. Aoki hoped that this kind of meticulous management would cause the process to gradually take root and become part of the factory's culture.

In 1981, the company introduced some simple Japanese-style group activities. Each group set its own goals and aimed to achieve them, and the best group was sent to a group activity presentation conference in Japan as a representative of Canon Taiwan.

Aoki also made efforts to improve employee retention. Every three months, the company would hold an event called the "Patriarch's Gathering," inviting family members of employees to tour the plant and attend a dinner party. Some of them came to shake Aoki's hand, saying they had not heard Japanese in decades. Nepotism is common in Taiwanese society, so the company uses a referral system for hiring employees, and allows the children of workers to join without pre-conditions.

The company began publishing a bimonthly in-house magazine called Jiayuan, about forty pages in length, with plans to make it a monthly publication.

A large autumn athletics festival was held once every two years. The team would march through the city, led by a brass band, from the plant to an elementary school a short distance away, where Aoki would welcome the athletes with a raised hand in salute. Each workplace had its own bake sale, which was very competitive. Snapshots of the field day were displayed in the factory cafeteria.

Masamitsu Miura (general manager of the General Affairs Department), who was transferred from Japan in November 1981, lamented that Taiwanese people did not have the custom of greeting each other, even within the company, and would say "Ni hao" as he walked around the plant and met people.

The union is a company-specific union called the Industrial Workers Association, which negotiates with the company on bonuses and other matters, but strikes are prohibited by law.

From July 1980 to June 1981, exports were USD 90.46 million to Taiwan Hitachi Electric, USD 60.26 million to Paisago Electric, USD 58.25 million to Taichung Funai Electric, and USD 57.07 million to Taiwan Canon Inc.

Shoji Aoki has promoted two local employees to executive positions since his arrival, and his goal was to manage the company with capital from Japan, the company from Taiwan, and not have Japanese employees on loan.

In the one-trillion-yen plan revealed by Ryuzaburo Kaku in 1980, he mentioned the following management philosophy for overseas operations.

"Based on the basic principle that local companies must contribute to the society of the country in which they operate, we would like to maintain our stance of contributing to the development of local industry by making appropriate profits, fulfilling our tax obligations, and ensuring stable employment. We would also like to move forward in the management of overseas companies by promoting local human resources who have the character, insight, and ability who could manage the company with confidence, and moving in the direction of entrusting them with the management of the company in the future."

Canon's overseas activities initially forced the company to adopt a distributor system, but as the market grew, the company switched to a policy of "raising their own children," and as we have seen, it developed direct sales channels in major markets around the world. Furthermore, the existence of the three overseas factories suggests a solution for the trade friction problem that Japanese companies are facing today (i.e.in the 1980s).

On March 11, 1981, the 10th anniversary party of Canon Taiwan was held at the National Hotel, the largest hotel in Taichung, and Mitarai, who had come for the celebration, was presented with a birthday gift. It was his 80th birthday.

On the following day, a dinner was held to which all employees were invited, and awards were presented for 3, 5, and 10 years of continuous service. Mitarai announced that March 15 would thereafter be a company holiday to celebrate Taiwan Canon's founding and that all employees would receive a special bonus in honor of the 10th anniversary.

Chapter 8

Takeshi Mitarai and Canon's Corporate Culture

Takeshi Mitarai and Canon's Corporate Culture

"Pipe Dream"

In his New Year's address in 1982, Mitarai said, "I have something to say to you all after reading the New Year's newspapers. By 1985, there will be fully electronic cameras, and by the 1990s, televisions will be hung on walls. In addition, uranium extracted seawater will be used in the field of energy, and artificial blood will be developed in the field of bioengineering. And by 2010, cancer will be completely conquered. Then, it will not be a dream to live to be 100 years old. I might be able to live long enough for that, just barely." Everyone laughed.

He continued, "One hour for a maglev train between Tokyo and Osaka is a little long, Suzukawa-kun …" again eliciting laughter from the audience with some sympathy for the difficulties imposed on Suzukawa, an employee at Canon. He concluded his address with the words, "It seems that a feast has been served…" and received a lively round of applause.

If Mitarai were to reach the age of 100 years, he would see the year 2001. Does that mean Mitarai harbored a longing for immortality, a longing that has existed since ancient times? As we will see later, Mitarai had already had his own grave for more than ten years. What Mitarai may have intended to convey in his half-joking, half-truthful words was his desire to see the "Canon family" that he has fostered grow and develop forever.

Born in 1901, in the middle of the Meiji era (1868–1912), when Japan was a small Asian nation trying to stand tall among the world powers, Mitarai came of age in the Taisho era (1912–1926), when Japan joined the ranks of modern capitalist nations in a single stroke during the era of World War I. The collapse of the Japanese Empire due to its defeat in the World War II and the abandonment of his life as a doctor, which he had intended to be his lifelong career, occurred at the same time, and this man who had aimed to be the best in the world in the postwar confusion of rubble and black markets, was now closer than ever, or has reached the point where it is possible, wants to see his dreams come true.

Japan's defeat on August 15, 1945 allowed Mitarai to cross a certain barrier. This was made possible by the fact that he had lived in a place that was neither nationalist nor anti-establishment but rather technocratic. Mitarai was able to participate in the postwar society in the same way that the prewar naval technical officers such as Hiroshi Kawaguchi and Hiroshi Suzukawa, who joined the company in the postwar era, were able to make use of their technical thinking in the postwar society — in particular, because Mitarai was also a doctor, which can be considered a kind of engineer.

Unlike ordinary engineers who deal with mechanical objects, Mitarai dealt with human beings. As symbolized by the fact that his young soul was inspired by William Smith Clark's slogan "Boys Be Ambitious," an inspiration he never let go of, Mitarai had a desire to dedicate himself to a goal, even if it were a fanciful, a "pipe dream," so to speak.

The goal of "defeating Leica" symbolized Mitarai's pipe dream, and his practical judgment as an engineer of people made it possible for Kawaguchi, Suzukawa, and others to join the company. Moreover, it was precisely because of Mitarai's pipe dream that he was able to bring in not only engineers but also talent who could be considered "first-class" at that time. This perfect balance of pragmatic judgment and imaginative thinking formed the foundation of Canon's technology-driven corporate culture.

Father with a Philosophy

However, you cannot create something with leading technology alone. There must be people behind the scenes to support it. The presence of craftsmen from the prewar period and down-to-earth people who made a virtue of hard work was also indispensable. It was only natural that Mitarai, while sometimes extending himself and proclaiming lofty ideals, adopted what could be called a mixed philosophy of new familialism and a health-first policy.

The engineers could follow the logic of technology and do as they were told even in unfavorable circumstances, but the craftsmen-type technicians had to absorb the new while abandoning the old (it can be said that it is themselves), and this was probably the generation that had the greatest difficulty adapting. There must have been a lot of drama over what these people had to abandon and what they had to learn in the process of introducing conveyor belts and advancing automated assembly, which were inevitable in the process of Canon's development into a modern company.

Perhaps it was these prewar workers who supported Canon's technological advancements behind the scenes until the mass production of the Canonet began, and Mitarai played a role as a conduit between the prewar and postwar groups.

For example, Shigeru Shinagawa, who joined the company before the war in 1941, had this to say about Mitarai.

"When we first gathered at the Shimomaruko Plant, the chairman's management philosophy was already in place. He instilled into his employees his way of thinking, and things were beginning to take shape. He was a man with a wonderful philosophy. He had the image of a man of deep sincerity, and I believe that some of the employees trusted him without the slightest hesitation. I see the philosophy of the chairman as if it were my own father's."

What is important here is that the embodiment of the "wonderful philosophy" is also captured in the familiar image of the "father." This is a good illustration of how people like Shinagawa viewed Mitarai. (A leader must be both a man of great philosophy and a father figure, which suggests that only such a man can be a true leader.)

The chairman's commitment to doing his best was evident in his body. It was as if he was saying, "I'll do my part, so you guys follow me," according to Fukutaro Tsuji (born in 1922 and joined the company in 1939), director of Canon Sales.

During the evacuation period, Mitarai had given Shoji Suzuki (born in 1913, joined the company in 1944) a boxed lunch on the train. "This person would never lie to me. I would follow him anyway," Suzuki thought.

The first person I met during my interviews for this book was Shuji Araki (né Tokunaga). Hideo Kondo, then the head of the secretarial office, had chosen him as the person who best embodied Canon's long history. During the interview, Kondo brought a Canon camera from the showroom at the Shinjuku headquarters and placed it in front of Araki.

Araki picked it up, took off his reading glasses, looked at it intently, and murmured, "This brings back some memories." Araki was sitting on the sofa in the parlor, and I was standing across the table from him, observing his actions. The way he looked at the camera at that moment was just like a parent looking at his child, as if a tear might come to his eye. I was moved. (Born in 1914, he had joined the company with the desire to assemble cameras with his own hands in 1937, and retired after serving as Director and Plant Manager. The impression I had at that time inspired me to try to capture the prewar days of Seiki Kogaku as carefully as possible.)

Tsuneo Misawa, born in 1921, worked at Nippon Kogaku's training school before the war and then as a fryer at Oi Manufacturing Company before joining Canon in 1946. He said, "I was impressed by the way the chairman always said that he would give everyone a goal, and when they achieved it, we would share the joy together."

"I Want Them to Be Happy Regardless of Profit or Loss."

However, their impressions may be unique and influenced by their ages. Therefore, I would like to present the views of two men who were born in the same year, 1927, but joined the company at very different times: Keizo Yamaji (managing director and general manager of the Office Equipment Division), who joined the company in 1951, and Tadashi Nakamura (currently director and general manager of the Fukushima Plant), who joined the company in 1949.

According to Yamaji, "We have a strong desire to please the Chairman regardless of profit or loss. It's strange. It's not about getting a pay raise or anything like that. It was the same when I was a low-level employee, and it's the same now. Even my wife says, 'If Mr. Mitarai says so, there is no doubt about it.'"

On the other hand, Nakamura said, "I really like the Chairman's personality. He is like a father. If I hear that there is some good fruit somewhere, I want to send him some, even if it's just a small amount, so he can try it. I'm not trying to curry favor. I really believe in the new familialism. My mother passed away at the age of 91, but from the first time she came to the company for her birthday party, she always looked forward to going to hear Mitarai speak."

Even though Yamaji and Nakamura were interviewed separately, they often expressed the same viewpoint. People born in 1927 belonged to a generation whose offspring had the chance to become part of Canon. However, there was a significant shift in values after Japan's defeat in 1945, and the postwar period commenced with a profound distrust towards the prevailing beliefs. Thus, it is crucial to note that this generation was considered the "newcomer" of the postwar era.

When Satoshi Nemoto (currently vice president of Canon Electronics) joined Canon Inc. in the same year as Yamaji, he found Mitarai to be a very autocratic leader. He noticed that everyone around him was tense. Hiroshi Nasu (currently managing director and the general managor of the Camera Division), who was born in 1930, joined Canon in 1952 and had a similar opinion. He said, "He was regarded as a god. I was told that when he got angry, I would not be able to defend myself even with a single word, and if I spoke carelessly, I would be shouted down. For better or for worse, such an image of Mitarai was prevalent in the company."

Anger and Execution

There was a good reason for his deification. Perhaps his tremendous anger was a great force to be reckoned with.

Fukutaro Tsuji, mentioned earlier, was once scolded over the phone when he worked at Akatsuki Musen (Akatsuki Radio) during the early postwar era. He was so angry that he could barely hold the phone.

In 1962, Canon introduced an 8-mm camera called the Motor Zoom 8EEE. It was a revolutionary camera with an electric motorized automatic aperture and zoom, but there were a number of malfunctions that resulted in the film getting stuck. At the time, most of the 8-mm cameras Canon produced were exported, and complaints were frequently received from overseas. Everyone who had worked on the project was summoned to Mitarai's office. Among them was Shigeru Nishioka, the assembly section chief. The president's office at the Shimomaruko Plant had a window on the east side, and Mitarai was sitting with his back to the window. Nishioka and the others sat in a dark place away from the window and hung their heads in front of Mitarai. "What do you guys think what work is?" Mitarai began, and then the angry voices flew one after another. Nishioka gingerly looked up at Mitarai and saw that each strand of his white hair stood on end.

Hiroshi Suzuki, who joined the company in 1950, served as the first secretary section chief for 11 years during his Shimomaruko days. Mitarai was very particular about food. For important dinners, he would instruct his staff to order the best fruits, even if it meant they had to be flown in, and examine them carefully when they arrived. If the catered food wasn't to his liking, Mitarai would call the restaurant the next morning to complain. "What did you serve us last night? You wouldn't serve that kind of food to your customers," he said in a harsh voice that could be heard beyond the walls of his office.

If an executive came to see Mitarai when he was in a bad mood, Suzuki would say, "It's better not to see him today." When Mitarai got upset, Suzuki hung his head and endured his tirade until the older man's anger subsided. If he kept his face up, Mitarai's angry voice would hit him squarely and hurt him. If he kept his head down, the angry sounds would fly over his head. When he glanced at Mitarai in between the rain of bullets, he saw his hair standing on end and the steam rising from his head.

It helped that Mitarai would be easygoing after unleashing all his frustrations. This is why he was sometimes called the "Squall of the South Seas," according to Shozo Takeuchi, the standing auditor.

Another factor that made Mitarai seem godlike was his keen intuition and quick judgment, as well as his ability to immediately implement what he thought was right, even in the face of opposition. There is a legendary story that when Seiichi Takigawa was president of Canon USA, he called Mitarai to ask for this type of person to be transferred to the U.S. Then, Mitarai immediately called the requested person, and this employee arrived in New York the very next day.

On New Year's Day in 1965, when Hiroshi Ito, who was greatly respected for his work on Canon's original lens design and had promoted the development of calculators, was deputy director of Tokki Seisakusho, Mitarai walked into Ito's room before he began his New Year's address to the staff and said, "I want you to become the head of the Optical Division." As was his usual style, Ito did not give an immediate answer. But during his New Year's address, Mitarai announced the change, shocking everyone who was listening. The reason was that the company-wide personnel changes had already been announced at the end of the previous year.

"Mitarai set a clear direction with his strong personality," according to Shotaro Furuya (born in 1926, joined the company in 1949), a good characterization of Mitarai's attitude.

Because of his quick temper, it was not unusual for him to return home from international trips a day early, or to take an earlier flight when traveling in Japan.

It was also common for Mitarai to make sudden change of destinations while abroad. Knowing this well, his secretary, Shozo Takeuchi, sometimes arranged for a flight to Paris in addition to the scheduled flight to London as a countermeasure. If he had taken such steps ahead of time, he generally have been able to avoid panicking. However, unlike in Japan, where you can just go to any travel agency and book a train or a flight, in other countries it is difficult to make sudden changes in schedules, and extraordinary things can happen.

One year, Mitarai and Maeda went to Rome a day earlier than scheduled to attend the launch of a new product before the start of Photokina. However, the hotel was completely booked because of a trade fair and they had to wait at the airport for five hours before they finally found a hotel. The next day, when Joji Kyodo went to pick them up at the hotel, they were standing there waiting with their luggage, even though there were still three days to go. "What's wrong?" he asked. "Well, Kyoudo-kun, it turns out that this is a love hotel with just one bed, and I had no choice but to sleep with Maeda-kun in a double bed."

If he thinks it's a good idea, he moves forward; if he thinks it's a bad idea, he quickly backs off.

Another example is the "London Conference" of 1966. Mitarai, who had been touring overseas agencies, gave Masaaki Kobayashi instructions to move to a larger building in Geneva because the office there had become overstretched, and then flew on to London. When he met with the executives of Japanese banks there, his instincts were clear. "The recession is sweeping across Europe."

With hardly any notice, Suzukawa, Matsui, and other executives were told to come to the hotel. "The situation in Europe is not right," Mitarai said. "We should rethink our aggressive measures." Kobayashi had been very excited, telling his employees that they were going to change offices, but the move was canceled. For a while, the "London Conference" became a topic of conversation in the export department at the headquarters, but just two years later in 1968, a new office was opened in Amsterdam.

I have already written about the time that Satoshi Nemoto blanched when Mitarai told everyone who was attending Photokina that they had to aim for the Hannover Messe.

As for Mitarai' characteristics, Nemoto said the following: "We may be too concerned about what goes on around us, but when the chairman feels that something is the right thing to do, he says it regardless of who he is talking to. He is not an expert in management or technology, so he is able to say whatever he thinks. If he had any expertise in those fields, he might have been more cautious. That's why he could give a direct order on what he thought of in any field."

Mitarai was very reluctant to have meetings, and when anyone went to him for advice on a project, he was reluctant to have the process leading up to it explained to him before the conclusion. According to Seiichi Takigawa, "You can't bring thick materials with you. It's best to start from the conclusion. If I bring three items, explain the first two items fully, keep the third one simple, and then try to get approval for all three, he would ask me about the third item.

When I explain something at length with absolute confidence, along with the documents, he would get angry and tell me to start with the conclusion. 'All right, just do it.' When I thought I'd discuss an item as an addition, he would start asking questions. That kind of good intuition is wonderful."

These examples are how the employees of Canon see him, and these accounts paint a fairly clear picture of Mitarai. But I wanted to ask the man himself to tell us about his image.

"Once We're Together…"

"If my sixth sense tells me it's a good idea, I do it. Then I go ahead and find it to be very difficult. Then, I said to myself, 'Well, there's nothing we can do, let's turn back.' I think this comes from my profession. Among physicians, internists and pediatricians are very cautious, but in surgery and in obstetrics and gynecology, we are the one holding the scalpel. A woman suddenly feels pain in the right side of her body on the eve of delivery, but we do not know the cause. Her white blood cell count is very high so there is a possibility of infection. We can't keep thinking that something is wrong for very long. If we wait too long to do something about, it will affect the fetus.

Then I decide to cut her open and see, and if there is no abnormality, I stitch her back together. But if there is an infected area, it must be removed.

"Such a way of thinking also comes into play in management," Mitarai says. "When the recession hit in 1965, the company immediately pulled its headquarters out of Ginza. I started the Synchroreader project because I thought I could venture out into a wider world and gather human resources from various fields. However, when it came to money, I thought I could handle it and didn't think about it too much. This was, simply put, the path I had taken. I don't like to complain. One year, I told the executives, 'If you complain more than twice, you will be fined.' But I was bad at business then, and I failed."

Takeshi Goshima (director of the Office Equipment Project Center; born in 1933, joined the company in 1956), pointed out that Mitarai's leadership was something that "moved people more by charisma than by orders," and this charisma was deeply related to the fact that he was a doctor.

The patient is naked in front of the doctor. Even if they do not physically remove their clothes, they are psychologically vulnerable. Mitarai often tells his employees, "Female patients are reluctant to answer questions. As a doctor, *anthroposcopy* is important." One must have the ability to gain insight into the problems of those who do not speak. When the company was headquartered in Ginza, Mitarai used to hold morning meetings. At around 7:30 a.m., the executives would gather in Mitarai's room for 20–30 minutes of tea and conversation.

As he looked at the faces of the executives who came into the room saying, "Good morning," Mitarai thought to himself, "You are in good spirits today, and I will ask for your help again today." If their eyes were red, he would think, "You drank too much last night." If they were somewhat listless, he would ask, "You don't look well. Is something wrong?" When the person replied, "My stomach is a little upset," he would tell them to take the rest of the day off.

I have previously mentioned that many employees, not just executives, were unexpectedly approached by Mitarai about their physical health. From the employees' perspective, they must feel that Mitarai is always looking after them.

The act of calling out to someone is an act that may not seem extraordinary, but when it was conveyed to employees in a way that overlapped with the human image of the leader, it helped to shape the corporate culture of the company. This may be reflected in the fact that Masamitsu Miura, who was assigned to Taiwan, never neglected to make an effort to say "Ni hao" to the local employees.

Tadashi Nakamura, the manager of the Fukushima Plan whose episode about wanting to share fruits with Mitarai reveals his affinity to the president, had this to say about the operation of the plant: "The foundation of a factory is to make things, and if you can't, it's not a factory. This must be done from the bottom of one's heart. Surprisingly, there are many cases where top management and workers are not of the same mind, even if they say they are. You have to really trust them. The top management must have a strong sense of love for the people and land of Fukushima.

"So how do we communicate the idea of prosperity with our employees to everyone?

"The same thing exists between the chairman and us. It may be naive to say, but if we do something just because we are told to do so, I believe that at some point, the employees will sense it."

Nakamura always attends the award ceremonies of zero defects (ZD), for example, because he does not have many opportunities to interact with people on the factory floor. Even if it's just a piece of cake, he eats with them. Two hundred people attend the ceremony twice a month, and no matter what happens, he always attends. It is easy to assume that if the factory manager attends the ceremony, the general managers of the production department or the general affairs department do not need to go, but the three of them always try to attend together. "That sends a message to everyone. How much dedication do the higher-ups have? People at the factory are sensitive to this. This has a strong effect on the growth of the factory."

You may not be able to talk to each female employee every year. However, even if it's just that one time that you greet Ms. A, she might tell others about it. She may not even say anything, but it may produce more effect. "Scholars say that a single factory manager can't handle 2,100 people..."

Nakamura also chaired the annual Bon Dance festival, continuing the tradition started by Nishioka, the plant's first manager. Nakamura invited neighbors and sent out invitations to employees' families, and the number of participants increased each year.

So, to put it simply, the "new familialism" is a theorization of Mitarai's sentiment of always asking his employees, "Hey, how are you?"

Hideharu Takemoto (born in 1934, joined the company in 1958), became head of the Personnel Section in 1969, but by then he had had many opportunities to meet with Mitarai while editing the company newsletter and was often told by him, "Think about how to apply the spirit of the new familialism to the modern world."

Takemoto noted that the company created a kind of social security system for employee welfare, including a property accumulation system and a stock ownership system, and also created a personnel system that respected workers as people, one that was centered on a merit-based, job-based salary system. "Canon's attitude is not just about how to utilize its human resources, but how to build an ideal company together."

This idea was expressed by Mitarai as follows.

"We will share our joys and our sorrows together."

One of Mitarai's dreams for the company was to build an alumni hall in the head office building once it was constructed, where employees who had left the company after reaching retirement age could gather with their grandchildren and play *go* or *shogi* (Japanese chess), or play pool. (In 1971, at Mitarai's suggestion, an association called Shuyu-kai was established, and its regular members are retired Canon employees or current employees have been working at Canon for more than 25 years. It also publishes a newsletter).

According to Mitarai, he is like a graduate of a school who is forever concerned about the well-being of the alma mater. "It would be sad to think that when one stops working at a company, it is the end of one's relationship with the company. Let's get together once a year and have a drink."

Mitarai said, "When he was with us, you might have thought he was a grumbling old man, but after he left, everyone has a feeling of nostalgia. Some may think that, thanks to Mitarai, we have come this far, and some may think that we could have gone even further, but since we have once been here together, let's keep our friendship for a long time."

He also said, "If you worked for a company, you will have a second alma mater, and there will be an alumni association. A mother is proud of the fact that she once worked for the company, and she wants the alumni to come to the reunion as well. How happy we are to visit our alma maters with our children and grandchildren!"

Free Culture

Although Mitarai's quick decision-making may at first glance appear to be his own initiative, as we have seen, he never forgot to make an effort to build bonds with his employees. He was not an expert in anything, except for being a doctor, so he left the specifics to the discretion of experts. This is how Canon's unique "free" culture was cultivated. Like air, it was invisible to the eye but definitely present, and was vital to Canon's development.

Masao Yamashita (born in 1939, joined the company in 1962), who previously worked for CBM in the U.K., received factory training for two months before joining the company. He was impressed by the openness of the employees and the youthfulness of the section managers and deputy section managers, and at the same time he thought, "There is room for me here."

Around 1965, while doing lens-related work at the Tamagawa Plant, Tadashi Nakamura (manager of the Fukushima Plant) was told by an outsider that "Canon's lens polishing methods are not standardized at all." At the time, Nakamura and his colleagues were struggling to find the most cost-effective method. While other manufacturers may have adopted a uniform and stable polishing method, Nakamura and his team were using trial and error, which was painful at the time but eventually produced a good product at a low price.

"Experimentation was allowed on site. If you try and fail, no one gets mad at you because it's better than not trying at all. That's why we made so many mistakes. You can do a certain amount of things even if you play very safe, but then you cannot go any further. So I was scolded the most when I didn't at least try to do something."

When Takeshi Goshima joined the company in 1956, and he was assigned to work under Hiroshi Suzukawa. He didn't like helping someone else do their job, so less than a month after joining the company, he asked Suzukawa if he could have a place where he could work by himself because he wanted to research automatic iris squeezers. Suzukawa readily agreed and brought Goshima various reference products. "At Canon, in such cases, they don't often say 'No, you can't do it,'" Goshima said. "They say, 'Let's try it and see.' That's why Canon is so quick to jump into new things. On the other hand, I've made so many mistakes that I'm surprised they let me stay here."

An engineer who joined the company mid-career from an electronics manufacturer once said to Takemoto, the personnel manager, "They tell us to do these things over such a long period of time with a liberal budget, but I wonder if they can leave us alone that long." Another example is a machine that cost tens of millions of yen, but it was not being used. "When I asked the person in charge the reason why, he replied, 'Because they have changed their way of thinking.' A mid-career employee saw this and said, 'That's inexcusable. They should be penalized under the performance-based system,' but in the end, they admitted, 'There is nothing we could do. You could throw it away.' The mid-career employee became angry, saying, 'This is unforgivable and a liability issue.'"

However, "You don't have to cut bonuses in half because of a mistake made by people with the best of intentions," Takemoto said. "Canon's freedom is based on the belief that human nature is fundamentally good. It is better to have people think about the future rather than about failures. We must quickly perfect technologies that others cannot, commercialize them, and sell them. Such creative work is an asset. We want to eliminate as much as possible any system that stifles imagination. We will not do anything backward-looking. There is a question of how far this will go in the management of a large organization, but if we are concerned about the nine failures, we will not be able to realize the one success."

As I examined the forty-five year history of Canon Inc., especially since Shimomaruko in 1951, I thought I could summarize it with the phrase "many failures, a few successes." I echoed this in every interview, and most employees did not deny it. However, Goto responded that "Doing various things is the source of Canon's vitality," while Takemoto said, "We have grown by making the most of our failures."

Seiichi Takigawa (born in 1931), who had served as president of Canon USA, was called back to Japan in January 1977 and appointed as president of Canon Sales. Mitarai said, "I'll leave it to you, I won't interfere at all. Go public." Takigawa said, "He doesn't go into detail. He gives us one area and tells us to do as much as we want. One phrase, 'go public,' which included everything."

In his New Year's address in 1972, Mitarai said, "Company life is built on mutual trust. The reason why timecards are still being pressed is because we do not yet trust each other." He then proposed abolishing time cards, starting with employees who had been with the company for five years or more (about half of them), and then abolishing them altogether in January of the following year.

Canon has the "Spirit of Three self's," namely, self-motivation, self-governance, and self-awareness. These are derived from the educational philosophy underlying the dormitory life in the old high school system. (This explains why Mitarai's new familialism is based on the desire for human relations that transcend interests.)

When Mitarai delegates an important task to someone, he always gives them autonomy ("self-governance") but asks them to proceed with caution.

This is exemplified by his telling Keishi Fukuda, who was going to Geneva, to "cultivate your strength," and Shuichi Ando, who was going to Australia, to "not be deceived by others."

When Masanori Seki (President of Canon Inc.) was nominated to the board of directors, Mitarai said, "It doesn't matter how hard you work, if you have not developed your full capacity as a human being." Seki remarked, "It is rare for a president to scold someone with the words, 'All you have is work.'"

"Everyone wants to be a director, but not everyone can be. Be careful what you say and do," Tadashi Nakamura was told. "He sees me being fidgety all the time."

When Yoshiaki Otake of Canon France was in doubt about a decision, he was scolded by Mitarai for hesitating. Mitarai said, "Do as you believe."

When Canon USA, under Takigawa's leadership, was soaring at a breakneck pace, Mitarai said, "Do whatever you want, but don't become the Kwantung Army," referencing the fact that the Kwantung Army, a unit of the Japanese Army stationed in Manchuria, often ignored the wishes of the home government. Another time, he said, "You know, it's not enough to be good at something; you have to improve your character."

"A Big Congratulations to You!"

The growth of the Canon organization, both internally and externally, may exceed Mitarai's expectations. However, he confidently asserts, "We have excellent human resources, and that's why the company has improved."

So, how does Mitarai himself regard his own life?

From 1935 to 1940, seven years after graduating from Hokkaido Imperial University, Mitarai worked as the head of the Department of Obstetrics and Gynecology at Seibo Hospital. It was a Catholic hospital and most of the patients were Europeans, so he picked up some words and phrases in several foreign languages. Foreign patients had money. And some of them arranged to have the money that was left over from their funeral expenses donated to the hospital after they died. Then, they would wait peacefully to enter Heaven. Mitarai was impressed by this way of thinking.

"It's good to have no anxiety at the time of death. This is what is called the power of religion."

In Japanese parlance, Mitarai mastered the art of "nothingness" by not being afraid of death and not being concerned with greed.

In 1959, something unusual happened to Mitarai. At that time, he had a villa in Odawara, Kanagawa Prefecture, where he enjoyed tilling the soil on his days off, but one day he picked up a flowerpot and felt a tightening pain in his chest.

He urgently returned to Tokyo and was examined by Dr. Fumio Otsuka, a friend and former classmate at Hokudai. Mitarai thought it might be intercostal neuralgia, but the medical staff took an electrocardiogram (EKG) to be sure. To his surprise, Dr. Otsuka said it was an early sign of myocardial infarction. Mitarai also went to the Jikei University Hospital, and the doctors there confirmed Dr. Otsuka's diagnosis. He was told, "Golf is fine, but don't play in the wind or rain. Having a glass or two of beer is fine, but not more."

The wedding of his second daughter took place that year, but according to Mitarai, the family of the bride-to-be wanted to show the luxurious wedding gifts to her relatives first out of "respect for the old customs." Mitarai, a rationalist who disliked such old customs, had to persuade the family of the bride-to-be to hold off, and there were other worrying events, such as his oldest daughter's husband being involved in an automobile accident. (When I asked him if anything was wrong with the company, he replied, "No, a company does not have stable years that last for so long. Profits don't come in, new products don't do so well. That's how it is with companies.")

"Then it occurred to me. This is precisely the kind of situation in which religion is needed. I am not religious in the ordinary sense of the word, and I am not a well-rounded person, nor am I enlightened in the Buddhist sense." A few months later, he went for a walk in the morning and evening to ponder the end of his life. He visited a cemetery at a temple called Kuhonbutsu not far from his home. He talked with the monks, received a Buddhist name, and had a grave erected.

"In the old days, when you crossed the Hakone Pass (a security checkpoint of strategic importance on the Tokaido highway), you could not pass through without a nameplate. In the same way, on the way to heaven or hell, the guard would ask you if you had your name or not, and if you didn't, you would go to hell," Mitarai said, smiling pleasantly.

He always carries nitroglycerin with him. A year later, the hospital took another EKG. The doctors and nurses were surprised to find that he was in much better condition than after the previous event.

"They didn't think that an EKG could change so quickly. But I really feel that there is a large mental component. I think I had overcome something during that time."

In October 1977, at Mitarai's initiative, the "Monument to Canon Pioneers" was erected at Koyasan in Wakayama Prefecture, and 75 deceased persons were enshrined there by 1982. Every year, the deceased who worked for Canon from the previous year are enshrined together and a memorial service is held.

Ultimately, human beings return to the earth. We return to nothing. However, as long as we live in this world, we should share the joy of being alive and drinking with others until our glasses are empty.

"I hope we can overcome the first half of this year as planned, and do the same in the second half. I am glad that I was able to be with you all at the right time. This is how we can celebrate our 30th anniversary with all our hearts, and let's use this as a foundation for the company to make great strides forward. Let us raise our cups and, in loud voices, congratulate the company on its future and pray for its prosperity." (1967, 30th anniversary celebration)

"My goal for the future is to make the 35th anniversary a festival. That is my wish. I want to get to the point where we can have a drink and eat red rice." (1968, commemorating the achievement of 20 billion yen in annual sales.)

"No matter how hard times have been for me, I have continued to do this award ceremony. This company does not belong to anyone. It's everyone's company. Please look forward to the next five years and persevere until then. I have never told a lie. If we work together, the company will surely prosper." (Long-service award ceremony in the same year.)

"Today is a particularly good day to celebrate. As mentioned in the president's speech earlier, the First Premier Company Plan has been completed, and to share the joy of this achievement, I am giving away a small envelope of money. Nothing could be more pleasant. However, we are headed for a great celebration in 1987, the year of the 50th anniversary, when the second phase of the plan will be accomplished." (New Year's Greetings for 1982)

"Boys be ambitious!"

A little over a century ago, in 1877, the 10th year of Meiji Era, William S. Clark, a man on horseback, whipped his horse with a crack of his whip and rode off in a single bound, kicking up snow and mud between the roads in the birch forest. The phrase he spoke still echoes in one person's mind.

The Man Who Made It Possible: Canon and Takeshi Mitarai (The end)

❋ Afterword

The interviews for this book were conducted mainly in Tokyo, but also in Osaka, Kobe, Oita, Hokkaido, and overseas. In principle, the interviews were tape-recorded and later transcribed, ultimately filling five 200-page university notebooks. There are many things that remained in my mind during the interviews but could not be included in the book, so I would like to mention some of them here.

The Interview began with a trip to Hokkaido. It was April 1981. The reason why I did not visit Oita, Mitarai's birthplace, for the first interview was because I felt that his most formative years were those he spent in Hokkaido. I stayed at a hotel near Hokkaido University and went to the campus around 10:00 a.m. I was surprised at the vastness of the grounds and the number of large trees.

It was possible to browse back issues of the *Hokudai Shimbun* (Hokkaido University News) (first published in May 1926) at the university library, which is called the Hoppo Room (The Northern Room). Mitarai was a student during the transition from the Taisho era to the Showa era, and various currents of thought were flowing into Japan, so it is quite interesting to see his life as a testimony of the times.

In the December 15, 1926 issue, there was an article written by someone named Sakai about the dormitory life. Although Mitarai was no longer there, the article gives us a glimpse of dormitory life at that time.

"In our spare time, we play tennis with the great plains of Ishikari in the background, and on winter days when we can't go outside because of a blizzard, we play table tennis all day long."

"Each room in the dormitory is equipped with steam to keep the temperature warm. On nights when there is a blizzard and a cold, snowy wind blows through the windows, we enjoy chatting with friends in the warm room or reading a book in solitude while listening to the sound of the steam."

"From the dormitory, the vast Ishikari Plain can be seen far away. The Keiteki Dormitory stands on the great Ishikari plain. When you step outside, you are in an area of beauty. In the morning, you can see the sun rise over Mt. Teine, far to the west of the dormitory, full of life, and in the evening, you can watch the sun set in all its majesty."

At the School of Medicine Library, I was able to see the faculty magazine *"Frate"* (first published in June 1925). I looked through every page of the 12 volumes published during Mitarai's school days to see if he had written something, but could not find anything. There were records of tennis and table tennis tournaments in which he participated, along with the scores. The wins and losses were almost 50–50.

According to a survey of University of Tokyo students published in the *Hokudai Shimbun* in 1927, tennis was the most popular sport at 34%, followed by baseball at 13%, swimming, horse-riding, judo, kendo, rowing, skiing, skating, music, travel. Their favorite hobbies were also listed: music, travel, drama, photography, tea, *ikebana* (flower arrangement), sword appraisal, *go* (a board game), movies, *shogi* (Japanese chess), *shakuhachi* (bamboo flute), billiards, *rakugo* (comic monologue), and *gidayu* (traditional Japanese ballads).

The Keiteki Dormitory looked almost like an abandoned building. Even when I was a student in the 1950s, dormitory students were known to be poor, but I found several motorcycles around the dormitory, muddy with thawing snow, and it made me feel the times.

After doing some research at the School of Medicine Library, I took a bus from Makomanai to Jozankei, one of the places Mitarai had visited as a student. The sound of bubbling snowdrift water hitting the rocks of various sizes in the valley remained in my ears. Poets Tekkan and Akiko Yosano visited this place in May 1931, and the sound of the river seemed to have made an impression on them as well. Akiko wrote a tanka poem:

A mountain villa in Jozankei, Ishikari

Only the river rumbling in the night and the morning

I stayed there overnight and took a bus to Lake Toya the next day. I was the only passenger on the bus, which departed from Sapporo, and the grandeur of the snow-covered landscape outside the window was amazing. The bus stopped briefly at Nakayama Pass, and the unobstructed view of Mt. Yotei, which is also known as Ezo Fuji, was breathtaking. I was impressed by the divine whiteness of the snowcap. I guess I was lucky, because the lady at the inn in Jozankei said, "You can't see the top of Ezo Fuji because it is always hidden by the clouds," and the bus driver kindly told me that we could see the mountain.

In fact, my first "interview" after arriving in Sapporo was at a beer hall directly run by Sapporo Beer in Tanuki Koji. It was now a multi-story dining building, and the restaurant on the basement floor served *robata-yaki*, a Japanese dish of grilled seafood and vegetables. I ate *hokke* (a kind of mackerel) and was surprised at its size, which was almost as big as a traditional Japanese straw sandal.

Dr. Seishichi Ohno, Mr. Mitarai's mentor from his days at Hokkaido Imperial University School of Medicine, was now 96 years old, a professor emeritus at Sapporo Medical University, and still went to work in his laboratory *every single day.*

When I entered the room, he was writing at his desk, and I sat down on the sofa at his request. After clearing his desk, he stood up and said, "Well then, let's say hello," and his humorous tone left a lasting impression on me. He put a starched white coat over his suit, and his posture was upright.

When the weather gets warm, he goes golfing twice a week with the 82-year-old president of Furuya Caramel, and once a week he goes to Higashi Nihon Gakuen (East Japan Academy), where he serves as honorary president. When he flies somewhere, he boards the airplane on his own, not revealing his real age, because he would need an escort if he did. As to why he is in such good health, he said that he had trained himself by swimming and skiing when he was young, that he had never smoked, and that he had quit drinking alcohol at some point in his life.

In the February 20, 1928 issue of the *Hokudai Shimbun*, there is an article entitled "Welcoming His Imperial Highness Prince Chichibu on His Visit to the University," and Dr. Ohno's name is mentioned as the guide. It can be said that there is no one in the ski world, either in Japan or abroad, who does not know of Dr. Ohno, thanks to his hard work promoting the sport.

When he was 70 years old, he escorted Prince Mikasa to Mt. Sapporo (1,200 meters high). As they descended the mountain, he felt that his legs were weaker than the previous year, so he asked someone else to lead the way and skied slowly on his own. Since then, he has stopped skiing. "I am an advocate of skiing," he said, "and I would be sorry if I injured myself skiing. I felt that if I continued skiing any longer, I would get hurt, so I stopped." I thought to myself, "There comes a time in every person's life when they have to break their attachments and give up on something once and for all."

Shuzo Imai, one of Mr. Mitarai's friends since his preparatory course days at Hokudai, lives in Tottori City, and I think he is probably the most excited about the publication of this book. When we met, his first words were, "I have to thank you. I always thought it was a shame that a great man like him remained so little known to the world. Thank you so much."

Minoru Nakao, who lives in Kobe, is a graduate of the Faculty of Engineering at Hokkaido Imperial University, one year Mitarai's junior. The two met when Nakao moved into Keiteki Dormitory. "He was a cultured person with a broad outlook and a love of contemporary plays. He was an admirable person, trustworthy without any pretensions. His sincerity was evident from every angle," Nakao said. When he met Mr. Mitarai again in 1948 after the war, Mitarai told him that Japan has become like this, but we have no resources, so we have no choice but to make do with what we can. Mr. Nakao said that Mitarai had suggested to him that he try shutter research. When I met him, Mr. Nakao was in the hospital due to illness, but he spoke fondly of his memories of the past and lent me a copy of *Shashinshu Hokudai Hyakunen* (100 Years of Photography at Hokkaido University). I had intended to meet him again, but I regret to say that he passed away before I could do so. My deepest condolences to him.

The story of Mitarai's eldest brother, Nobuo (born in 1890), whom he describes as "like a benevolent father," could fill another volume.

Nobuo's father, Taizo, was a graduate of the first Oita Prefectural Normal School, and Nobuo entered junior high school in Oita with the intention of becoming a teacher. However, his older sister was married to a doctor, and he left for Tokyo to take the entrance exam to become a doctor himself, but failed.

During his second year preparing for the university entrance exam, he learned that Jikei Idai (currently the Jikei University School of Medicne) was establishing a preparatory course, and he enrolled at the age of 19. His father had taught him the Chinese classics, and he felt that he had to rebuild the Mitarai family, so he was determined to take care of his younger brothers and sisters. At the age of six, he visited another house as a representative of the family, and his father also allowed him to attend small celebrations in the town as a representative of the family. His father often told him, "That mountain used to be our mountain and that land used to be our land," and he felt that his father was investing a lot in me. When he was in elementary school, he read Kenjiro Tokutomi's memoir *Footprints in the Snow*, which inspired him greatly.

Their father passed away in 1911, and upon graduation, Nobuo started working in in a hospital as a surgeon. In 1915, he opened his own practice in their hometown of Kamae, but his mentor told him, "Doctors are not supposed to advertise. Don't put a signboard on the street." For a long time, he did not even advertise in newspapers.

In the fifth year of middle school, Nobuo studied Christianity and attended the church of Masahisa Uemura for a while, and was finally baptized. However, as he studied medicine, he began to think that religion might not be necessary if science continued to develop. Eventually, he stopped attending church, believing that God is hypothetical and that science is the only way to explain civilization.

One of his dormmates during his preparatory course days at Jikei was the socialist Iwasaburo Okino (born in 1876), for whom Nobuo wrote the preface to his book *Treading on White Ice* in his later years. He read with great enthusiasm *A Village where Milk and Honey Flow* by Toyohiko Kagawa (born in 1888, a Christian minister famous for his social work), and under the influence of this book, he devoted himself to organizing an industrial union while working as a doctor in Kamae.

About his brother, Nobuo said, "Takeshi was a mild-mannered, benevolent, and gentle person from the time he was born. Our mother loved him very much, and he was very devoted to her. (Their mother, Tora, died in Kamae in June 1945, just before in the end of the war, at the age of 82.) When you become like that, you tend to become overbearing and arrogant, and act in ways that are not from your hearts, but that was never the case with him," he said.

Toyoroku Ando (born in 1905), advisor to Onoda Cement, is from Oita and was one of the first students of Mr. Sakichi Kishino at Saiki Junior High School. He is three years Mitarai's senior. During his high school days, when Taisho Democracy was at its peak, he was free to read anything he wanted, even books by Marx.

About Mitarai as a manager, he says, "Things like 'Go Home Quickly' are very good, but they are not easy to do. He takes care of the health of his employees and draws out all of their individual strengths."

Mr. Heihachiro Kondo, who worked as a secretary at Zeon, told me about Mr. Kishino and loaned me some of his materials.

For research and interviews overseas, I left Narita Airport on November 3, 1981, and returned to Itami Airport in Osaka on December 6, 1981. I traveled to 13 cities in 9 countries in 33 days. I was told it was "crazy schedule" everywhere I went.

I went to a wrong place for an appointment in Amsterdam and almost got lost in Giessen, Germany when I was supposed to spend only 20 minutes walking around the city, but found myself in an unexpected place. I forgot my camera at the Toronto airport (fortunately I got it back). I left my shoes outside my room to get them cleaned at a hotel in Canada and they were stolen. I bought very expensive shoes at a shoe shop in Little Tokyo, Los Angeles, recommended by a beautiful Korean woman with good Japanese. I was almost robbed by an immigrant mother with several children near the Louvre Museum in Paris. However, thanks to the kind assistance of the Japanese employees at Canon's overseas branches, I was able to conduct most of the interviews I had planned. The following is a sketch of some of the problems Japanese companies encounter overseas.

First, in Europe, socialist measures are used to redistribute wealth, and progressive taxation has had a negative effect on the incentive to work, since no more income remains in the hands of those who earn more than a certain amount. Taxes on overtime wages are particularly high, so people demand vacation time instead of overtime pay. They do not save much because their pensions are guaranteed. For these reasons, it is very difficult to motivate European workers, said Mr. Fukuda, president of Canon Amsterdam.

In other words, they are not hungry and have little sense of competition. Life is stable at each level. While parents in Japan tend to expect their children to achieve more than they did, those in Europe are not eager to spend huge amounts of money on tuition fees to send their children to university, and thus the number of students who go on to university is limited.

The British are obsessed with cars to an unthinkable extent for the Japanese. This is because cars are a status symbol. Canon CBM in the UK mainly leases Ford cars, ranging from the Granada at the top to the Escort at the bottom, and the car corresponds exactly to one's position in the company. To attract the best people, you have to provide them with a good car. This is the second most important thing after salary.

In addition, parking spaces are assigned according to the company's hierarchy, and if they overflow, the cars are placed on the street. Japanese employees would prefer driving smaller, more fuel-efficient Japanese cars, but they would not be allowed to say so, even as a joke. They might be told, "People in a lower rank think that if they work hard and get to a certain position, they can drive around in those cars. Do you want to ruin their motivation?"

Australians are just like the British in that they care about appearances in every way. When they become managers, they demand better cars, and when they attend parties, they even say, "It would ruin my reputation if I came with that guy." It is not like in Japan, where the department head goes drinking with his subordinates.

The story of Los Angeles plant manager Kenzo Seki (born in 1936) and his children is a good illustration of the problems faced by Japanese employees working overseas in educating their children.

He came to Los Angeles when his children (both boys) were in the fourth and fifth grades of an elementary school and now they are in a middle school. In the elementary school, they did well in math and were called "Superman," which made them happy. But in the middle school, they begin to have problems understanding the questions. Also, they were bullied by their classmates because they couldn't understand what their classmates were saying to them.

They had practiced karate in Japan, so they would have been able to defend themselves one-on-one, but they were bullied and attacked by a group of boys. Mr. Seki had to persuade them when they didn't want to go to school. They wanted to go back to Japan, but even if they did, they wouldn't be able to compete in the entrance examinations for Japanese universities. Mr. Seki had heard of a case in which a junior high school student returned to Japan, but fell behind his classmates and became so neurotic that he feared for his life. He only recovered once he returned to the U.S.

In some cases, the wives of the employees sent overseas experience discriminatory attitudes. A wife of a Japanese expatriate was actively involved in various groups, but an American who came to a party said, "Oh, there is a Japanese person here. I'll never come to a party like this again" and left. In another case, a Japanese woman kindly offered to lend something to a neighbor, but they said, "What the Japs used is dirty." If adults are like that, it is even worse when it comes to children. "We can be a good manager despite the language barrier, and our wives can stay at home, but our children are thrown into a foreign culture, and they are bullied by other children, and there is nowhere for them to hide," Mr. Seki points out. Many Japanese children overseas must deal these problems on their own with little or no help.

Hiroto Kagami once had a problem as his wife was unable to communicate with her own daughter. Their daughter was four when the family came to New York, and there was no all-day Japanese School until she was in the third grade. She attended a local elementary school, so she could barely speak Japanese. His wife and daughter could not have a conversation without Mr. Kagami interpreting. At that time, Canon USA had just started direct sales, and all the Japanese staff at the company were extremely busy. On weekdays and weekends alike, he would return home drunk after drinking with his subordinates, but his wife and daughter would still be up, waiting for him to come home. Then he would pull himself together and help his daughter with her homework.

When I met Mr. Nagata in Giessen, his two children were in the second grade and pre-school. He teaches them German and math after he gets home from work. He has also arranged for his children to study Japanese through a correspondence course for children overseas. The amount of study is much greater than in Japan.

Mr. Miyazaki's three children in the UK are all "foreign-born" and have never been to school in Japan. The older of the three, who is eleven years old, has finally started speaking Japanese at home, but his reading and writing are not up to the level of his peers in Japan, and he shies away from books written in Japanese. He often does look at *manga*, although he probably does not read the characters. Nevertheless, Mr. Miyazaki still gives his children *manga* because it is an opportunity for them to come into contact with the Japanese language.

If Mr. Nagata and Mr. Miyazaki were in Japan, they would not have to spend extra time on these matters. Like most Japanese fathers, they would leave their children to their wives. However, neither of them have much choice but to devote themselves to their children's education. Because they are forced to worry about their children's problems together, there is a possibility that a much deeper parent–child relationship will be formed than if they were in Japan. In this sense, I feel that it is not necessarily a negative thing, but perhaps that is just my opinion as an outside observer.

However, the question remains whether companies can continue to take the attitude that children's education issues are merely the personal affairs of their employees. Aren't the children the ones who will experience the most difficulties? It remains to be seen how they will deal with this issue.

As I wrote in the section about the Taiwan plant, Mr. Miura, the general manager of the General Affairs Department, made an effort to say *"Ni hao"* (Hello) to the local employees, which gave me the impression at the time that this effort was very valuable. However, the article "Reading Body Language 1" in the July 1982 issue of *Taiyo* (The Sun) magazine explains that, in China, words of greeting were originally scarce and *'Ni hao'* may have been patterned after Russian or Western words. In pre-revolutionary China, there were few opportunities for people to meet for the first time, and people were not eager to meet strangers. [...] Even among acquaintances, the custom of greeting people was not very common." It was also said that from ancient times, it was considered polite to walk past a socially superior person in a short run. It will be very interesting to see whether Mr. Miura's efforts in cross-cultural communication bear fruit or not.

In general, I am not sure how effective Japanese egalitarianism has in the management overseas, and whether this is simply a matter of management methods or whether it is deeply connected to culture and ideology must be considered over a long period of time.

Finally, I would like to thank all the people who helped me with the interviews. Here I will mention the names of those who were not mentioned earlier in this postscript.

Among Mr. Mitarai's friends are Yukio Kishimura (né Iwatsuru) (resident of Kishiwada, Osaka Prefecture), Kiyoshi Kojima (president of Marubishi Oil Chemical, Osaka), Kumazo Nagata (Tokyo), Ryosaku Mitarai (Saiki), and Gen-ichi Ogawa (Professor Emeritus of Hokkaido University, Sapporo).

Canon-related (including head office, sales companies and other affiliated companies, and former employees): Yoshiya Agari, Shuji Araki, Saichiro Amano, Hiroshi Ito, Ryuzaburo Kaku, Hiroshi Kawaguchi, Morimasa Kaneko, Kinji Kikuchi, Takeshi Goshima, Shigeru Shinagawa, Hiroshi Suzukawa, Hiroshi Suzuki, Shoji Suzuki, Yoshifumi Suzuki, Michihiko Senoo, Masanori Seki, Seiichi Takigawa, Hidehiko Taguchi, Susumu Tazawa, Shuji Takemoto,

Tetsuro Tamanuki, Fukutaro Tsuji, Nobuo Terai, Kazuo Naito, Hayao Nakahara, Tadashi Nakamura, Saburo Nagata, Hiroshi Nasu, Shigeru Nishioka, Hiroshi Nishigaki, Satoshi Nemoto, Tsuneo Nozaki, Yoshiyuki Hayashi, Muneo Hirai, Takashi Fujimura, Ryozo Furukawa, Tomomasa Matsui, Takeshi Mitarai, Hajime Mitarai, Tsuneo Misawa, Kazuo Mizukoshi, Matao Mitsui, Ryoichiro Yamagata, Keizo Yamaji, Hideo Yamamoto, and Torakiyo Yamanaka.

Outside Japan, in addition to the people I interviewed, many people helped me with local guidance and other matters. In the order of their locations, Keishi Fukuda, Yuichi Endo, Naoki Nambu, Naoki Himeno, E. Magnus, J. Doorn, and J. Linden in Amsterdam; Yukio Yamashita, Yasuyuki Matsuda, Masayuki Miyazaki, P. Benham, and R. Cosgroff in the U.K.; Yoshiaki Otake and Ryozo Hiramitsu in France; Tsuneo Enome, Kunihiro Nagata, Hiroshi Iizuka, and K. Hansen in Giessen; Fujio Mitarai, Hiroto Kagami, Hiroshi Hagiwara, Nakamura, Ken'ichi Mori, D. Farr, Joji Kyodo, and Susumu Mitarai in New York; Haruhiko Takano, Mamoru Maeda, and D. Phillips in Toronto; Junichi Tominaga in Chicago; Shigeru Hayashi and Katsumi Takizawa in Atlanta; Toshizo Tanaka, Yasuharu Sato, Tomio Hirao, Yoshio Katayama (Attorney at Law), Mr. and Mrs. Yamada and Mr. and Mrs. Masumura from Oita Prefecture, and Noriyoshi Kawasaki in Los Angeles; Haruo Odagawa in Hawaii; Shuichi Ando, Yosuke Motai, Hideo Tsushima, Teruo Kobayashi, Sadao Fukazawa, and Masahiro Okamoto in Australia; Hiroshi Saito, Tetsuo Kawamura, Kiyoshi Uehara, Yuji Sugie, Masatatsu Murotomi, and Kenji Miura in Singapore. Shoji Aoki, Touhei Matsuo, Kanenojo Nakamura, Masamitsu Miura, Takamoto Kyo, Hiroaki Kou, and Koichi Wang in Taiwan; Kinya Uchida from Latin America, whom I met in Tokyo. We asked Ms. Nojiri and Ms. Namiki, both long-time employees of the Secretarial Office at Canon Inc. to give us their impressions of the Chairman from the perspectives of female secretaries. During the more than one year of research, I was greatly indebted to the women in the secretarial office, as well as to Hideo Kondo, former head of the secretarial office; Yoshimi Iwata, current head; and Takeo Takahashi, deputy head, for their detailed research of documents and other information. In addition, I am sure that there are many other people who contributed to the research for this book without my knowledge. This book was made possible with their help as well. I would like to express my sincere gratitude to all of them.

December 5, 1982

The Man Who Made It Possible:
Canon and TAKESHI MITARAI

2024 年 3 月 31 日　初版第 1 刷　発行

著　　者　加藤　勝美
発　行　人　浅田　厚志
発　行　所　出版文化社

〈東京カンパニー〉
〒104-0033 東京都中央区新川 1-8-8　アクロス新川ビル 4 階
TEL：03-6822-9200　FAX：03-6822-9202
E-mail：book@shuppanbunka.com

［埼玉オフィス］　　〒363-0001 埼玉県桶川市加納 1764-5

〈大阪カンパニー〉
〒532-0011 大阪府大阪市淀川区西中島 5 丁目 13-9　新大阪 MT ビル 1 号館 9 階
TEL：06-7777-9730（代表）　FAX：06-7777-9737

〈名古屋支社〉
〒456-0016 愛知県名古屋市熱田区五本松町 7-30　熱田メディアウイング 3 階
TEL：052-990-9090（代表）　FAX：052-683-8880

https://www.shuppanbunka.com

取材協力：キヤノン株式会社
翻訳アドバイザー：河野至恩　　翻訳協力：ThinkSCIENCE